WALL STREET REVALUED

Imperfect Markets and Inept Central Bankers

ANDREW SMITHERS

A John Wiley & Sons, Ltd., Publication

Published in 2009 by John Wiley & Sons, Ltd

Registered office
John Wiley & Sons Ltd, The Atrium, Southern Gate, Chichester, West Sussex, PO19 8SQ, United Kingdom

For details of our global editorial offices, for customer services and for information about how to apply for permission to reuse the copyright material in this book please see our website at www.wiley.com.

Library of Congress Cataloging-in-Publication Data

Smithers, Andrew.
    Wall Street revalued : imperfect markets and inept central bankers / Andrew Smithers.
        p. cm.
    ISBN 978-0-470-75005-6
    1. Capital market–United States.   2. Monetary policy–United States.   3. Finance–United States.   4. Banks and banking, Central–United States.   I. Title.
    HG4910.S565 2009
    332'.04150973–dc22

                                                                                                    2009019921

A catalogue record for this book is available from the British Library.

ISBN 978-0-470-75005-6

Set in 11.5/13.5 pt Bembo by SNP Best-set Typesetter Ltd., Hong Kong
Printed in Great Britain by TJ International Ltd, Padstow, Cornwall

Contents

Foreword

by Jeremy Grantham

Rumor has it that the first time I met Andrew Smithers when he came into my office almost 20 years ago, I offered him a job, which he gleefully declined as preposterous since he already had a job he was perfectly suited to and was quite happy being an independent financial economist. Andrew is a unique mix of professional, analytical, skeptical, independent and crusty. No one quite like him had come my way until then. He goes straight for the point and attempts to beat it to death, usually successfully. He has complete disdain for any hint of self–interest, of which he finds bucket loads in what he describes as "stockbroker economics," always written in a manner that implies a curled lip.

The first important experience we went through together was the breaking of the Japanese bubble. We had arrived independently at the same point of considering Japan the biggest equity and real estate double bubble of all time. It was not the last time we agreed. In fact, my only complaint with Andrew is just that. We don't get to argue with each other enough. Arguing with Andrew is not an experience you would want to miss. If you could imagine being attacked by an eight-armed Indian god equipped with eight razor-sharp swords, you would get the picture. After speaking at one of our client conferences in London, for example, he answered a question by pointing out the three or four implicit fallacies in the question!

As Japan crashed and crashed some more, Andrew would come up with ever more rigorous arguments for leaving it alone. Half price: not even close. Six years into a decline: just warming up. Twelve years into the decline with Japan's Nikkei blown to 15¢ on the S&P 500's dollar, and Andrew's merciless logic was still keeping our enthusiasm for Japan down, and rightly so. He helped give us confidence for one of the largest, longest, and most profitable bets of our career. What is more remarkable is that he more or less said how it would unfold nearly 20 years ago and told everyone it would be the longest running bear event in history, which it has indeed been.

Of other coups, I will highlight "Valuing Wall Street," co-authored with Stephen Wright. This book came out with impeccable timing in early 2000, and explained the doom that awaited us. (Together with Robert Shiller's "Irrational Exuberance" they made the best-timed and most accurate 1-2 punch in financial history!)

Now, in this volume, he is attempting something even more important: to wage war on both the retreating efficient market academic establishment and the recently proved incompetent central bankers who were in its thrall.

Andrew rips the basic tenets of the Efficient Market Hypothesis to shreds, and that is the easier part. Much more difficult, he replaces it with a new, more complete and more complex theory of Imperfect Markets, which he holds to the far more stringent tests of being useful in investing and *testable*. The current theory of Market Efficiency fails each of these. Along the way, he skewers central bankers everywhere.

Established academic schools of thought have an enormous reluctance to change their theories. They have careers, awards and reputations involved and they defend their work tenaciously. Very, very few senior academics change their minds profoundly. Max Planck, the physicist, described this process succinctly: "Science advances one funeral at a time." One can imagine that theories in the softer sciences like economics are even harder to move. One theory in particular – the Efficient Market Hypothesis (EMH) – has dug in its heels. It has proven resistant to decades of data that are incompatible with its theory of efficiency … data that suggest that in real life markets are jungles of behavioral excesses that can result in manias and panics. The theory holds fast to the belief in "rational expectations" that investors are cool, collected, rational machines optimizing their economic vitality at every turn. The EMH ruled the academic waves for 50 years, and for the majority of the time – say, 1968 to 1998 – it was found to be nearly impossible to get tenure or peer reviewed articles published in prestigious journals if you espoused views deemed heretical by the high church of "rational expectations!" The assumption of rationality meant that markets were always efficient and, as such, econometricians could build precise mathematical models, just like physicists. Indeed, the theory was described as suffering from Physics Envy. But the models had a drawback: they were precise, but unfortunately precisely wrong. The EMH therefore led generations of researchers away from messy reality to precisely modeled assumptions. As we have seen recently, though, a world modeled on such profoundly wrong assumptions can be extremely dangerous to economic wellbeing. The EMH has been described as the most expensive mistake – or simply the biggest mistake – in the history of finance. (This assessment has been attributed to Summers and to Shiller but, if neither want it, I'm sure Smithers or I will be pleased to accept it.) Since the EMH is so at odds with the historical facts of irrational booms and busts, it has not played well with economic historians. The Dean of this group, Charles Kindleberger, in his famous "Manias, Panics, and Crashes" fingered the EMH in his last paragraph. He said, "Dismissing financial crisis on the grounds that bubbles and busts cannot take place because that would imply irrationality is to ignore a condition for the sake of a theory."

At this brick wall of belief in the EMH, a few score of us have tilted, shattering our lances time and time again. Solid data documenting inefficiency was ignored, bouncing off their defenses. All these little behavioral twitches can never amount to a useful comprehensive theory the academic establishment seemed to say, so let us ignore them, for what we have now is a neat and useful theory.

For people who worship hard data and intellectual rigor, this dismissiveness has been irritating and frustrating for a long time, but in the last 10 years even the high priests of the EMH have begun to notice a few nicks in their brick wall. But now they should really worry, for the remorseless argument presented by Smithers in this book resembles a large sledge hammer rather than a lance. Starting with the proposal that the EMH in its strong form is probably wrong and in its weak form can never be tested and is therefore not science, Smithers sets about building an alternative case. He calls it the Imperfectly Efficient Market Hypothesis, and it is both testable and useful. His theory holds that prices wander around fair value – the efficient price – sometimes as far away as in the 2000 tech bubble described in the previously mentioned "Valuing Wall Street." It was here that he and Wright argued that in early 2000 the US market was – astonishingly to most readers – over twice fair value. (Adjusted for inflation it indeed passed way below half its 2000 peak early this year.) In contrast to such an extreme event as 2000, much of the time the market is merely moderately away from fair value and every few years it indeed passes through fair value. In this sense the market is occasionally efficient. As Smithers points out, the market does not fly out of orbit entirely, moving to hundreds of times earnings or approaching zero. Rather, it behaves as if tethered to a central value, loosely controlled by longer-term economic arbitrage. Sometimes this gravitational pull of value works quickly, but sometimes very slowly, reflecting the nature of a necessarily uncertain future and, occasionally, very irrational players. When it is slow in reverting to fair value, Smithers argues that it produces amazing risk for professional investors – who hate to lose business – as impatient clients leave.

Central to Smithers' concept is that valuing markets is entirely possible and useful. It is useful for predicting future returns for careful, very long-term investors: buying more when stocks are occasionally very cheap and less when very expensive not only increases returns, but lowers risk. In a mean reverting world, over-pricing is indeed a risk and a badly underestimated and understudied one at that.

Smithers points out that the crushing consensus behind the EMH in earlier years – it is now finally creaking and cracking – diverted serious work in the financial end of economics away from the concept of value. (Franco Modigliani, one of a tiny half handful of my heroes, told a conference in Boston in 1982 that a market at 8 times depressed earnings was below half price, and in 2000 he sat [very frail] and told the Boston Quant Society that the market at 35 times above normal earnings was over twice fair price. But he had bigger or at least more interesting theoretical fish to fry, and unfortunately never seriously wrote this up, nor was anyone of his stature around to take up his cudgel. In a nutshell Modigliani implied that markets could be valued.) Now Smithers returns to the central point of "Valuing Wall Street": the market does have a fair value that can be measured. Such a value is provably useful as the market will fluctuate around it allowing profitable investment decisions to be made.

This leads Smithers to the associated key thought in this book: that Greenspan's and Bernanke's belief in EMH and the resulting belief that bubbles cannot be identified led us into our current grief. My own favorite illustration of their views was Bernanke's comment in late 2006 at the height of a 3-sigma (100-year) event in a US housing market that had had *no* prior housing bubbles: "The US housing market merely reflects a strong US economy." He was surrounded by statisticians and yet could not see the data. My view, reflected in the Kindleberger quote, is that his profound faith in market efficiency, and therefore a world where bubbles could not exist, made it impossible for him to see what was in front of his eyes.

Greenspan before him was also not sure – at least from time to time – that bubbles could exist, and even if they might, who was he, he argued, to contest the views of tens of thousands of well informed individuals? To be safe, they both adopted the Greenspan Put position: With all our doubts, let us see how the market plays out – bubble or not – and we can still deal with the downside consequences of any bubble bursting by rushing in to provide liquidity. Today we are dealing with the results of that policy.

So these are the two critical monsters of misunderstanding that Smithers has to slay: first, that the market is efficient and valuing it is therefore irrelevant, even if it could be done, which it can't; and second, the Fed and central bankers everywhere can ignore the consequences of asset class bubbles forming, and simply deal with the consequences, if any, when they come along. For all of us, unfortunately, the main consequence is that asset bubbles *always* break, and their breaking can have terrible economic repercussions, as we found out in the US in the 30s and the 70s and in Japan in the 90s. We are relearning this lesson as we speak.

In my opinion, Smithers nails these two monsters in their coffins along with a swarm of their smaller progeny. I certainly hope they stay there. I look forward to a more complicated future where we can start to build on the messy real world as Smithers proposes, and avoid the substantial pain that comes from dangerous oversimplifications.

Jeremy Grantham, Chief Strategist and Chairman,
Grantham, Mayo, Van Otterloo

1

Introduction

This book is based on two principles: first, that assets can be objectively valued and, second, that it is extremely important that central bankers should adjust their policies when asset prices get substantially out of line with their underlying values. I seek to show that it was the denial of these two principles that led to the errors by central bankers which are the fundamental cause of our current troubles. The assets which are most liable to be badly mispriced are shares, houses, and private sector debts, including bonds and bank loans. In 2002, Stephen Wright and I wrote a paper explaining why the Federal Reserve should adjust its policy, not only in the light of expected inflation, but also if stock market prices reached excessive levels. But at that time we doubted whether "this view would yet receive support from the majority of economists".[1] As I write, in March 2009, it is quite hard to find economists who disagree. Opinions tend to be moved more quickly by events than by arguments, and this change is no doubt the result of financial turmoil and the threat of a severe recession. I aim to show, however, that the change is sensible, soundly backed by evidence and capable of being supported by theory.

Financial turmoil and recessions are closely linked. Crashes do not occur randomly, but generally follow the booms which are

---

[1] *World Economics* Vol. 3 No. 1 Jan–Mar 2002. "Stock Markets and Central Bankers – The Economic Consequences of Alan Greenspan" by Andrew Smithers and Stephen Wright.

associated with asset bubbles. When these are extreme, the subsequent turmoil is most severe. The three most extreme examples of modern times are today, Japan after 1990 and the US in the 1930s. Falling asset prices, among their many undesirable consequences, make it difficult and sometimes impossible for central banks to control their economies simply through changes in short-term interest rates. The current turmoil has its origin in the series of asset bubbles which began with the stock market in the latter part of the 20th century. If the agreed policy of central banks had been to restrain asset bubbles, and they had acted to do so, the current pain could – and probably would – have been avoided. But while the view that we were then putting forward seems to have been justified in retrospect, it will not command, and should not command, the necessary authority to influence future policy decisions unless it has the support of a coherent and testable economic theory, which it is the purpose of this book to provide.

The symptoms of the financial mania, which began in the 1990s, were many. Not only were asset prices driven to absurd levels, but bankers and others believed that these prices had some fundamental validity and, on the basis of this confidence, created complicated additional structures whose assumed values became, in turn, articles of faith and the basis for further leverage. Loans were extended on the assumption that the assets which backed them were reasonably valued and, in the resulting boom in business, it was the bankers who believed in these follies who were most likely to be rewarded with extravagant bonuses. It has been well remarked that the most successful sellers of snake oil believe wholeheartedly in the virtues of their product, and in recent times bankers became the quintessential sellers of snake oil. When asset prices fell, the whole house of cards came tumbling down and there is a tendency to see the fundamental problem in terms of these symptoms of absurd asset prices, complicated financial structures, extravagant bonuses and undisciplined bank lending. But these symptoms were not the fundamental cause of the mania, although the asset prices alone should have given sufficient warning of the looming problems. Human nature doesn't change quickly, and people respond to opportunities and incentives. Bankers and other financiers will always hang themselves, and us with them, if provided with sufficient rope. The excessive rope provided by central bankers was not only a necessary condition of the current turmoil, it was a sufficient one. We have a world of fiat money – that is, money which can be created at the whim of our central bankers, as distinct from one based on gold, for example, and if their whims are wayward, the results will be disastrous, without any other conditions for disaster being required except the normal human responses and frailties.

The cause of our present troubles was the actions of incompetent central bankers, who provided excessive liquidity on which the asset price bubbles and their associated absurdities were built. When too much liquidity is being created, the results will appear either in consumer or asset prices. Central bankers were alert to the former and, if the symptoms of excess liquidity had appeared in consumer prices, they would no doubt have responded to dampen them down, even at the cost of having a much earlier recession than the one which is deepening as I write. But an earlier recession would have been relatively mild with a limited loss of output and welfare. Unfortunately, it was in asset rather than consumer prices that the excesses were revealed and, equally unfortunately, the Federal Reserve, which in this instance deserves far more opprobrium than other central bankers, announced that this did not matter.

The central concerns of this book are why the Federal Reserve held this view, why it was wrong and how things could and should be managed better in the future. The single most important element in the Federal Reserve's view was the claim that asset prices cannot be valued. This was modified at various times and different arguments were regularly trotted out as changing circumstances made each previous claim less credible. But the ability to value assets is the central issue and claims that it can be done run against the long-held view that, while the real economy operates in a less than fully efficient way, financial markets are different. This view is no longer widely held in its starkest form but, in practice, many of the arguments that are produced about financial markets involve the same underlying assumptions, even though those who are making them seldom recognize the implicit, rather than explicit, assumptions that they are making. It is therefore necessary to show that assets can be valued and that financial markets are not perfectly efficient. But this is not enough. It is also necessary to expose arguments which rely implicitly on these assumptions. Otherwise the same follies will return by the back door. For example, as I will show, almost all arguments that involve the Equity Risk Premium and its so-called "Puzzle" include in practice an implied assumption that financial markets are perfectly efficient.

The ability to value asset prices is obviously important for investors, fund managers, actuaries, pension consultants and those concerned with the regulation of financial institutions, as well as for central bankers. This book is therefore addressed to all these audiences.

Shares are not the only assets with which central bankers need to be concerned. House, bond and loan prices are also extremely important. Even assuming that agreement can be reached on the importance of asset prices and how they should be valued, it is necessary to consider the actions that central banks, investors and consultants should take or recommend in the event that assets become markedly misevaluated.

While many people have poured justifiable scorn on the idea that financial markets are perfectly efficient, it is necessary not just to debunk the theory but to put an alternative in its place. I call this alternative the Imperfectly Efficient Market Hypothesis. One aspect of this book is therefore to show that the Efficient Market Hypothesis is not testable but that the Imperfectly Efficient Hypothesis is and proves robust under testing. This involves the ability to value markets and here I am helped by the useful circumstantial evidence provided by having claimed in 2000 that shares were extremely overvalued and by their subsequent fall. In March 2000, Stephen Wright and I published *Valuing Wall Street* in which we explained that the stock markets were far from being perfectly efficient, and that it was possible to value them. We also expected the results of the overvaluation of the market to be dire. The last sentence of the book was "We therefore doubt whether it will be possible to act promptly and strongly enough to stop a major recession developing in the USA in the new millennium".

As we showed, the US stock market could be valued by using the q ratio. At the same time Professor Robert Shiller published a book claiming that markets could be valued by using the cyclically adjusted PE ratio ("CAPE").[2] Both books showed that the US stock

---

[2] *Valuing Wall Street – Protecting Wealth in Turbulent Markets* by Andrew Smithers and Stephen Wright was published by McGraw-Hill and *Irrational Exuberance* by Robert J. Shiller was published by Princeton University Press, both in March 2000.

market was extremely over-priced and were published at the peak of the bubble. The precise timing, which was (at least in our case), a matter of luck, thus proved to be extremely fortunate since the market, as measured by the S&P 500 index, had by early 2009 halved from its 2000 peak in nominal terms and fallen even more in real ones. These two separate approaches to value produce very similar results and this has great advantages. Not only must two valid answers to the same question agree, but CAPE is unaffected by the issue of valuing intangibles. This has been used as an objection to q, which in turn is unaffected by claims raised as an objection to CAPE that the long-term returns on equity and thus the equilibrium PE are not stable. The way in which the two metrics of q and CAPE agree is evidence against both these objections, though I will also show in other ways that neither are valid.

I shall show that it follows that the stock market can be valued and that this is essential if central bankers are to take note of asset prices. They must know the warning signs. But there are other vital elements that must be explained. One is why asset prices matter for the economy and central bankers, as well as for investors. To do this I demonstrate that interest rates affect asset prices and, as asset prices affect the economy, this is a major transmission mechanism whereby central banks influence demand in the real economy. I show, however, that the impact of interest rates on asset prices is ephemeral. The result is that this transmission mechanism breaks down if share prices rise too high. Ideally, therefore, central banks need to be able to use interest rates to control demand in some way which does not involve the impact of interest rates on asset prices. This reinforces the logically straightforward case that if central banks are asked to have two targets, in this instance both consumer and asset prices, they need more than one policy weapon to deal with them. We must hope that the provision of such an additional weapon will be agreed and will improve central bankers' ability to manage the economy by not allowing asset prices to be seriously misvalued.[3] But whether or not such an additional policy

---

[3] It is only aggregate prices that matter in this context, not individual share prices. There is indeed strong evidence that the pricing of shares, relative to one another, is performed with considerable efficiency; it is only in the aggregate that serious inefficiencies can be shown to occur.

instrument can be agreed and will prove useful, we must be prepared to consider the possibility that periodic mild recessions are a necessary price for avoiding major ones and, if this is correct, to accept the consequences.

If the market is not perfectly efficient, it is necessary to show why this doesn't provide an easy way to make money. Demonstrating that imperfectly efficient markets are not a "free lunch", due to the practical limits of arbitrage, is thus an important element in this book. Associated with this is the question of leverage. The gap between the return on equities and the return on bonds or cash on deposit has been large, and this has led people to question how this gap is not reduced by the simple expedient of investors borrowing and leveraging their equity portfolios. I show that these arguments contain an implicit, rather than explicit, assumption about the way in which such leverage works which involves ignoring the fact that market returns are less volatile over the longer term than they would be if share prices behaved in a more random way.

Partly no doubt because of its fortunate timing, *Valuing Wall Street* has resulted in many letters of thanks from readers who took our advice and saved themselves from major losses as a result. But there were a number of issues regarding value which we did not discuss or only touched on briefly and which I seek to cover more fully here. For example, I treat in greater detail the alternative approach to value, to which I refer as CAPE, taken by Robert Shiller. This produces very similar answers to those that resulted from our use of q and this element of agreement is itself important. Another is the issue of intangibles. Since 2000, Stephen and I have been teaching a regular course to fund managers, MBA students and others, on how to value stock markets, and questions about intangibles are the ones raised most frequently. In addition, when teaching this course I have encountered a whole string of doubts, problems and interesting questions, which I have also sought to address. As well as dealing with issues not previously or fully covered in *Valuing Wall Street*, this book is concerned with the interaction of the central banking policy with share prices, with their interaction with the economy and with the responses to misvalued asset prices which should sensibly be taken by investors and consultants.

The issues discussed are therefore important at both the personal, national and, indeed, international levels. Investing in overvalued assets often brings loss, pain and misery and it would clearly be better if these results can be avoided, or at least modified. But violent fluctuations in asset prices also produce more general misfortune, through their impact on the real economy. Asset prices are one of the key transmission mechanisms through which changes in interest rates by central banks influence the real economy. But the more overvalued they are, the weaker this influence becomes. As I write, the Federal Reserve seems, under the impact of falling asset prices, to have lost control of the US economy at least temporarily, and become unable to prevent a recession through its control of interest rates. Fortunately, I expect them to be able to regain it with the help of fiscal stimulus and a large-scale refinancing of the banks. Nonetheless, it would have been better, even if my optimism proves justified, if the Fed had remained in better control, if the economy had been less volatile and if massive additions to the US public sector debt had not been required.

Working on stock market valuation seems never to have been fashionable among economists. One unfortunate side effect has been that otherwise well-informed economists and central bankers often appear to have been ill acquainted with the subject and this has led them to make erroneous and ill considered pronouncements about the difficulty or even impossibility of valuing stock markets. Had the matter been the subject of wide and serious debate, it is likely that they would have studied the subject more thoroughly before pronouncing upon it. This lack of debate was a significant cause of the indifference, or worse, that the Federal Reserve showed towards the stock market bubble as it rose to its peak in 2000. The Federal Reserve was, nonetheless, mildly sensitive to criticism and responded by a series of claims that varied over time. The first was that assets could not be valued and their prices should therefore be ignored.[4] Furthermore, that any adverse consequences resulting from the collapse of asset bubbles could readily be prevented by monetary policy – if necessary, by sprinkling money from helicopters. When it was pointed out that monetary policy had not been ignoring asset prices, but had been responding to falls but not rises, the argument shifted

---

[4] See, for example, *Monetary Policy and Asset Price Volatility* by B. Bernanke and M. Gertler, published in the *Federal Reserve Bank of Kansas City Economic Review* 1999 4th Quarter pp. 17–51.

and the excuse was made that the Fed need only respond to asset price falls since these were much more violent than the rises.[5] It seems to me to be a valid observation and criticism that the way the debate developed showed that the Federal Reserve's determination to ignore asset prices had driven their arguments rather than, as things should have been, that the strength of the case determined their policy.

The financial turmoil that burst in 2008 appears to have had its origin in the stock market bubble which broke in 2000, and the Federal Reserve policy to offset the impact of this on the real economy fuelled the excesses of the subsequent asset bubbles. These, which took share prices back to their previous nominal heights and house prices to new real ones, finally broke in 2007. It seems likely that the Fed's policy response, after the stock market fell from its 2000 peak, was all the more excessive for fear that those who criticized its indifference to the stock market bubble would have had added ammunition if the economy had fallen into a marked recession shortly afterwards. The result of the Fed's policy, whatever its motivation, was that the stock market bubble of 2000 became by 2007 a bubble which was not confined to shares but common to all asset prices. This chain of causality cannot of course be proved; we cannot tell what might have happened had monetary policy been different or whether those implementing it had unrecorded or even unacknowledged motivations. It could be, though it seems to me unlikely, that the excesses of the 2007 bubble were due to errors unconnected with the stock market bubble that broke in 2000. The sequence of events is, however, clear. The break in the stock market in 2000 was followed by a recession and then by monetary conditions which allowed and encouraged the asset price excesses which peaked in 2007.

Events change views. The slump of the 1930s probably contributed as much as Keynes's arguments to today's widespread, though sadly by no means universal, acceptance that intentions to save and

---

[5] Examples of the Fed easing in response to asset price declines include the cuts in interest rates made when Russia defaulted in 1998 and the hedge fund LTCM was saved from liquidation. This anxiety to preserve overvalued asset prices became known as the "Greenspan put" and contributed both to further market madness and to subsequent collapse.

to invest are not automatically balanced under conditions of full employment and that such a balance cannot necessarily be achieved by monetary policy alone. The problems of the late 1970s and early 1980s led to renewed emphasis on monetary policy and the recognition that unchecked inflation could, through its impact on expectations, lead to an unpleasant combination of inflation and lost output, which became known as stagflation. The financial turmoil of 2008 is likely to bring about another reassessment. I hope that the importance of asset as well consumer prices for central banks will be increasingly recognized. Already there are encouraging signs, notably in reports, that even the Federal Reserve has decided to reconsider its attitude.[6]

While I naturally find evidence of such a change of heart welcome, it will not have any practical influence on policy unless some broad agreement can be established as to how assets can be valued. This is not going to be easy, as any discussion encounters strong prejudice in both popular and academic debate. Central banking is subject to strong political pressure and a degree of popular understanding and discussion in the financial press is essential rather than just desirable. This book is therefore addressed to a wider audience than academics. I hope that it will prove useful to those with a broad interest in finance and macroeconomics. This aim is reflected in the book's structure. In the main text I set out the arguments in a non-technical way, with the algebra and technical details set out in the appendices. I have also made extensive use of Charts as I find that these are often a telling way to communicate important points. The heroine of *Alice in Wonderland* wonders "what is the use of a book without pictures or conversation". In this book the absence of conversation is at least offset by many pictures.

In presenting a serious debate on value I find myself in opposition to the majority of the views that I have encountered from stockbrokers and investment bankers. While there are some admirable exceptions, I have come to the harsh conclusion that they are a major source of misinformation encouraged, perhaps, by concerns that a general understanding of the issues involved was unlikely to

---

[6] As reported, for example, in "Troubled by bubbles" by Krishna Guha in the *Financial Times*, 16 May 2008.

be helpful for business. Except in rare and extreme times, value has very little influence on the way share prices move, looking even three or more years ahead. However, the claim that "shares today are good value" is believed to be an aid to sales. If it becomes generally understood how shares can be valued, then it must follow that this claim will be known to be nonsense around 50% of the time. In practice, this would be unlikely to matter very much, as the stock market is often a sensible place to invest, giving a higher return than other possible choices among asset classes, even if mildly overvalued. But the stock market, while not wholly irrational, encourages irrationality in its participants, whose instincts are to see reason as a threat to their livelihood.

Financial journalists can seldom afford the time to engage in their own research and are therefore dependent on the work of others. They receive most of their information from stockbrokers and investment bankers and only a few can therefore be expected to offer a view which is independent of these sources. Popular views on value, which are largely derived from the media, are thus naturally biased towards irrational claims whose sole aim is to be always, under any circumstance, amenable to demonstrating that "shares are cheap". It is therefore no surprise to find that among investment bankers and financial journalists the two most common claims to value are, as I plan to show, unadulterated nonsense. One of these is that "Shares are cheap given the level of current (or forecast) PE multiples" and the other is that "Shares are cheap relative to interest rates". As popular views influence economic policy, it is important that popular nonsense should be exposed rather than ignored, and by doing so I hope to add some lighter touches, which can often be in short supply in any discussion of the dismal science of economics, particularly in the current economic climate.

While the problems of opening up a serious debate on asset value among academics have been reduced by the recent turmoil in financial markets, they remain powerful. Because the fluctuations of financial markets are of vital importance to the real economy, policy makers need a soundly based and broadly shared understanding of financial markets. No such paradigm exists today. The various theories that are held by academics and financial practitioners cannot be readily pulled together and no simple statement can be made that "As generally agreed this is the way that markets work".

Financial economics today has similarities with macroeconomics in the earlier part of the 20th century, when it became increasingly clear that markets did not necessarily work without friction on the lines assumed by perfect competition and some modifications to the model were therefore needed. In the 19th and even in the early 20th centuries, neither governments nor central banks were held responsible for managing the economy and, even if such responsibility had been acknowledged, there was no agreed economic theory on which such management could be based. There were no agreed methods for offsetting the consequences of policy errors or boosting the economy in the face of sharp contractions in demand. Today there is a large degree of agreement on how to respond to macroeconomic problems of this sort, though recent debates show we are well short of unanimity. But financial economics is without a broad basis of agreed theory on how to prevent or respond to financial turbulence and as the output of the financial sector has increased as a proportion of total GDP, the consequent potential for misfortune has risen.

In academia, the main problem is the hangover from the Efficient Market Hypothesis (EMH). Despite the doubts and scepticism that it aroused even at its peak of popularity, its one-time dominance has left a feeling that discussion of value is not a serious activity for economists. This has been reinforced by a concern that if value could be ascertained it must somehow involve money making and this was beneath the dignity of economists even if they succeeded and, even more, if they failed.

The article[7] which set out the opinions of Stephen Wright and myself on the importance of equity prices for central banking, while more detailed than any previous comments we had made on the subject, reflected views that we had been expressing as the US stock market went to its peak in 2000. When the market fell the following recession was quite mild, partly due to fiscal stimulus and partly to the Federal Reserve's policy of extreme monetary ease. While this was successful in achieving the short-term aim of moderating the weakness of demand, it did so by driving up asset prices, including houses, and virtually all forms of risky assets as well as equities. As asset prices are one of the main transmission mechanisms by which

---

[7] Footnote 1 op. cit.

monetary policy affects the economy, it is common, but by no means invariable, for the prices of different types of assets to move together. This was, for example, the experience of Japan in its asset bubble of the 1980s. But one bubble differs from another and there are often bubbles on bubbles in which one particular asset class, or sub-group, becomes even more absurdly priced than others. Tele-communication and internet companies were particularly prone to overvaluation in 2000, real estate companies were exceptional in the Japanese market of the late 1980s and leveraged investment trusts stood out in the US in 1929. These particular excesses have provided a source of euphemism and excuse for those who like to assume that the problem was specific rather than general. Thus the 2000 stock market bubble, which led to the greatest recorded overvalua-tion of the US stock market in general, has its apologists who like to refer to it as the "high tech or dotcom bubble". Central banks therefore need to look at asset prices in a broad way and consider how excesses may be reflected in house and other property prices, as well as in the prices of risky financial assets such as equities and credit sensitive debts. Robert Shiller has also emphasized this. In *Irrational Exuberance,* he wrote in part 5, "A Call to Action": "It is a serious mistake for public figures to acquiesce in the stock market valuations we have seen recently and to remain silent about the implications... The valuation of the stock market is an important national – indeed international – issue."

Economists have sometimes been accused of such attachment to their theories that they take a cavalier attitude to conflicting evidence. Although I have found occasions when this critique has had some measure of justification, I doubt whether economists' attachment to their theories and their response to threats to them are as a rule any worse than those found in other sciences. But it is clearly vital that such excess attachment should be avoided and I will therefore support the arguments set out in this book with a careful study of the data. But in order to prevent the detail that this involves from distracting attention from the central case, I first set out a synopsis in Chapter 2 and then seek to show that each of the key points are supported by evidence.[8]

---

[8] The data sources and other essential help for this book are set out in Appendix 1 Sources and Obligations.

The neglect from which asset value analysis has suffered is reflected in the limited amount of work that has been devoted to the construction of reliable long-term data series for stock markets and, as a result, there are marked weaknesses in the available statistics. For example, share prices are available in many stock markets for over 200 years but, with the exception of Professor Siegel's admirable compilation of US data, I have not been able to find reliable indices dating before the 20th century. Even for data since 1899, it is only as recently as 2002 that the excellent work by Elroy Dimson, Paul Marsh and Mike Staunton[9] has resulted in reliable figures on financial market returns covering a wide range of countries being published. I make extensive use of both these sources and I hope that one benefit from the higher profile that the subject is now beginning to receive will be an improvement in stock market data over long periods. Unfortunately, such statistics are little prized by market participants, with the result that important data series which cover more than the past 20 or even 10 years are often unavailable from internet data providers such as Bloomberg and Reuters. For the study of value, short-term data series are generally useless, because if they revealed regular patterns of mispricing, these would be arbitraged away. Over long periods, however, arbitrage is highly risky and so patterns of mispricing, if not too regular, may be observed and still survive. Only very long-term data are thus capable of providing insights into market behaviour. It is perhaps unkind – but not, I think, unjustified – to ascribe this indifference to data which covers a long period to the sharp reduction in the ability to misuse data by "data mining" which results. As I shall show, particularly when dealing with how not to value the stock market, data mining is a common and egregious fault of "stockbroker economics".

Even when long-term data are available, the nature of statistical evidence provides problems with its testing, as market values become most important and interesting when they are at extreme values. In these circumstances, the probabilities as shown by statistical tests, for example for mean reversion, tend to be less strong than when values are around average. Happily, as more data become available from the work of statistical archeologists and the efflux of time, the statistical evidence should improve.

---

[9] *The Triumph of the Optimists* published by Princeton University Press.

If my claims are correct they will tend to be supported as additional data become available. I hope, however, to persuade readers on the basis of the evidence and arguments set out now. I recognize that the claims I am making are large ones. Although the EMH is largely discredited, an alternative is not readily available and this I aim to supply. However, not only am I seeking to show that asset markets are not perfectly efficient, I aim to show that they can be valued not only in theory, but with a fair degree of accuracy in practice. This ability is not only important for investors, fund managers, and actuaries, but crucially for central bankers. Furthermore, if they take note of asset prices and adjust policy when prices move towards excess, the management of economies will improve and large benefits to our welfare should then be attainable by avoiding a repetition of the problems from which we are currently suffering.

2

Synopsis

In this chapter I set out the key issues which this book addresses and a summary of the arguments I use to support my conclusions. I also refer, at each step, to the chapters in which I provide the supporting evidence for the case that I am making.

The importance of share prices for central banks depends on two separate points. The first is that the stock market responds to changes in interest rates, and the second is that this response is ephemeral. As interest rates affect the stock market, which in turn affects the real economy, this is one way in which the policies of central banks, and in particular of the Federal Reserve, are effective. Their changes in interest rates have these temporary impacts on the market, acting as a transmission mechanism whereby the actions of central bankers affect the real economy. But as the impacts of these changes are ephemeral and stock markets are influenced by other things as well, the effectiveness of this transmission mechanism varies; in certain circumstances it can become useless thus weakening significantly the effectiveness of monetary policy. To demonstrate these qualities it is necessary to show three things. First, that interest rates have no long-term relationship with the level of share markets, which I discuss in Chapter 3; second, that share prices respond temporarily to changes in interest rates, which I show in Chapter 4; and third, explained in Chapter 5, that the level of share prices affects the real economy.

The level that the stock market would have if it were efficiently priced is its fair value.[10] When interest rates change they may stabilize the economy by pushing share prices towards this fair value or destabilize it by pushing them away. But the greater the distance between price and value, the stronger are the forces pulling price back to value. The transmission mechanism provided by the relationship between changes in interest rates and share prices must not therefore be misused because its power diminishes when the stock market moves away from fair value. If share prices are driven too far from their underlying value, the ability of central banks to influence the real economy can become seriously impaired. (Chapter 3 deals with interest rates and the level of stock markets, Chapter 4 with changes in interest rates and changes in share prices and Chapter 5 with the impact of asset prices on household savings.)

It seems improbable that a perfectly efficient stock market would respond in the way it does to changes in short-term interest rates. It would also not be pulled back towards its underlying value if it were simply a mad and irrational casino. It is therefore likely that the stock market is neither perfectly efficient nor totally inefficient, but could be called "moderately", or "imperfectly", or "long-term" efficient. The evidence that this is the case thus supports the relationship between stock markets and interest rates and is in turn consistent with it. Moderately efficient stock markets are not always at fair value, nor completely independent of value, but rotate around it.

The timing of market peaks and troughs is highly uncertain, as are the returns that can be made from holding cash unless investors know in advance that they will shortly be reinvesting their liquidity. This means that it does not normally pay investors to sell overpriced markets and buy underpriced ones. But the likely returns from doing so rise the more markets become misvalued and therefore, as the market diverges from value, the forces pulling it back to value become stronger. This is very different from the idea that the stock market is an irrational casino, moved entirely by the wayward excitements and irrational behaviour of investors. (Chapter 6 describes the hypothesis that markets are moderately efficient or imperfectly efficient and

---

[10] A glossary of this and other terms which may not be familiar to all readers is included in Appendix 2.

shows that this is very different from both the perfectly efficient and casino models.)

Because central banks should therefore be concerned with asset prices, they need to be able to judge how current prices relate to value. I therefore explain how equity markets can be valued and this leads on to a discussion showing why the Efficient Market Hypothesis (EMH) should be discarded in favour of the view that markets are moderately efficient. This view is itself a hypothesis and I therefore both show that it is testable, in sharp contrast to the EMH, and that it is robust under testing. This does not mean that the model should not be open to being discarded if it is shown to fail tests, which I should have considered but omitted to do, and which can be shown to be necessary for its validity. It must also be open to improvement. It may, for example, prove possible to improve the forecasting ability of q and CAPE by adding refinements to their measurement or finding other and better metrics which are even more robust under testing. The claim I am making for the Imperfectly Efficient Hypothesis is not that it is the best model that is possible, but that it is an improvement on what is currently available. (Chapter 7 examines the EMH and Chapter 8 shows the degree to which the Imperfectly Efficient Hypothesis is robust under testing.)

In addition to the valid methods of valuing equities, namely q and CAPE, numerous claims are made about others, which prove on inspection to be without merit. Having already, in Chapter 3, dismissed claims that shares can be valued relative to interest rates, I look in Chapter 9 at two other commonly used but invalid approaches to value. These are the approaches which use either current PEs or trend fitting. The last approach uses only the history of past returns to value the market and, although the trend fitting approach is not valid, past returns can be useful if the data are analyzed in other ways. Serial correlation is the technical term which describes many series in which the past has an impact on the future. If high figures in the past have a tendency to be followed by poor ones and vice versa, the series exhibits negative serial correlation and mathematicians have shown that such series contain within themselves some forecast of their own future. As this negative serial correlation is a characteristic of the real returns from equity markets, it follows that, to some extent at least, an analysis of past returns provides a guide to future returns to a greater degree than would be the case if markets followed a more random pattern. In Chapter 10 I look at a way of using this characteristic, not to value the market directly, but indirectly at least from the resulting forecast of equity returns.[11] This approach has potential for other markets than the US, because unfortunately the data for most stock markets on earnings per share, needed to calculate CAPE, and for net worth adjusted for inflation, needed to calculate q, are poor or nonexistent. It does, however, have limitations and problems which I set out and, while these should become less important over time, I am happier to use another approach, which is set out in Chapter 11. If we have sufficient information we can rank times in the past by their relative subsequent returns. From this we can establish times when the various markets were at fair value. If they subsequently gave average returns up to, say, the end of 2008, it is reasonable to assume that the market in question was fair value at that time. One advantage of this method is that its accuracy can be tested by comparing the results for the US market with those given by q and CAPE, and it is encouraging that the results are very similar.

Recent events have shown that equities are not the only assets whose value should be a matter of concern to central bankers. Land and house prices are clearly important, and economists seem to have been less shy of looking at the difference between house prices and values than they have at share prices and values. The result of greater attention has not yet led to complete agreement, but there is a growing consensus that prices can and have diverged from equilibrium levels and that the equilibria in different countries have different levels and causes. I discuss these issues in Chapter 12.

Both shares and houses represent titles to the ownership of real assets but, as we have recently seen only too clearly, financial assets with only nominal values can also become overpriced and a source of financial instability. This occurs when the level of risk aversion falls to dangerously low levels and the reward to investors that they receive from buying less liquid assets is very low. The level of this reward is important in providing a guide to the level of risk aversion, and is another aspect of asset pricing which central banks need

[11] This approach is set out by Donald Robertson and Stephen Wright, in "Testing for Redundant Predictor Variables" (working paper downloadable from http://www.econ.bbk.ac.uk/faculty/wright).

to watch. As there is no generally agreed term for this reward for sacrificing liquidity and I need to refer to it regularly, I have termed it the "liquidity price". Assets which can be readily realized at short notice without significant sacrifice in terms of price are naturally more valuable than others which have in other respects similar characteristics. The price put on this liquidity varies and it falls as investors become increasingly willing to assume risk. The price of liquidity thus provides a very important general warning signal. Low prices mean low levels of risk aversion and, when investors are insufficiently concerned with the risks they are running, their decisions become increasingly foolish. Low prices for liquidity are often associated with the overpricing of all risky assets, including shares and houses, and changes in the willingness to accept risk can be sudden and thus induce sharp and dramatic changes in the prices of all financial assets (Chapter 13).

The standard and very reasonable convention for calculating returns on equities is to assume that dividend income is reinvested in the stock market. While this is the sensible and even natural response of those who are saving for their retirement, other investors usually behave in a different way since they will often wish to spend their income and some part of their capital gains. The time when investors spend their income or capital gains has an important impact on the return they get from equity portfolios. In Chapter 14 I show how different "the returns on equities" can be from "the returns from equity portfolios". This distinction, so far as I can find, has been ignored in academic papers which deal with the Equity Risk Premium (ERP), which is the difference between the returns that investors expect to receive from equities and those which they expect from less risky assets such as bonds or bank deposits.

It has been argued that this premium has historically been so large that it constitutes a paradox. It has also been claimed that being so large it should have been arbitraged away by leveraging equity portfolios with debt. Both these arguments rest on the implicit and unstated assumption that equity returns are unaffected by income being spent or reinvested. I show that if the market is imperfectly rather than perfectly efficient, this assumption is unjustified both in theory and in practice. If income is spent on consumption, it cannot be reinvested and as the "return on equities" assumes that income is reinvested, it is clear that the "return on equities" should not be used to calculate the equity risk premium when the model under consideration assumes that income will be consumed. The actual return on equity portfolios will differ when income is spent from that which will be earned when income is reinvested and models which ignore this important difference are not properly constructed. A similar issue arises when the returns from leveraged portfolios are being considered. Debt has to be serviced by interest payments, which must be paid by any investor who wishes to leverage an equity portfolio. It follows that the income from the equity portfolio cannot be automatically reinvested, so that the return on a leveraged portfolio of equities will differ from the "return on equities". This becomes extremely important when looking at the likely returns and risks involved in leverage. In Chapter 15 I look at the impact of leveraging equity portfolios either with long-dated or short-term debt. Although there are occasions in the past when this has proved to be advantageous, I show that the results in general have been poor in terms of the returns and the risks being run. This explains why the gap between equity returns and those on short-term deposits and bonds has not been arbitraged away through the investors borrowing money to buy shares.

With the benefit of hindsight it has, of course, been possible to choose times when large profits would have been made from leveraging an equity portfolio. The unusually low level to which long-term interest rates fell in 2008 raised the question of whether it might be possible to choose, with foresight, suitable times to do this. In Chapter 16 I explain how under these extraordinarily favourable conditions the risks of investing in a leveraged portfolio of equities became, in my view, attractive towards the end of 2008. An essential element in this was that the interest payments were so low that their adverse effect was very small and the return on the particular equity portfolio was much closer to the "return on equities" than would have been the case under more normal circumstances.

In Chapter 17 I show that profits have been habitually overstated by US companies and probably by companies in other countries. This is of course important in itself, but it is also crucial for the discussion about intangibles which is the subject of Chapter 18 and which has been the source of more questions than any other from students during our course on stock market value. We can show, via the return to investors and thus independently from any convention regarding the way profits are defined, that profits reported by companies have been over- rather than understated. It follows that they cannot be increased by changing, in aggregate at least, the conventions which are applied to the value of intangibles. This does not mean that the current convention might not be changed with some advantage. For example, a greater value could be ascribed to intangibles, in aggregate, than is done today. But as profits and net worth are over- rather than understated, a compensating reduction will need to be made to the value of tangible assets. If this is not done, profits after tax and net worth would be even more overstated than is currently the case.

There are other important accounting issues, in addition to the habitual overstatement of profits. One of these is the growing use, over the past one or two decades, of marking assets to market values rather than maintaining their value at book cost. This has led to a growing divergence between profits as published by companies and profits as normally defined in the national accounts, which is the subject of Chapter 19. The official data on the aggregate values of nonfinancial company balance sheets are treated differently in the UK and the US. In the latter, compiled by the Federal Reserve, the difference between the aggregate corporate balance sheets that result from the national account data and those that come from companies is adjusted to conform with the latter, while in the UK this is not done. The official data thus appear to show that UK companies have become much more highly leveraged than US ones. I show that this is a misleading representation of the true situation. In general, the change in company accounting has meant that today's balance sheet "apples" should not be compared with the balance sheet "pears" of earlier years. This is, however, regularly done and the resulting misinformation has probably contributed to current financial problems, since it has misled commercial banks, central banks and finance ministries into believing that corporate balance sheets have been less highly leveraged than has in fact been the case. I show that if alternative measures of corporate leverage are used, either by adjusting balance sheet data to national accounting rather than corporate accounting standards or by comparing debt with output, nonfinancial leverage today is at an all-time record level in the US, surpassing even the previous peak of 2002.

The change in accounting practice, and the way the Federal Reserve adjusts the data on company leverage, also has the effect of changing the net worth data on which q is based. In Chapter 20 I conclude that this has had the effect of producing an additional overstatement of current net worth figures, in addition to the long-term one that results from the historic overstatement of profits. Happily, the Federal Reserve publishes data which make it possible to remove this distortion. In broad terms, the US stock market, which in mid-March was rotating around 700 on the S&P 500 index, has fallen back to below fair value for the first time in over 20 years, and is thus cheap again. History shows, however, that it has a high chance of becoming quite a lot cheaper still, illustrating that value is not a good guide to short-term market performance.

If central banks start to be concerned with asset as well as consumer prices they will face practical problems, in addition to the measurement of value. Some comment, rather than a detailed discussion, on these issues seems needed and this is the subject of Chapter 21. Central banks have today only one policy instrument – their ability to change short-term interest rates – with which they can try to influence the economy and try to meet their inflation target. There is a strong case that if they are to be charged with achieving two different objectives, first to maintain a low and stable rate of consumer price inflation and second to prevent serious misevaluations of asset prices, then they will need additional powers. One suggestion that appeals to me is the ability to vary banks' minimum capital ratios, which has been proposed as a way of offsetting the tendency of banks to exaggerate cycles.[12] This pro-cyclical behaviour has been described as the equivalent of lenders of umbrellas wanting their loans back when it starts to rain. In addition to helping to moderate banks' pro-cyclical behaviour, the suggestion has the advantage of providing the sort of additional policy weapon that should make it easier for central banks to manage the economy if they are to enlarge their concerns to cover asset as well as consumer prices.

---

[12] For a description of these proposals, see *The Fundamental Principles of Financial Regulation* by Markus Brunnermeier, Andrew Crocket, Charles Goodhart, Avinash Persaud and Hyun Shin. Geneva Reports on the World Economy 11.

If they had this additional policy weapon, central banks would be in a practical position to respond to asset prices if they become too far divorced from fundamental values, without having to change interest rates when this would seem inappropriate from the viewpoint of consumer inflation. They would then have an alternative policy available and might not have to act in a way which has been called "leaning against the wind".[13] This addition to central banks' armory can only be effective if the impact of interest rate changes on economies does not only come solely via their impact on asset prices. If it does, a successful instrument for depressing asset prices would have the same impact on demand as a change in interest rates. Fortunately, it is likely that interest rates affect economies in other ways and not solely via asset prices.

Central bankers are not the only people who need to respond to asset prices. They are clearly of great importance to investors, fund managers, actuaries, pension trustees and pension consultants. In Chapter 23 I consider the actions that should be taken by these various groups at different levels of asset prices. In particular, I consider whether they should vary their exposure to equities and even, in the unusual circumstances outlined in Chapter 16, be prepared to leverage an equity portfolio.

In Chapter 24 I look at the problem of international imbalances, which are reflected in both current account surpluses and deficits and in domestic savings imbalances. I point out that this is not an alternative explanation to our current troubles, but part of the general disequilibria in which excess liquidity creation in the US, absurd asset prices, and current account imbalances are all related. Finally, in Chapter 25 I seek to summarize the key points I wish to stress. I refer to the fact that when asset prices fall from excessive levels, central banks then lose control of their economies. It is therefore essential that central banks understand how to value assets and respond before they become exorbitant.

---

[13] For example, Sushil Wadhwani, a former member of the Bank of England's Monetary Policy Committee, argues the case for "leaning against the wind" in *Should Monetary Policy Respond to Asset Price Bubbles? Revisiting the Debate.* National Institute Economic Review No. 206, October 2008.

3

Interest Rate Levels and the Stock Market[14]

In Chapter 2 I wrote that changes in interest rates affect changes in share prices, but that there is no evidence of a relationship between the levels of interest rates and the level of share prices. These separate characteristics reveal how central banks influence the real economy and how, when markets become overvalued, changes in interest rates, which are the mechanism for exerting that influence, can become ineffectual. These points are best demonstrated by three separate approaches. The first is to look at the nonexistent relationship between nominal bond yields and PEs. The second is to show that there is no apparent relationship between real interest rates and either PEs or the future return on equities. As variations in rationally expected future returns must be an indication of value, it follows that there also seems to be no long-term relationship between real interest rates and share values. I deal with both these issues in this chapter. The third is to consider the relationship between changes in interest rates, both real and nominal, which have usually moved quite closely together, and changes in share prices, which I do in Chapter 4.

[14] See Appendix 3 "Interest Rates, Profits and Share Prices" for the mathematical background to Chapters 3 and 4.

3.1 Nominal Bond Yields and PEs

As conventional bonds are a title to interest and capital payments which are fixed in nominal terms, while equities are a title to the ownership of real assets, it is inherently improbable that there should be any connection between bond yields and PEs. There have, however, been so many claims to the contrary that it is necessary to show that they are without any practical as well as any theoretical justification. The usual claim is that there is a stable relationship between bond yields and average earnings yields[15] or, less usually, dividend yields. This is often designated as the Fed Model. This seems to be an unjustified aspersion on the Federal Reserve, which has never endorsed its use, though it might be criticized in not having pointed out that the US central bank had no connection with the model.

The popularity of the Fed Model is due to the relationship which ruled between 1981 and 1997 and which I illustrate in Chart 1. That it was accidental is shown by looking at the same relationships over other time periods; for example in Chart 2 I show how

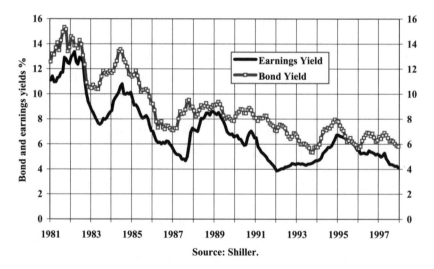

Chart 1. US Bond and Earnings Yields 1981–1997.
All charts in this book are reproduced in colour. See plate sections at page 86 and 182.

[15] Earnings yields are another way, in addition to PEs, of expressing the relationship between share prices and earnings per share. Earnings yields are equal to 100/PEs.

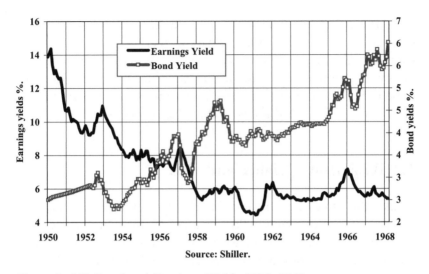

Chart 2. US Bond and Earnings Yields 1950–1968.

the exact opposite relationship held from 1950 to 1968. If long-term data are used, then it is clear that there is no correlation whatever between nominal bond yields and either dividend or earnings yields.[16]

Theoretical justification for the Fed Model has been claimed on the grounds that changes in interest rates alter the value of future streams of income because the rate at which the income in years to come should be discounted ought to change with the bond yield. There are, however, numerous defects with this claim. One is that it assumes that the future stream of income to be expected from equities will not vary with the change in the nominal bond yield. As equities represent titles to the ownership of real assets, this assumption is clearly unjustified. Many changes in bond yields, particularly large ones, reflect changes in expectations about future inflation and, if inflation does change, then the nominal return from real assets, and thus to equities, will also change.

The Fed Model is nonsense in practice as well as in theory and simply represents a triumph of what is known as data mining. This

---

[16] Using data from January 1871 to December 2008, the correlation coefficient between bond yields and dividend yields is −0.19, and between bond yields and earnings yields is +0.13, i.e. there is no relationship.

is the use of carefully selected data to support a story which has no
real justification. It has been remarked that "If data are tortured
hard enough, they will always confess".[17] When seeking to test a
theory it is important to use all the available data rather than just
some of it. When this is not done, it often provides a useful warning
that data may be being mined rather than properly employed.

3.2 Real Bond Yields and PEs

Unlike the nonexistent relationship between nominal bond yields
and the PEs or dividend yields on equities, for which there is no
theoretical justification, the idea that there should be some relationship between equities and real interest rates and bond yields is at
least reasonable on a priori grounds. Investors have a choice between
holding equities or bonds, and if the prospective return on bonds
is relatively high or low, it is reasonable to assume that this will be
reflected in prospective returns on equities, as investors will be
inclined to sell the asset with the lower prospective return in favour
of the other. It is common to find references in the financial press
and academic papers to the Equity Risk Premium (ERP), which is
the additional return which investors expect from investing in equities compared with the return that they expect from investment in
cash or bonds. Almost invariably the comments which accompany
such references involve the assumption, usually implicit rather than
explicit, that equity returns are not independent of real bond yields,
i.e. that even if the ERP varies, it needs to be considered when
estimating probable equity returns.

Real returns on bonds and equities are calculated on the basis of
their total returns, including both income and capital and adjusting
for inflation, and it is relatively easy to test whether the difference
between them has been stable in the past. Chart 3 compares the difference between the real returns on equities and real bonds over
15-year periods, beginning in 1801 for the US and 1899 for the UK.
The chart shows that the ERP, defined in terms of actual results, has
not been stable nor does it show any clear indication of rotating
around some stable long-term average (i.e. mean reverting).

---

[17] The comment is generally credited to Nobel Laureate, Ronald Coase.

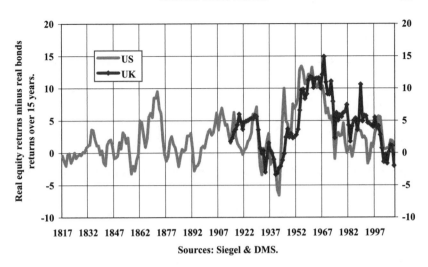

Chart 3. UK & US Real Equity Minus Real Bond Returns.

Table 1. Real Returns on UK Long Bonds and Inflation.

Period	Real return to investors	Inflation
1840–2007	1.80	2.51
1840–1900	3.99	−0.50
1900–2007	1.00	3.65

If we assume that investors often make errors but that such errors should cancel out over time, then the instability of ERP shown by hindsight would indicate that the prospective ERP is also unstable. But it looks as if investors have been very bad at forecasting future inflation and that these past errors have not cancelled out, or at least that it has required up to 200 years for them to do so.

This is illustrated in Table 1 for the UK and Table 2 for the US. In both countries the periods which gave the best real return on bonds have been those when inflation was particularly low and returns have varied with inflation. If the rate of inflation had been expected, this should have been reflected in the bond yields, and the data therefore indicate strongly that fluctuations in inflation have been largely unanticipated.

Table 2. Real Returns on US Long Bonds and Inflation.

Period	Real return to investors	Inflation
1802–2007	3.32	1.53
1802–1900	5.24	0.01
1900–2007	1.95	3.12

Table 3. Correlation Coefficients Between Bond Returns and Inflation for UK.

Period	Current yield minus current inflation	Real return to investors
1840–2007	−0.61	−0.51
1840–1900	−0.99	−0.98
1900–2007	−0.44	−0.38

Table 4. Correlation Coefficients Between Bond Returns and Inflation for US.

Period	Current yield minus current inflation	Real return to investors
1802–2007	−0.95	−0.63
1802–1900	−0.99	−0.92
1900–2007	−0.87	−0.28

This interpretation is reinforced by the data shown in Tables 3 and 4. Investors will naturally seek compensation, in the form of higher nominal yields, if they expect inflation in the future. The correlations between the current yields on bonds and inflation, shown in the second columns of the tables, were much more negative during the 19th century, in both the UK and US, than in the 20th century. This suggests that investors in the 19th century did not expect the current level of inflation to be reflected in future years. This expectation was fully justified as 19th-century inflation was highly volatile in the short term but stable at around zero over time. As a result the correlation between inflation and poor returns

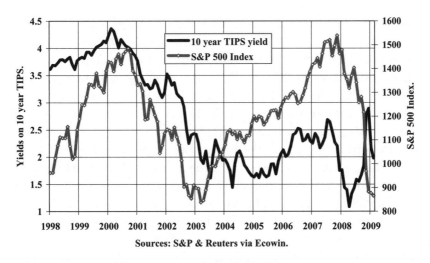

Sources: S&P & Reuters via Ecowin.

Chart 4. US Yields on TIPS and the S&P 500.

to bond holders over one year was particularly strong during the 19th century.[18]

We can readily test whether the ERP has been stable in practice (ex-post) and, as Chart 3 shows, it has not. But, given investors' poor record at forecasting real bond returns, this does not, however, necessarily mean that the expected ERP (ex-ante) has not been stable.

The introduction of government bonds in which the principal and interest are linked to the rate of inflation should help provide useful information about the expected ERP. These bonds, which are known as Index-linked in the UK and Treasury Inflation Protected (TIPS) in the US, are only a relatively recent innovation. We only have around 20 years of data for them, but this is long enough for some tentative conclusions to be drawn from the variations in their yields. Chart 4 shows the way in which the yield

[18] The data sources used in Chart 3 are from Siegel for the US from 1801 to 1997, updated from the S&P 500 Index for nominal equity returns, Federal Reserve for bonds and adjusted for inflation using the BLS data on consumer prices. For the UK the data are from DMS from 1899 to 2007 updated for 2008 using the FT All Share Index for equities, and Reuters, via Ecowin, for long bond returns; both updates adjust for inflation using the ONS data on the retail price index. The data in Tables 1, 2, 3 and 4 are the same for the US, but for the UK I have used bond returns and inflation data from the US NBER's website from 1840 to 2000, updated from the Reuters and ONS data. I have used different data sources for the UK because the DMS data are not available before 1899.

on TIPS has moved and compares these changes with those that
have taken place in the stock market. From 1998 to 2000 the
returns on TIPS rose at the same time as the stock market; they
then both fell from 2000 to 2003 and then again both rose from
2003 to 2008. In the US, TIPS have been in issue since 1997. At
the peak of the stock market in 2000 they gave a real return of 4%
p.a. and this has since fallen to under 2%.

Because TIPS are, as the name implies, protected against inflation, these changes indicate that if the expected ERP is stable, then
returns to investors in the stock market were expected to rise as
the market rose and to fall as the stock market fell. While this will
present no surprise to those who do not expect short-term changes
in the stock market to be driven by rational expectations, it is only
with considerable difficulty that it can be seen to be consistent with
the view that the stock market is perfectly efficient and that expectations for future stock market returns vary in a rational way. This
makes it testing, and perhaps impossible, to construct a convincing
model in which the ERP, defined in terms of expectations, and the
return on equities are both stable and that they move together.

The case for the expected long-term return on bonds being
stable is nonetheless quite good. David Miles in his analysis of long-
term UK bond rates concluded that "Real interest rates from year
to year are rather volatile, but there has been a strong tendency for
them to return to a long run average which is close to 3%".[19] This
conclusion was derived from data from 1700 to 1998, and required
some assumption about the variations in inflation that investors
had expected. The one David Miles used was to take "...a five year
moving average of inflation as a simple, but probably quite reasonable, measure of what people would have expected the average rate
of future inflation to be". Using a different approach, based on the
returns which were achieved when expectations appeared to match
outturns, Stephen Wright has shown that the expected real return
from government bonds in the US has been around 4% p.a.[20] The
gap between these two figures is quite large and to some extent
probably reflects the difference in the way that inflationary

---

[19] *Interest Rates from the 17th to the 21st Century* by Professor David Miles published
by Merrill Lynch, 8 June 1998.
[20] See Appendix 6 for details.

expectations have been estimated. To some extent, however, it may represent the difference between the UK, which was a capital exporting nation over much of the period being considered, and the US, which was a capital importing one. An incentive is needed to persuade capital to flow from an exporter to an importer, as the exporter will consider that he has greater risks if he invests in assets denominated in a foreign currency. This incentive will be provided by the returns on bonds in the importing nation being higher than on those of the capital exporter.

Even if we accept that the expected long-term return on bonds and equities have both been stable, this does not necessarily imply that there have been variations in these expectations nor, if there have been, that they have moved together. There are three basic possibilities:

1. That expected long-term returns are absolutely stable and that the actual variations simply reflect the poor forecasting of investors. This is not compatible with the large fluctuations in the returns on TIPS shown in Chart 4.
2. That expected returns revolve around these long-term stable averages and that they move together, so that when expected returns are high for bonds they are also high for equities.
3. That expected returns revolve around these long-term stable averages but that they move independently for bonds and equities, so that high or low expectations for bond returns have no implications for equity returns and vice versa.

Stephen Wright's work shows that when expectations of inflation have proved to be accurate, the return on US bonds has averaged around 4% but, as Table 5 shows, actual returns during these periods have varied between 2.27% and 5.67%. Table 5 also shows, however, that when these periods have produced below average returns on bonds, they have been more often associated with above than below average returns on equities. These differences could be the result of bad forecasting of equity returns, and it therefore remains possible that expected returns on bonds and equities do fluctuate together around their averages, but the data are evidence against such a relationship.

Of the three possibilities outlined above, 3. is therefore the most likely. If there are variations in the expected real returns on both bonds and equities, then such variations move independently of

Table 5. Real Returns % p.a. on US Bonds and Equities, During Periods when the Error in Forecasting Inflation was Minimal.

From	To	Bond returns	Equity returns	Mean expectational error
1801	1818	5.67	5.93	−0.0688
1824	1861	4.39	5.29	0.0028
1887	1913	2.74	5.96	0.0007
1916	1940	4.01	4.77	−0.0548
1951	1955	2.27	20.54	−0.1836
1976	1998	4.80	10.48	0.0411

each other and there is no connection between them. As illustrated in Chart 4, the experience of the last 20 years shows that if the expected ERP is stable, then expectations of equity returns seem to rise when the stock market has risen and fall when it has fallen. But as the long-term real return on equities is stable, rational expectations should change in the opposite manner with rising markets leading to falls in expected returns.

The evidence is clear that the ex-post ERP has not been stable. The expected ERP could be, but on the limited evidence available it seems more likely that it isn't.

The historical independence of real bond and equity returns has been great but not complete. This is because inflation has had a negative impact on real equity returns as well as real bond ones and this marginally complicates the issue. But as the impact of inflation on real equity returns has been far less than on real bond returns, this leaves the historic independence of the two returns largely unaffected. Furthermore, as inflation has been largely unanticipated, as Tables 1 to 4 show, it also leaves the probable independence of anticipated returns unaffected.

The way that unanticipated inflation affects real bond returns is straightforward. Nominal bond yields when issued reflect the current anticipated rate of inflation and the interest payments do not change during the life of the bond. If inflation is higher than expected, the real returns will then be lower. The reason why unanticipated inflation has any impact, even a relatively small one, on equity returns is more complicated. It is probably caused by the interaction between inflation and profit margins. As I will show in more detail in

Chapter 8, profit margins are strongly mean reverting, but they appear nonetheless to have some negative shorter-term correlation with inflation.[21] Thus, if inflation is low, profit margins will benefit, for a short time at least. This is probably the result of the way that inflationary expectations respond to inflation. If inflation falls, it is common for inflationary expectations to fall with it. If they do, the economy is capable of operating for a time at a higher level of output, relative to the normal limits imposed by the availability of labour and capital, without causing inflation to pick up. If central banks are targeting a stable level of consumer price inflation, they will naturally respond to this by setting lower interest rates than would otherwise be likely as these are consistent with the higher level of output. As long as inflationary expectations keep falling, this will allow the economy to operate at a higher level of capacity utilization than was previously compatible with stable inflation. As profit margins move with capacity utilization, falls in inflation, accompanied as they are likely to be by falls in inflationary expectations, provide a boost to profits and rises in inflation have a negative impact. Expectations for inflation cannot, of course, fall indefinitely and over time the division of output between returns to labour and returns to capital will revert to their longer-term stable mean.

I have shown in this chapter that in practice the gaps between both real and nominal returns on bonds and equities have been very unstable. As there is no reason to expect this to change, it is not sensible to try to estimate the prospective returns on equities, and thus their value, from the current returns on bonds, either nominal or real. This does not necessarily mean that the ERP, defined as the difference between expected returns on bonds and equities, is not stable, but the limited evidence we have is that it is not.

---

[21] See *Inflation Dynamics and the Labour Share in the UK* by Nicoletta Batini, Brian Jackson and Stephen Nickell, Bank of England External MPC Paper No. 2.

4

Interest Rate Changes and Share Price Changes

Chapter 3 showed that neither the level of nominal nor real interest rates seems to have any relationship with the level of share prices. This in any event seems likely provided that financial markets are not assumed to be perfectly efficient. When economies are weak, central banks respond by lowering interest rates, but investors have low expectations and stock markets tend to be depressed, with the result that their prospective returns are particularly good, with the 1930s providing an outstanding example of this. If this were the only consideration, it would mean that returns on equities and bonds would be negatively rather than positively correlated, as low interest rates mean poor bond returns and low stock markets give high ones. But there are other factors involved, one of which is that the stock market as well as the bond market usually responds, if only temporarily, to changes in short-term interest rates.

While there is no long-run relationship between interest rates and the level of share prices, this does not mean that changes in interest rates cannot influence changes in the stock market. There could be a significant short-term impact which decayed over time.[22] Checking this is not, however, entirely straightforward. As an example of how difficult this might be to unravel, it could be that falls in interest rates would set off a rise in the stock market six months later, which would then fall away again over the next six months. In these circumstances there would be an important relationship between interest rate and share prices changes, but no apparent one if the changes are measured over one year.

To examine the possibilities we need to look at the relationships between interest rates, profits, and share prices and try to isolate the impact of changes in profits from the impact of changes in interest rates. Profits and interest rates tend to move together, as both respond to economic strength and weakness.[23] If, therefore, we look independently at the separate impact of profit and interest rate changes on share prices, we might find that a relationship which appears to exist between interest rates and share prices is really due to a change in profits. It is therefore necessary to examine these relationships simultaneously rather than separately or on a bilateral basis. This requires the use of multiple regression analysis, specifically using so-called Vector Autoregressive (VAR) models.[24]

As the aim is to see whether it is likely that there is some relationship between changes in interest rates and share prices, even if these relationships tend to change over time, our first step is to look at the likelihood that changes in interest rates affect changes in share prices without seeking to gauge whether such effects are positive or negative. The results that we get from this exercise are illustrated in Chart 5, on which the vertical y-axis shows the probability of interest rates having an effect with 0 indicating none and 1 indicating certainty, at least in the statistical sense. The chart shows that changes in interest rates are very likely to be associated with changes

---

[22] For example, *An International Analysis of Earnings, Stock Prices and Bond Yields*, ECB Working Paper 515, by Alain Durré and Pierre Giot (2005), concludes that while there is no relationship between bond yields and the level of the stock market, changes in interest rates are related to changes in share prices. This ECB paper thus supports the conclusions set out here, which use, inter alia, data over a longer time period.

[23] The correlation coefficient is 0.40.

[24] The details and equations of this analysis are set out in Appendix 3.

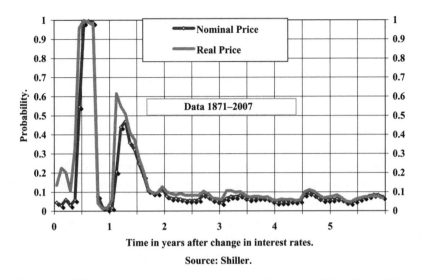

Chart 5. US Probability that Interest Rate Changes Affect Share Price Changes.

in share prices with the impact coming 6–9 months after the change in interest rates. However, after 18 months there is a very low likelihood that changes in interest rates have any impact on share prices.

Having established the probability that interest rate and share price changes are related, the next step is to establish the form that the relationship takes; i.e. conditional on interest rates affecting share prices, what is the probability that changes in interest rates and share prices move in opposite directions? As might be expected (see Appendix A3.2), there is a high conditional probability that the short-term impact of falls in short-term interest rates is helpful to the stock market and rises tend to be inimical. After nine months the impact becomes less certain but remains highly probable. It seems, therefore, reasonable to expect that changes in interest rates, assuming no other offsetting changes, will have a positive impact on the stock market within 6–9 months after they occur. The high (conditional) probability that falling interest rates help to push up share prices in fact extends over several years, but this is of no significance looking out beyond 18 months, as Chart 5 shows that the impact of interest rate changes either to push up or lower share prices is very limited over longer horizons.[25] That is, over longer horizons the (joint) probability that interest rates affect share prices, and that this effect is helpful to share prices, is low.

As interest rates affect short-term changes in share prices, but their levels are not associated, it is clear that other factors must be the dominant influences on share prices over the longer term. I will show later that the key influence is "value" around which prices rotate.

The fact that short-term changes in interest rates and share prices are associated is very important as it provides a transmission mechanism through which monetary policy affects the real economy. But it becomes even more important, as I will show in Chapter 5, when this short-term impact of interest rates on asset prices is, as I showed in Chapter 3, an ephemeral one without any long-term significance.

[25] The data for interest rates, share prices and inflation used in Chart 5 are from Shiller. They have not been updated for 2008 data which became available after the calculations were made but which are unlikely to affect the conclusions.

5

Household Savings and the Stock Market

I have shown that there is strong evidence that changes in interest rates affect the stock market, but that the level of interest rates is not related to future equity returns and thus to the value of the equity market. I will now seek to show that the stock market has an important impact on the real economy, so that these features provide central banks with a powerful influence on the economy, but one that needs to be used with care. The impact of changes in interest rates on the stock market will decline if the market becomes seriously overvalued as there will then be a strong force pulling the market back to fair value and the more overvalued the market becomes, the stronger this force will be. At a certain point this will dominate over interest rate changes and the stock market will tend to fall despite any declines in interest rates, thus weakening the impact of monetary policy. The evidence of history is that this is a practical, as well as a theoretical, possibility. We have one example with us today, Japan's economy after its stock market fell from 1990 onwards and that of the US after the post-1929 collapse is another.

The savings of the household sector may be usefully divided into two parts: those which come from pension savings, either from defined contribution or defined benefit plans or from personal pension schemes, and the balance from other sources, which I name "discretionary" savings (though there is a contracted element also

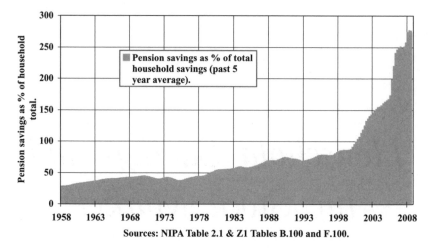

Sources: NIPA Table 2.1 & Z1 Tables B.100 and F.100.

Chart 6. US Pension Savings as % of Total Household Savings.

in these, notably through insurance schemes). Chart 6 illustrates the importance of making the distinction between the two types of savings, because their relative importance has changed so much in recent years. Whereas pensions contributed less than one-third of the total in the 1950s, in the 21st century they have become the dominant factor.[26]

Chart 7 shows that pension savings tend to rise and fall with the stock market.[27] I do this by comparing the proportion of household disposable income which is saved via pension funds with a ratio of the value of US equities, as shown by the S&P 500 index and disposable incomes.[28] Pension funds are heavily invested in

---

[26] Payments by corporations or government to pension funds are included in household savings. The change in pension reserves is shown in Z1 Table F.100 and household savings in NIPA Table 2.1. The former is shown in Chart 7 as a percentage of the latter, using a 5-year average to smooth the swings from year to year which have been marked at times.

[27] The correlation coefficient between the stock market and pension savings over 12 months, using the quarterly data available since 1952, has been 0.72. It rises to 0.73 if the stock market is related to pension savings two years later, but then falls away. Twelve month averages are used because pension data are only available without seasonal adjustment.

[28] Employee contributions to pension funds are included in disposable income, in Lines 7 and 8 of NIPA Table 2.1.

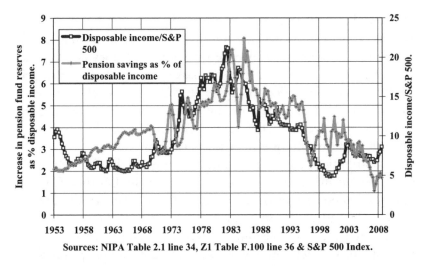

Chart 7. US Pension Savings and the Stock Market.

equities, and the proportion has risen in the post-war period from 6% of pension liabilities in 1953 to 66% in 2008.[29] When share prices rise faster than disposable incomes, so does stock market wealth owned both directly and via pension funds. As the typical reason for savings is to have enough wealth to provide a comfortable income in retirement, contribution to individual pension accounts will naturally tend to fall when the stock market is strong and a similar decline in pension fund contributions by employers occurs when actuaries and pension consultants judge that the rise in pension assets makes reductions appropriate. It is not surprising that weak stock markets are associated with rising pension contributions and vice versa.

I will show later that sustained periods of good equity returns are followed by poor ones. Savers should be less responsive than they are to the fluctuations in share prices since after a period of high returns the apparent rise in wealth is likely to dissipate and

[29] Z1 tables L.118, L.199 and L.120 show the equity holdings and total liabilities of private, state and local government and Federal government pension funds. L.117 shows the data for insurance companies, some 50% of whose liabilities are represented by pension reserves. No data are available on the attribution of equities in L.117 to pensions or life insurance reserves. If life insurance and pension tables are combined, the ratio of equities to pension reserves rises from 4% to 55%.

future savings will receive poor returns in line with low real equity returns. If allowance is made for this, the level of savings needed to produce a satisfactory income on retirement does not fluctuate anything like as much as the stock market. It is perhaps not surprising that individuals do not generally have the level of financial expertise needed to adjust for this. It is, however, disturbing that actuaries and pension consultants seem to have shown a weak understanding of this aspect of financial economics.

Contributions to pension funds were generally reduced as the stock market moved to its peak in 2000. In the US they fell from 5.43% of disposable income in Q3 1997 to 2.26% in Q3 2000, a fall of 58%. With the subsequent fall in the stock market, many pension schemes have become underfunded and this has increased the risks that beneficiaries will not receive their full pensions. In the UK, actual losses have been sustained and a system of insurance, which already existed in the US, has been introduced. I have personal experience of the ignorance of financial economics shown by pension consultants. To give one example, in 1999 I was Chairman of a UK company with a substantial pension fund, which had the majority of its assets invested in equities. As the stock market was moving to ludicrous levels, the board of directors agreed that we should recommend to the trustees that they sell the equity holdings and thereby reduce the risk to the fund. Although this was in time done, resulting in a great benefit to the fund, action was delayed and the benefits somewhat reduced by the opposition of our consultants. They argued that if we made such a change in our investment policy we would need to increase the pension contributions, because the returns which we would get in the future would be lower than if we remained in equities. Their advice was bad; not only in theory, but in practice as events have shown, as today the stock market is still well below the level at which we sold. It may be, therefore, that if actuaries and pension consultants read this book or, by some other route, become better trained in financial economics, household savings would become less sensitive to the level of the stock market.

Economists have, I think, tended to underestimate the influence of the stock market on household savings. As far as I know, other economists have looked at savings in total, rather than breaking the sources down between pension and other savings, and they have looked at the relationship over the post–World War II period as a whole, thereby failing to make allowance for the much greater importance of pensions savings towards the end of the 20th century. Large recent revisions to the data have also resulted in a rise in the importance of pension savings and in the sensitivity of these savings to changes in the stock market.[30]

If pension consultants made due allowance for the negative serial correlation of real equity returns then pension contributions would be more stable than they have been, because the value of the existing investments would rise as prospective returns fall and the two changes would largely compensate for one another. They tend, however, to be appointed by the sponsors of the pension funds, who naturally welcome the idea that pension contributions should be cut if the fund appears to have a surplus over its liabilities. This unfortunately creates conflicts of interest. If pension consultants become better educated in financial economics, or their judgements become less distorted by conflicts of interest, the ability of central banks to influence demand by variations in interest rates would probably be less than it is. This would have the bizarre effect of making the economy less responsive to monetary policy than it has been.

Equities are not the only asset which influences household savings. Individuals respond to changes in their apparent wealth, of which houses are a large component. During the post-war period, changes in the value of house property have been much less volatile than those of equities.[31] Some studies have suggested that house prices are the more influential of the two, and while the correlation between house prices and "discretionary" savings is even stronger than the correlation between pension savings and share prices,[32] the greater volatility of the stock market and, in recent years, the dominant role of pension savings make this far from certain. Both share and house prices are very important and when they move in the

[30] The changes were particularly large in the Flow of Funds of the United States (Z1) for Q3 2008, published in December 2008.
[31] The standard deviation of log changes in the value of household equities from 1952 to Q3 2008 was 6.2 times that of log changes in house property values.
[32] The correlation coefficient between changes in "discretionary" savings and the value of house property is 0.843.

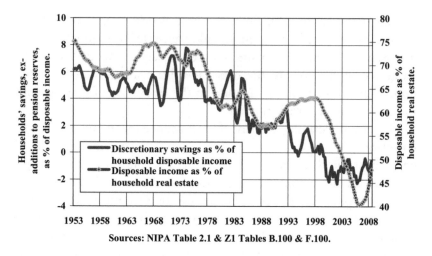

Sources: NIPA Table 2.1 & Z1 Tables B.100 & F.100.

Chart 8. US Household "Discretionary Savings" and the Value of House Property.

same direction they reinforce each other's impact on household savings.

The importance of house prices is illustrated in Chart 8 which shows that household savings, excluding those made via pension funds, have moved in line with the value of house property, comparing both with disposable income. Changes in household savings have a marked impact on consumption. From the peak of 12.5% of disposable income, household savings fell to less than 1% in 2007 and this boosted consumption by around 7% of GDP. Changes in asset prices which, as the data show, have had a major impact on savings have therefore been a very important influence on total demand and since share prices respond, at least temporarily, to changes in interest rates, this provides an important way in which the Federal Reserve has been able to stimulate or depress demand by cutting or raising interest rates.

Interest rates have a strong influence on house prices, with the availability of credit as well as its cost being very important. The boom in house prices which peaked in 2007 was due as much to an easing of credit conditions as to the low level of interest rates. Instead of only lending, say, 70% of the appraised value of a house, banks were prepared to lend up to 100% and there were similar reductions in other requirements, such as the income of the borrower.

The short-term risk-free rate of interest, as represented by the assets which have no risk of default in nominal terms, such as Treasury bills, is controlled by the Federal Reserve and other central banks. But the availability and cost of credit to private sector borrowers, such as households and companies, are in many ways even more important. Credit conditions can vary a lot between one period and another, even if risk-free interest rates are the same, and the price and availability of credit to the private sector, as well as share and house prices, have an important influence on savings. Although I have discussed household savings in terms of its average ratio to income, this represents a wide spread of behaviour between those who save a lot and those who spend more than their income. When credit conditions tighten, as they have today, the second group find it impossible to borrow with the same ease as before, or even at all, and as the high savers have no incentive to save less, a tightening of credit has the effect of pushing up the savings rate.

Credit conditions can be tightened by central banks increasing interest rates, but we are currently experiencing a situation in which it is the actions of commercial banks and other lenders which are causing the credit crunch. Even if central banks are not powerless in these conditions, their ability to control the economy is massively reduced. It is relatively rare for credit to be tightened by the actions of commercial rather than central banks, and current conditions resemble those of the US in 1930 and Japan in 1990 rather than the periodic squeezes that have regularly resulted from rises in short-term risk-free interest rates. Even the very high rates of up to 14% which occurred under Paul Volker's Chairmanship of the Federal Reserve did not produce a credit crunch as tough as today's. As these conditions lead to a very weak economy over which central banks have limited influence, they should be avoided.

Falling share and house prices are one aspect of this, as they undermine the security against which many bank loans have been extended, and the increased losses that banks suffer as a result make them cautious of extending new loans. Another major cause of bank losses, which in turn leads to credit reductions, comes from a fall in the value of interest-bearing assets, such as loans and fixed interest securities. These vary in price, not only with concerns about the risk that the borrowers will default, but with the rewards that lenders demand for holding less liquid assets. This reward for a loss of liquidity has varied greatly in recent years, from very low levels a year or two ago to very high ones today. When a sharp rise occurs, the value of many assets held in banks' balance sheets falls to levels well below their book value. When this happens, banks have to rein in their lending as they risk having their capital ratios fall below the requirements of bank regulators, and in the prevailing climate of uncertainty they will usually wish for a larger than usual margin of safety between their preferred capital ratios and those actually required by the regulators. This is particularly true today, when it is clear that the capital ratios currently required by regulation have been too low and will need to be raised in the future.

The three most important asset prices, whose price changes can have a dramatic impact on credit conditions, are shares, houses and the "price of liquidity", which varies with the reward that lenders require when they purchase assets of limited liquidity. It is therefore these prices which central banks need to watch closely and which they need to be able to value, lest they rise too much. I shall therefore be concentrating on these three asset prices later when I consider how they can be valued.

6

A Moderately Rather than a Perfectly Efficient Market

In Chapter 4, I remarked that while there was a reasonable a priori case for the level of real, though not nominal, interest rates to be related to future share returns, no such relationship actually appears to exist. This is important evidence about the way that financial markets work and when models are constructed to explain their behaviour they must be consistent with the lack of any observed relationship between interest rates, either real or nominal, and the returns on equities.

There are a number of possible models that can be constructed to explain the way that returns from the stock market vary over time but, as there are only two variables which affect these returns, the models fall within a limited range. (At least until the factors that can influence those variables are introduced to complicate matters.) Companies can finance themselves in one of two ways: either by debt, such as loans from banks and long-term bonds, or by the equity capital owned by shareholders. The total value of companies' capital, less their debt, is thus their equity, which is also known as net worth. The returns to investors who buy the market and then sell a few years later will be determined by the return made on the equity capital of companies and by variations in the ratio between share prices and companies' equity capital. If, for example, the stock market were priced, both at the time of investment and at the time of sale, at a level equal to net worth, then the return that the shareholders would receive would be equal to the return that the companies made on their net worth. Thus it would not matter whether this return was paid out to shareholders as dividends, used to buyback part of the share capital, or invested by the companies in expanding their business.

If, however, the stock market valued companies at the beginning of the period at net worth but at the end at, say, 20% more than net worth, then the return to investors would be the return on net worth plus an additional return due to the rise in the price of shares relative to the net worth of the companies.

Returns to investors are determined solely by these two variables, which are the return on corporate net worth and on the ratio between the value that the stock market puts on corporate net worth at any time and its underlying value. As a result, the range of possible models which account for the return to investors is limited and falls between two extremes, which I shall call Model A and Model B. With Model A, returns vary solely because the returns on corporate equity vary, while share prices always remain equal to corporate net worth. At the other extreme, Model B, variations in the returns depend solely on variations in share prices with the return on corporate equity being stable. If the stock market was truly efficient and expectations were, on average, soundly based and thus justified by results, then Model A would be a good description of the market. Returns to investors would vary with returns on corporate net worth and it might then be reasonable to expect these to fluctuate with real interest rates. It is this implied model that appears to underlie the common expectation that the ERP is stable and that it should therefore be possible to value the stock market by reference to real interest rates.

We can test how well Model A does as a description of the stock market by comparing the returns made by companies to those made by shareholders. If shares were always valued at the net worth of companies, these returns would be the same. As the returns to both companies and shareholders vary quite a lot from year to year, these short-term variations can hide the underlying situation. To

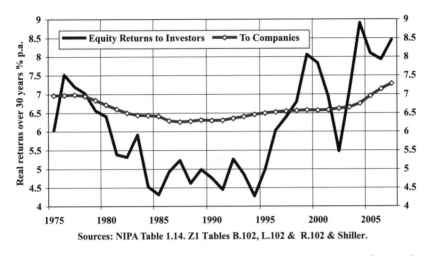

Sources: NIPA Table 1.14. Z1 Tables B.102, L.102 & R.102 & Shiller.

Chart 9. 30 Year Real Returns to Shareholders and on (Nonfinancial) Corporate Net Worth.

avoid this, in Chart 9 I show the returns on corporate equity over 30-year periods up to the year shown on the x-axis of the chart, with the returns that investors calculated in the same way.[33]

It is immediately clear from Chart 9 that the returns to investors and to companies have been very different, even when measured over 30 years. It is therefore clear that Model A is not a good description of the stock market's behaviour. If it had been even a moderately good description, the equity returns to investors would have been much closer to those made by companies and would have been much more stable than they have been.[34]

---

[33] The data used here are from the Flow of Funds Accounts and these are only available for the post-war period. Thus the chart starts in the 1970s when 30-year data first become available.

[34] Returns on US corporate equity are derived from the NIPA and Flow of Funds data, and are only available for nonfinancials and from 1945 onwards. I have adjusted the corporate returns for the overvaluation of net worth, which I discuss more fully in Chapter 16. The adjustment being consistent for all years leaves the stability unaffected. The chart shows domestic nonfinancial corporate profits after tax, including the inventory and capital consumption adjustments (NIPA Table 1.14 line 29) as a percentage of domestic net worth, which is calculated by deducting from net worth (Z1 Table B.102 line 32) the amounts attributable to US investment abroad (Z1 Table L.102 line 17) and the accumulated value of statistical discontinuities (Z1 Table R.102 line 20).

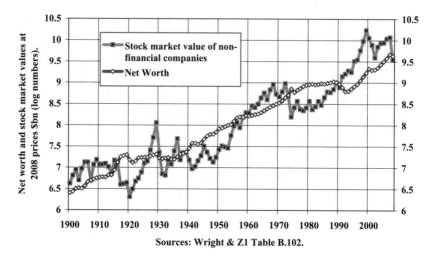

Sources: Wright & Z1 Table B.102.

Chart 10. US Nonfinancial Companies Net Worth and Market Value at Constant Prices.

We have long-term data for the net worth of nonfinancial companies,[35] and there are strong grounds for expecting that return to be stable. This is not only because of the stability shown in the relatively recent data (Chart 9) but because, as I will show later, the long-term return to shareholders has been stable as has, over the very long term, the value of the stock market relative to corporate net worth. If this assumption is correct then a "Model A" stock market would have shown very stable returns over 30-year periods as corporate net worth has grown at very stable rates since 1900 (Chart 10), particularly when compared with the fluctuations in the stock market value of nonfinancial companies.

While Chart 10 shows that corporate net worth has grown at a relatively stable rate, the return to investors (Chart 11) has been far from stable even when measured over 30 years. However, the returns appear to move around a stable average, indicating that very long-term returns measured over, say, 100 years will have been stable. It is therefore clear that the stock market's behaviour is incompatible

[35] Stephen Wright has assembled pre-1947 data from a variety of sources and the Z1 data are available from there on. See "Measures of Stock Market Value for the US Nonfinancial Corporate Sector" published in the *Review of Income and Wealth,* December 2004.

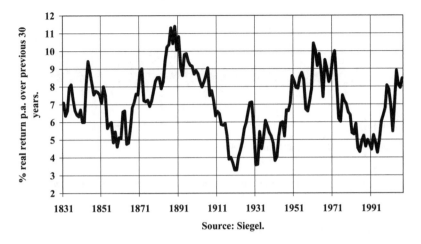

Source: Siegel.

Chart 11. US Real Equity Returns over Previous 30 Years 1831–2007.

with the assumptions underlying Model A, at least if we are looking to describe that behaviour over less than 100-year periods.

At the other extreme from Model A is Model B, in which variations in returns to shareholders are determined solely by fluctuations in share prices, as the return on corporate net worth does not change from year to year. Model B fits the data much better than Model A, but is far from a perfect description. Returns to shareholders over the very long term are stable, as can be seen from Chart 11, in which the 30-year returns rotate around a stable average, and in Chart 12, where the same phenomenon is seen for annual returns. It appears, therefore, that they are subject to a force which brings them back over the very long term. While share prices are seldom at the level they would be if the market was perfectly efficient, they rotate around that level.

It appears from the evidence that I have assembled so far that neither Model A nor Model B provides the best possible description of the stock market, but there lies something somewhere between the two, though closer to Model B over periods of 30 years or more. The model, which seems best to describe stock market real returns, is one in which a distinction is made between short-term and longer-term returns. In the short term, returns are mainly determined by fluctuations in the level of the stock market, but the importance of these fluctuations, while still crucial over 30 years,

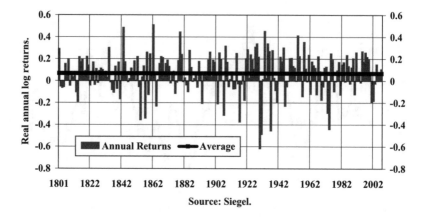

Chart 12. US Annual Real Returns on Equities (1801–2007).

becomes increasingly unimportant over the very long term, when returns to both shareholders and on companies' net worth are stable and must ultimately be the same.

If the market were perfectly efficient, then there would be no difference between price and value, as the market would always be "correctly" priced. Judged at least by foresight, the market cannot be perfectly efficient and at the same time ever mispriced. Subject to other evidence, therefore, the most likely model of the stock market is not one of perfect efficiency or of complete chaos, but one in which the market is imperfectly efficient. It shows this by rotating around its slowly rising fundamental value, represented by corporate equity, in cycles of around 30 years so that the predominant influence on returns within these cycles is share price fluctuations modified by, and in the long term equal to, the stable long-term return on corporate equity.

The model that I am proposing lies between two extremes. One extreme description of the stock market, which is the subject of the next chapter, is that it is perfectly efficient, so that its price is always correct and thus equal to its value. Another is that the market is just a wild casino in which prices are determined by the unpredictable and random enthusiasms and fears of investors. In neither case does value, as distinct from price, have any real meaning, nor are returns influenced by the past behaviour of share prices. However, in the model described in this chapter, value is represented by the underlying net worth of companies around which prices revolve. Over the short term, prices move in an almost unpredictable way but over the long term, since they rotate around fair value, their returns are far from random but are quite predictable, being determined by a combination of the stable long-term return on corporate net worth modified by the extent to which they are at any time away from fair value, as the pull back to that value over time will add to or subtract from that long-term return. If we can measure the degree to which the market has diverged from that fair value and the speed at which it is likely to return, we will be able to predict stock market returns with greater accuracy than would result from simply assuming that the returns at any time will be the same as their long-term average.

I have sought to show in Chapter 3 that interest rates have no long-term relationship with stock market values but, in Chapter 4, that they had an important short-term relationship. If, in addition, as explained in Chapter 5, asset values have an important influence on the real economy and, as seems likely from the analysis in Chapter 6, they can swing around their fair value, it must be very important for those in charge of economic policy that they measure these swings and the degree to which asset prices at any time diverge from them. If they fail to do this, they will risk finding that changes in asset prices, over which they will at times have no control, dominate over changes in interest rates and monetary policy ceases to be able to control the economy.

7

The Efficient Market Hypothesis

The Efficient Market Hypothesis says something extremely simple, which is that shares are always correctly priced. In a world of perfectly efficient markets, stock prices only change because new information becomes available, which rationally changes investors' assessment of markets' current value. The idea, set out in Chapter 6, that asset prices rotate around their fair value rather than remain always at that level, thus runs contrary to the EMH which was for a long time the dominant, though by no means universally accepted, view of the way financial markets worked. In this chapter, I will therefore look at this hypothesis and the remnants of its influence, even if the more extreme versions of it are seldom held.

It has long been accepted that markets in the real economy do not always behave, at least in the shorter term, as they would under conditions of perfect competition. It is therefore somewhat odd that there has been some reluctance to accept that financial markets suffer from similar imperfections. If, however, the issue is placed in an historic context, the original attachment to the EMH is more easily appreciated. When the EMH was originally put forward, it appeared to be supported by evidence and to accord with the simple view that if financial markets were not efficient, they would provide opportunities for profit which would be exploited until they no longer existed. Since then, however, the evidence against the hypothesis has mounted.

The EMH does not depend on the simple idea that anything but perfect market efficiency would allow unexploited opportunities for profit, though it is sometimes assumed to do so. This idea is logically unsound as it is dependent on a circular argument. If we know that a market will be correctly priced at some known date in the future, then it should be correctly priced today, as the reward from selling an overpriced asset can be readily calculated and, if adequate, will be exploited. But only in a perfectly efficient market will this condition apply. Markets can rotate around their true value, without offering a free lunch to anyone, provided that the extent and timing of the rotations are unpredictable.

A more serious objection is that information has a cost, and there must be sufficient incentive in terms of the return to cover this, so that complete efficiency is not logically possible.[36]

Markets could, however, show a close approximation to perfect efficiency even if there is therefore no logical necessity for them to do so. There is no a priori reason why they should not be and, if the evidence supported such a hypothesis, it would and should be accepted. The support which the EMH received when it appeared to accord with the evidence was therefore perfectly reasonable. What is unreasonable is a reluctance to discard it in the face of new evidence. But this reluctance is as common as it is unjustified. Changes in assumptions which underlie our understanding of the world frequently meet these problems and the process has been famously set out by T.S. Kuhn,[37] who describes the importance of paradigms in science and the difficulty of shifting them. Paradigms, which encompass the broadly agreed assumptions generally held at any time about branches of knowledge, can both help and hinder. A commonly agreed basis for new research is a help when a subject is progressing well, but it stifles development when the assumptions

---

[36] I pointed out this paradox in an article "Index Funds and Capital Market Theory" published in *Investment Analyst* in September 1978. The paper most commonly quoted by economists is "On the Impossibility of Informationally Efficient Markets" by Sanford Grossman and Joseph Stiglitz, published in the *American Economic Review* (Vol 79, pp. 293–408, December 1980).

[37] Notably in *The Structure of Scientific Revolutions*, University of Chicago Press, 2nd edn 1970, first published 1962.

behind it need to be replaced by a new vision. The EMH has become an obstacle to progress in financial economics. While its inadequacies have become increasingly recognized, it retains some residual support, even among some senior academics whose disapproval is unhelpful for the careers of younger people. This is one reason for the reluctance that economists have shown in suggesting an alternative. Another possible reason is that the construction of such a theory is a wide-ranging enterprise, which is not readily suited to the limited scale and concentrated precision of academic papers.

A story which supports and illustrates Kuhn's theory is provided by Andrew Lo and Craig MacKinlay. They recount the disbelief shown by an eminent economist who was acting as moderator to a seminar at which they presented evidence that was incompatible with the EMH in its then accepted form. The discussant was so loath to accept the evidence that he felt sure that there must have been some mistake in the data or their calculations.[38]

Data on US equities, as shown in Charts 11 and 12, illustrate a key feature of stock markets, which is that they have given stable long-term returns.[39] If markets are efficiently priced, shares must always be at fair value and it follows that there can then be no difference between price and value. This does not mean that returns cannot vary, but that changes in these returns can have only two possible sources. One is that the returns required by investors change, the other is that there will be differences between the returns which investors expect and the returns that they actually receive. If investors are prone to errors in their forecasts which, as set out in Chapter 3, they seem to have been with regard to inflation, then realized returns will differ from those expected. But the returns that companies earn on their net worth are, for the most part, unaffected by variations in inflation and as long-term equity returns have been stable, it is reasonable to assume that, although expectations may often have proved wrong, the errors of optimism and pessimism have cancelled out. The observed variations in returns around the

---

[38] See the introduction to *A Non-Random Walk down Wall Street*, by Andrew Lo and Craig MacKinlay, Princeton University Press, 1999.

[39] At least in the absence of catastrophes; the French, German and Japanese markets, which have suffered from them, have given lower returns.

long-term average can then be the result either of forecasting errors or of swings in expected returns. Without additional evidence there is no way of telling which of these two possibilities have either dominated in general or have been responsible for any particular deviation of returns from their long-term average.

If the returns required by investors are stable, in the short as well as the long run, as is indicated by the long-term stability of real equity returns, then future returns in an efficient market would be unaffected by past changes in share prices. But even in a perfectly efficient market, the future is unknowable, so prices can vary with new information. Unexpected news will be constantly coming forward and markets will respond to it. The returns that investors receive will not necessarily be those they expected. Markets can be perfectly efficient without having perfect foresight.

Unless forecasts are biased so that returns are persistently greater or less than those expected, past returns will vary in line with the balance of unexpected events. Looking forward, the balance between good and bad news will be random and will be neutral in aggregate over time. Unless the returns that investors are looking for vary, and the past stability of returns suggests this is unlikely, a natural corollary of the EMH is that future returns will be unaffected by past changes in share prices. These will rise on good news and fall on bad, and as the chances of good and bad news in the future will be equal, future returns after a bout of good news will be no different from those after a bout of bad. Share prices will thus follow what is known as a "random walk", being determined by chance as good or bad news follows. Like gains and losses at roulette, the market would not be influenced by past events.

The EMH thus leads naturally to the Random Walk Hypothesis (RWH), if expected returns are constant and the RWH and the constant expected returns version of the EMH are identical. The RWH was for some time assumed to be the way markets worked. Subsequent research[40] has, however, showed that this assumption is unjustified.

Stock markets are notoriously volatile. Research into this volatility has shown that the markets do not follow a random walk. If they did, their past behaviour would have no influence on their future and

---

[40] Including that of Andrew Lo and Craig MacKinlay, which was presented in the seminar to which I referred in footnote 38.

the analysis of volatility shows that this is unlikely to be the case. If markets follow a random walk, and their past has no influence on their future, then this would be true of their volatility; and if this were measured over relatively long periods of 20 to 30 years, the volatility when measured over these long periods could be forecast from their volatility over short periods, such as one year. But this is not how volatility actually behaves. Markets were less volatile over longer periods than they would be if the RWH held. The variance,[41] which is a measure of volatility, has fallen by more over time than it would have done had stock prices followed a random walk. It can be shown mathematically that this "variance compression" means that stock market returns exhibit "negative serial correlation", i.e. that high returns will be followed by lower ones and vice versa. As the observed behaviour of markets exhibits "variance compression", with returns varying less over longer time periods than they do over shorter ones, it is less risky for investors to hold equities if they expect to invest for, say, 30 years than it is for those who are saving for their next year's holiday or who have short-term time horizons for similar reasons.

Chart 13 illustrates the variance compression that has been shown in the US stock market, using data from 1801. The observed

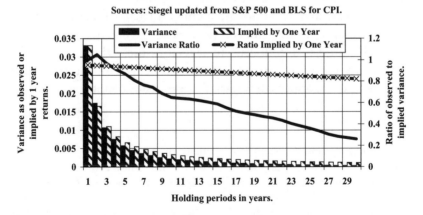

Chart 13. Variance Compression in US Real Equity Returns 1801–2008.

---

[41] Variance is defined as the average of the squared differences between the actual returns and their mean. It is therefore the square of the standard deviation.

variance in the returns is shown by the dark gray bars. These variances fall steadily with the length of time that the investor holds equities, as shown on the horizontal x-axis by the numbers which indicate the length of time in years that the investors stay in the market. These dark gray bars may be compared with the bars with diagonal stripes which show how the variances would have changed had the RWH held and the longer-term variances been determined simply by the one-year variance of the stock market. The solid line moving diagonally down the page gives the ratio between the striped and dark gray bars. It falls steadily as the number of years over which investors hold shares rises. If the RWH had held, then the ratio between the striped and dark gray bars would have fallen much less than it actually did and this ratio is shown by the top line (with crosses) which slopes slightly down over time, but by far less than the solid line does. If returns followed a random walk, then the solid line would be very similar to the top line.[42]

The evidence for variance compression is strong. Not only is it shown for the US, using all the data that we have, but also shown separately for the 19th century on its own and again using data from 1900 onwards. It is also shown for all the 17 individual stock markets for which data are available from 1900 onwards, as illustrated in Chart 14. It is shown in all markets when measured in their own currency (even for Belgium and Japan, though it is weak in each of those cases), and for all markets except the Netherlands when measured in US dollars. In several of these there is evidence of volatility expansion in the early years.[43] Chart 14 illustrates that the timing of volatility compression varies from country to country.

---

[42] If we had an infinite number of observations, the top line (crosses) would equal 1 on the right-hand scale and move across the chart parallel to the x-axis. The slight downward trend of the actual top line is because it is adjusted for the limited number of observations available.

This can also be observed in the US over some time periods if quarterly rather than annual data are used. During periods when stock returns exhibit positive serial correlation, bets that a rising stock market will continue to do so prove correct. This no doubt accounts for the popularity of so-called "momentum investing". The unpredictability of the point of time at which positive serial correlation turns to a negative correlation also accounts for the large and sudden periodic losses which result from this approach to fund management.

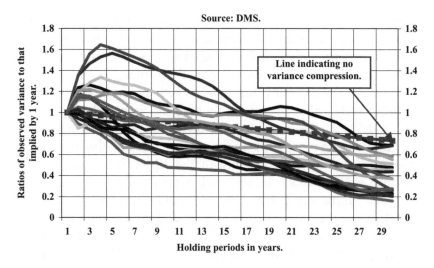

Chart 14. Variance Compression in 17 Markets + World 1900–2007.

It also varies over different time periods in any one country. It has sometimes been argued that the way in which volatility compression varies over time is evidence that the conclusion that markets exhibit variance compression is unreliable. This does not seem to me to be a sound argument. If the pattern of variance compression was constant, it would be possible to predict when it would start to operate and this would provide a strong guide to market timing, by giving a strong indication of when an overvalued market would start to fall and an undervalued one would start to rise. If such an indication were available, then markets would not be able to become over- or undervalued. Markets would indeed be perfectly efficient and the RWH would hold.

As already mentioned, variance compression can be shown mathematically to signify that over the longer term stock market returns must exhibit negative serial correlation, which means that after sustained periods of good returns we must expect bad ones and vice versa. The simplest explanation for variance compression, and the negative serial correlation of returns, is that markets rotate around fair value. This rotation naturally causes returns to swing around their average, so that after periods of above or below average returns the opposite occurs. Being pulled back to value also has the effect of dampening volatility over time, so that variance is less over the longer than over the shorter term. As price swings around value, rather than remaining at it, such markets are not completely efficient. But equally they are not completely inefficient, as they are fairly valued on average, even if not all the time.

Like the real economy, financial markets appear to be moderately or imperfectly rather than perfectly efficient, in line therefore with the model which seems to fit the evidence we produced in Chapter 6. This additional evidence reinforces the case for this model and thus casts doubt on the validity of the EMH. The evidence for variance compression is incompatible with the RWH, which must therefore be discarded, but it is only indirect evidence against the EMH. While the observation that the RWH did not hold was therefore a blow to the EMH, it was the RWH which was tested and found wanting, not the EMH directly. Faced with the evidence of variance compression, there were two possible ways forward. One was to drop the EMH and put something else in its place. The other was to reformulate the EMH so that it did not require market returns to follow a random walk.

Dropping the EMH was the obvious step to take in view of the evidence against the RWH. However, to many economists this seemed a radical move and it was resisted, in particular by those who had produced papers in which the validity of the EMH had been assumed. Ditching the EMH amounted to the sort of revolutionary change which T.S. Kuhn has termed a paradigm shift, and it has met with the opposition usual to such shifts. Some economists were therefore keen to adjust rather than discard the EMH; this meant that the hypothesis had to be modified sufficiently to allow for the observation that real returns on equities rotated around their long-term average level. In order to make this observation compatible with perfect efficiency, it was necessary to assume that these fluctuations reflected changes in the wishes and expectations of investors. This avoided the obvious assumption, which would have been incompatible with the EMH: that markets rotated around fair value and that there was therefore a difference between price and value. If investors at one time required a real return of 4% and at another a real return of 8%, then a perfectly efficient market would price the market consistently with these returns. In broad terms it would at least need to be matched by similar fluctuations in the return on net worth,[44] though this second requirement was, so far as I am aware, never spelt out by the proponents of this modified version of the EMH. Given sufficient time for errors in forecasting to be cancelled, these fluctuations in the returns required by investors would average out to match the observed long-term average return.

When the EMH was first proposed it was assumed that the hypothesis implied that stock market prices followed a random walk. This was a testable hypothesis and was shown to be false by the evidence for variance compression. If the EMH in its new form were to be acceptable then it needed to be tested, and this involved finding a way to show that investors' expectations changed in line with the changes in their returns. No one has yet found a way of doing this. We know the returns that have occurred, but unless we can measure expectations for equity returns, we cannot know whether the fluctuations in these returns are the result of the imperfect pricing of the market or changes in the returns that investors require.[45]

The alternatives of revising the EMH or replacing it with the hypothesis that financial markets are imperfectly efficient can be compared. Once the evidence showed that returns exhibited negative serial correlation around a stable long-term return, the simplest and most obvious explanation was that long-term returns on net worth were stable and markets rotated around net worth, which was also fair value; in short, that stock markets were imperfectly rather than perfectly efficient. This has the great advantage of simplicity and, according to the principle of parsimony – also known as Occam's razor – it is generally agreed that simple explanations should be preferred to more complex ones. An even more important issue is testability. No hypothesis can be valid unless it is both

---

[43] Capital takes time to create, so that short-term fluctuations in returns on corporate equity do not need to vary instantaneously to match changes in the returns required by investors.

[44] The problem is usually described as that of the joint hypothesis. To test the EMH in revised form requires additional assumptions which amount to other hypotheses. If the joint package is tested and found wanting, then it cannot be said that the EMH has itself been falsified, as it might be the other hypothesis which is at fault.

testable and robust under testing. When the EMH was held in its
Random Walk version, it was a testable hypothesis, but it was not
robust. In its revised form it has ceased to be testable. It therefore
falls the wrong side of Karl Popper's demarcation between science
and non-science.[46]

The case against the EMH leads naturally to the idea that
markets rotate around value rather than remain perfectly tied to it.
For this concept, which I have termed the Imperfectly Efficient
Market Hypothesis, to be demonstrably superior it needs to provide
a better account of the way in which markets work and to be both
testable and robust under testing. I have already shown in Chapter
6 that the Imperfectly Efficient Hypothesis is compatible with the
independence of interest rates and stock market levels, and fits
readily and parsimoniously with the evidence for variance compression. In the next chapter I will show that the concept is robust
under testing.

---

[45] "It must be possible for an empirical scientific system to be refuted by experience ..." and "I do not demand that every scientific statement must have in fact
been tested before it is accepted, I only demand that every such statement is
capable of being tested." From *The Logic of Scientific Discovery* by Karl Popper,
English edition published by Hutchinson & Co. 1959.

8

Testing the Imperfectly Efficient Market Hypothesis

As a preliminary to testing the Imperfectly Efficient Market hypothesis, it is important to understand the nature of equities and in particular their dual nature, which comes from the fact that equities are both financial assets and titles to the ownership of real assets. This dual aspect has the advantage that it presents us with two separate but equally valid approaches to valuing them. One important test for any valid hypothesis of equity valuation is that both approaches must produce the same answer if correctly applied. Like all financial assets, the value of equities is the discounted value of all future income or other cash payments that will accrue to their owners. If these future cash payments and the correct rate at which they should be discounted are both known, then the present value of financial assets is also known. For equities, this involves seeking to estimate the future cash payments and the interest rate at which they should be discounted and this approach has received the vast bulk of the attention given to the value of equities by financial economists. But as titles to the ownership of real assets, equities cannot, in a reasonably competitive economy, diverge far from the cost of creating those assets. These costs need to include the financing of those assets whose construction takes an appreciable length of time, although as I will show later this is not in practice a significant factor. Equities thus have a fundamental value which in practice is independent of the rate of interest.

In considering the appropriate rate for equities at which the future income payments should be discounted, it is important to appreciate that the return on capital must in equilibrium equal its cost and that this is true of both debt and equity. This is more obvious for bonds than it is perhaps for equities. If a company issues a bond to yield 8%, then this will be its cost to the company and also the return to investors who buy at the time of issue and hold it to maturity. But the return to investors who buy the bond after issue or sell it before maturity may be very different. If, for example, the bond falls in price after issue, then investors who buy it at its lower price and hold it to maturity will have a return which is higher than 8%. In aggregate, however, the winners and losers will be matched; the average return to investors will be the same as the cost to the company.

The same considerations apply to equities, although less obviously so. The average return to investors must over time be the same as the return made by companies on their equity (net worth) and this will also be the equilibrium return over time when on average shares are neither over- nor underpriced. Equally, the cost of equity to companies must be the same as the return that shareholders get from holding it. As the long-term real return on equities has been stable, this identity between cost and return provides us with an essential piece of information about valuing equities, which is the right discount rate to use provided it is also measured in real terms.

I showed in Chapter 7 that the EMH is not robust under testing in its RWH form and does not qualify as a valid hypothesis in its revised form. We must therefore provide a new hypothesis. We need to establish a coherent model of financial markets which is testable and robust under testing. If markets are not perfectly efficient, then their current price will often diverge from their underlying value. They may do so in a random and chaotic way or in some more organized form. The concept of value is therefore a natural starting point in the search for market models involving imperfection but not total disorder, and these imply there is a measure, which I call the fundamental, that determines the value that markets should have in contrast to their current price.

Many claims have been made about how the stock market can be valued. Such claims have been made at various times by all sorts of people, including economists and investment bankers. To see whether any models that claimed to measure value were valid, Stephen Wright and I considered the criteria with which they would have to comply.[47] I will explain each of these more fully later, but in summary we showed that the following tests were those which a valid criterion of value would need to pass.

1. There needs to be a fundamental against which price can be compared and this fundamental must be reasonably stable.
2. The ratio of price to value must not wander all over the place. It must rotate around its average and must be shown to revert to this average, i.e. to be "mean reverting".
3. It must be understandable in terms of economic theory.
4. It must have a moderate, but limited, ability to forecast future returns.

I should emphasize that we developed these criteria before we set out to find whether there were any valuation metrics that were robust – we did not choose the tests which could be passed by a particular metric which we favoured. In the event, only two of the various metrics we considered successfully passed these tests. The successful ones were q, which is the ratio of the market value of equities to the net worth of the companies, and the cyclically adjusted price/earnings ratio (CAPE). The data used for these two ratios measure slightly different groups of companies, as q measures only nonfinancials, but includes unquoted companies, while CAPE measures all quoted companies. Having found two valid metrics, it was important that they should prove to be compatible. If they had failed to agree with each other it would have been likely that there was an additional test which we had failed to identify, one which q or CAPE would have failed to pass.[48] However, not only did both

---

[47] Set out also in Chapter 20 of *Valuing Wall Street*.

[48] Among the metrics we considered and which proved not to be robust were: (i) the dividend yield; (ii) the cash flow dividend yield, which includes buybacks and all other forms of cash transfers to shareholders, either positive or negative; (iii) the current or "prospective" PE; and (iv) bond yield ratios (the Fed Model).

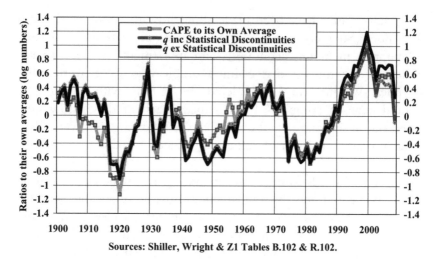

Chart 15. US Stock Market Value at End 2008.

these metrics satisfy all the tests, but they also agree with each other, as illustrated in Chart 15.[49]

8.1 The Test of a Measurable and Relatively Stable "Fundamental"

The need for a fundamental is fairly obvious, as without one there is no basis against which the current price can be compared. The need for it to be relatively stable is equally clear, as without this value could become volatile. It would, for example, be hard to justify the validity of any metric if a stock market did not become cheaper as it fell and more expensive when it rose and this would occur regularly if the fundamental was not much more stable than share prices. The fundamentals of both q (the net worth at current prices of the nonfinancial corporate sector), and of CAPE (the average for the past 10 years of earnings per share, also at current prices) are

---

[49] The coefficient of correlation between q and CAPE from 1899 to 2008, the period for which we have data for both, is 0.90 when q is measured to include the statistical discontinuities and 0.91 when they are excluded.

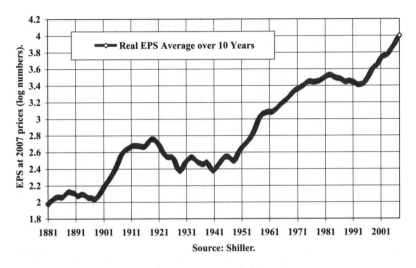

Chart 16. US Real EPS Average over 10 Years.

measurable and relatively stable. I showed this for q in Chart 10 in Chapter 6, and now for CAPE in Chart 16.[50]

8.2 Testing Whether the Ratio of Price/ Fundamental is Mean Reverting

The ratio of the current price to the fundamental measures the degree to which the stock market is currently misvalued. It is fairly valued whenever this ratio is at its average and it follows that this ratio must rotate around this unchanging average. It must therefore revert to its mean. Chart 15 shows that this appears to be the case for both q and CAPE and this is confirmed by the standard statistical tests.[51]

---

[50] The stability of q's fundamental is more impressive, not only by comparing the two charts, but because it is derived straight from the data, while 10-year average EPS in constant prices is a series which is smoothed by its construction. See also Appendix 3.

[51] ADF statistics using the data from the end of 1900 to the end of 2008 are −2.58 (90%) for CAPE, −2.79 (94%) for q including statistical discrepancies, and −2.39 (85%) for q excluding the statistical discrepancies. Using the data from 1871, which are available for CAPE but not for q, the ADF statistic is −2.82 (95%). The figures in parenthesis show the probability of mean reversion and these vary between 85%

8.3 Testing Whether the Criterion Is Justified in Terms of Economic Theory

The justification in terms of economic theory is straightforward in the case of q, as the price of all produced assets in a moderately competitive economy will be the cost of producing them. Thus the net worth of companies, measured by the cost of producing their assets, after depreciation but adjusted for inflation, should in equilibrium equal their market value. When the cost of an investment is calculated it is common, but not universal, practice to allow for the financing costs as well as those of materials and labour and the rate of interest assumed in the calculation of financing costs tends to vary. The time taken before an investment project becomes operational also varies, so the differences in the treatment of financing costs and the allowance made for them may produce some variation in the measurement of net worth over time. This is unlikely to be of any significance unless there has been a marked change in the average length of time over which new capital projects become operational and there is no evidence, even anecdotal, that any significant change of this sort has occurred.

If the value of net worth in official data was precisely accurate, the fair value of nonfinancial corporations would be identical with this net worth and the ratio of stock market value to net worth would be 1 when the market was at fair value. This would also be the average value of q. In practice there has been a persistent tendency to overstate the value of net worth in official data. One result is that the q ratio averages around 0.63 rather than 1.00. Fortunately, the degree of overstatement appears to be consistent so that q can be used to measure the value of companies by comparing the value at any time with its long-term average. This overstatement of net worth arises from a persistent overstatement of profits which can be demonstrated in a variety of ways, which I address in detail in Chapter 16.

---

and 95%. There is a very strong probability that all the ratios of price to the fundamental are mean reverting, though the test passes the conventional requirement of being 95% probable only for the data on CAPE since 1871. This is, however, only a convention and does not mean, as it is sometimes assumed to do, that series are not mean reverting if the ADF statistic does not indicate this level of probability. The distinction between the two definitions of q is explained in detail in Chapter 20.

The economic justification for CAPE is also reasonably straightforward. As the long-term average of the PE multiple is stable, we know that the market will be at fair value provided two conditions are satisfied. The first is that profits must be at their equilibrium level and the second is that the market is selling at its average multiple. CAPE is basically a way of calculating the equilibrium rather than the current level of earnings. The value of the stock market can then be derived by comparing this equilibrium PE with the long-term average PE of the stock market.

The method used effectively assumes that the equilibrium level of earnings per share, as distinct from the current level, can be calculated by averaging the earnings per share of the stock market for each of the past 10 years. The calculation is done by adjusting the past data on earnings per share to current prices, thereby avoiding distortions arising from variations in the rate of inflation. When the current price of the market is divided by this average of past earnings per share, the result is the PE that the market would have if earnings per share were currently at their equilibrium level. This Cyclically Adjusted PE (CAPE) can then be compared with its long-term average and the ratio of CAPE to its average measures the degree to which the market currently diverges from its fair value.

The crucial assumption is that this averaging for 10 years' earnings per share will provide a good guide to the current equilibrium level. Although the use of 10 years is somewhat arbitrary, the result can readily be justified due to the strong mean reversion of profit margins, which are the main cause of short-term profit fluctuations.

Chart 17 illustrates the strong tendency for profit margins to revert to their mean over quite short cycles in which the average period between peaks and troughs has been around 3–4 years.[52] Averaging earnings over 10 years thus achieves in practice the desired result of providing at any time an approximate value for the equilibrium level of earnings, rather than the current level. The choice of 10 years is arbitrary and another number, such as 12, might reasonably be preferred and would have the advantage of producing an even more stable fundamental than that shown in Chart 16. However, the

---

[52] The ADF statistic for US profit margins from 1929 to 2007, which are all the years for which the data are available, is −5.49. In statistical terms at least this indicates a 100% probability that margins are mean reverting.

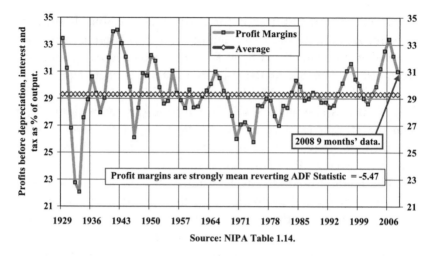

Source: NIPA Table 1.14.

Chart 17. US Corporate Profit Margins Annual Data from 1929.

use of 10 years has become the industry standard[53] and keeping to that has the considerable advantages of being familiar and avoiding the confusion that would arise if different definitions were used.

There are, of course, other factors in addition to margins that cause earnings per share to fluctuate. These include the rate of corporation tax, the extent to which companies are financed by debt rather than equity, and the level of interest payments. But in the past these have not been subject to sudden falls or jumps sufficient to invalidate the assumption that margins are the main short-term determinant of changes in earnings per share. While interest rates are quite volatile, much corporate debt is financed over the medium to long term, so that corporate interest payments fluctuate much less than short- or long-term interest rates.

8.4 Testing if It Has a Weak Ability to Forecast Future Returns

Our fourth test is that the valuation metric should have a limited ability to forecast returns and it needs to be stressed that both the

---

[53] This seems to have its origin in a suggestion by Graham and Dodd that 10-year average earnings should be used for valuing individual companies (Graham, Benjamin and Dodd, David L., *Security Analysis*, McGraw-Hill 1934).

forecasting ability and its limitations are important. The former can be demonstrated in a number of ways. One is to compare the valuation of the stock market shown by q and CAPE at different times in the past and with the real returns that investors have received when investing at those times. If on any occasion the market was shown to be expensive, then subsequent returns should have been poor and, if cheap, they should have been good. Provided that we have sufficient subsequent data, we can measure the value of a market at any given time by hindsight. For example, we can calculate the returns from any given starting point over the next 1 to 30 years and average these returns. This will give us the average return that investors with different time horizons would have received from the given starting point. These average returns can then be compared with the long-term average real returns over the whole period covered by the data available. We can, for example, calculate the returns that investors would have received had they bought the market at the end of 1929 with those received by investors who bought at the end of 1932. In each case we would calculate the returns that would have occurred had investors sold at any year later between 1 and 30 years. The average of each of these returns would give us a return for a whole range of investors. We could then compare the average return for investors who bought in 1929 with those who bought in 1932. The latter was far greater than the former and this provides solid evidence that the market in 1932 was much cheaper than it was in 1929. By doing this for all years for which we have at least 30 years of subsequent returns, we can rank the years relative to one another in terms of these subsequent returns and thus in terms of their relative cheapness.

Using the Shiller data from 1871 to July 2008, I have used this method for all holding periods of 1 to 30 years up to July 1978, when the calculations were made. Cheap markets are those which have given, with hindsight, above average returns and expensive ones those that have given below average ones. The extent of their misevaluation can be measured by ranking each period in terms of the subsequent returns that investors received on average over the following 1 to 30 years.

Chart 18 compares the value of the US stock market using CAPE with the values that I have derived from hindsight. The high degree of correlation shown by the two metrics demonstrates that CAPE is a good predictor of future returns.

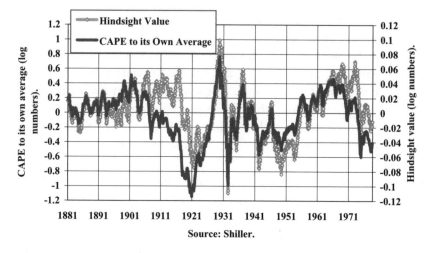

Chart 18. US Stock Market. Comparing CAPE with Hindsight Value.

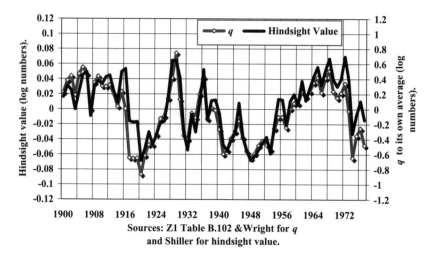

Chart 19. US Stock Market. Comparing q with Hindsight Value.

Chart 19 illustrates a similar comparison between q and hindsight values. As q data are only available on an annual basis from 1900 to 1925 and there are no earlier data, the period covered is rather shorter than that shown in Chart 18, which also uses monthly data. As a result the two cannot be directly compared but the appearance of a better fit between q and hindsight value is supported by the correlation which is even greater than that between CAPE and hindsight value.[54]

Other statistical methods can be used to check on the ability of q and CAPE to predict future returns. When this is done it appears that both q and CAPE have a weak ability to predict future market returns, with q rather better than CAPE and the current PE being useless.[55]

The ability to forecast future returns is an essential feature of a valid criterion of value, but it is also both odd and illuminating. Its oddity lies in the necessity that its forecasting should not be too efficient. If returns are too predictable, then the information will be exploited. Investors will leverage their portfolios when prospective returns are high and sell when they are low and in doing so will prevent markets becoming misvalued.

But this arbitrage will only occur if the rewards are commensurate with the risks involved. The returns on nearly all assets are risky, in that expectations seldom match the uncertain outcomes, although of course they can exceed as well as fall short of those hopes. Even the real returns on Treasury bills vary over time with fluctuations in nominal interest rates and inflation. The nearest thing to a risk-free return is a zero coupon government bond, indexed to be paid at a constant real value at a fixed date, provided it is held to maturity. But even this is risky for investors to hold in preference to equities when these are overvalued, because they will wish to reinvest in equities when they have fallen sufficiently. This moment cannot be forecast and the value of the bond in which they are invested will at that moment also be uncertain. Selling equities when they are overvalued can be sensible, but only if the prospective returns from the sanctuary asset, in which the funds previously invested in equities are temporarily lodged, will exceed those on equities over the uncertain time period in question. The uncertainty about the time when the investor will wish to return

---

[54] The correlation coefficient between q and hindsight value is 0.90 and that between CAPE and hindsight value is 0.72.

[55] This is the conclusion of "Rational Pessimism: Predicting Equity Returns using Tobin's q and Price/Earnings Ratios" by Matthew Harney and Ed Tower, published in *The Journal of Investing,* January 2003 and, with regard to the comparison between q and CAPE, the working paper by Robertson and Wright (op. cit.).

to equities makes cash (or its equivalent, such as money on short-term deposit), the most likely and generally sensible choice as a sanctuary asset. Although real cash returns vary, the asset can at least be realized in the short term at its original nominal value. Bonds have an even greater exposure to inflation and even if that is stable the nominal value at any time prior to maturity is uncertain.

The need for rewards to be commensurate with risk before arbitrage can be sensibly attempted provides a guide to the limits within which shares can normally become overvalued without offering opportunities for investors to have a high probability of improving their returns. The limits depend on the long-term real return on equities, the variations in the time taken for the market to swing around fair value, and the likely return on alternative assets. Historically, there have been only five peaks in the market's overvaluation since 1900, as can be seen from Chart 15. The average time between peaks has been 24 years but the average is far from regular and each of the last two swings has taken over 30 years from peak to peak. Cash has given very variable real returns, but generally in the 20th century these were between 1 and 2% p.a. while the US stock market has had a long-term average real return somewhere between 6% and 7%. From these data we can estimate roughly the extent to which the stock market can become overvalued without it being worthwhile for investors to reduce their equity holdings in order to improve their returns. If, for example, the real return on equities is normally 6%, Treasury bills can be expected to give at least a 1% real return and the stock market has an equal chance of being over- or undervalued in 15 years' time, then the limits of overvaluation given a limited number of rational investors will be just over twice. This is equivalent to 0.69 in natural logs. The calculations are not particularly sensitive to the assumptions made. For example, if we assume long-term real returns of 6.5% on equities and 2% on cash, then the limits of overvaluation become 1.92 (0.65 in natural logs).

A glance at Chart 15 shows that, during the period for which we have adequate data, only twice has the market become so over-valued that it was worth while selling on either of these assumptions: the first time being prior to its 1929 peak and the next prior to the peak in 2000. But even if the stock market has rarely been at levels at which arbitrage was open to rewards commensurate with risk, a rational investor would have expected even less overvalued markets to give below average returns and vice versa and a valid criterion of value would have been able to indicate when returns were likely to be good or poor. The eagerness of investors to hold shares is thus unlikely to be very sensitive to even quite large swings away from value, but should become stronger as such swings become pronounced. On such occasions, particularly if reinforced by a change in expectations regarding the economy, changes in interest rates will have less influence than usual on changes in share prices and the effectiveness of monetary policy will then be reduced.

8.5 The Close Accord of q and CAPE

Although it was not included as one of the four tests, I mentioned that if we found that there was more than one criterion of value which satisfied them, then the measures of value shown by the different tests should agree. This additional test is amply satisfied, as shown in Chart 15, and as the two approaches are based on different data sources, their agreement provides us with additional information. For example, it reinforces the probability that the real return on equities is stable. Valuing the market via q makes no assumption about the level of the stability of real equity returns. CAPE, however, effectively assumes that real returns are stable, as this is implied by comparing the current value of CAPE with its long-term average. It is therefore improbable that the values given by q and CAPE would be so similar if this assumption were not amply justified. Equally, valuing the stock market via CAPE makes no assumptions about the net worth of companies, so the similarity of the values given by q and CAPE makes it highly likely that net worth figures used for q represent a consistent degree of overvaluation and can thus be used for the calculation of market value. This also indicates that the use of q is not invalidated by the absence of any intangible assets, which is a subject I deal with at greater length in Chapter 17.

9

Other Claims for Valuing Equities

In Chapter 8, I sought to show that stock market value can be measured and that central bankers, investors and others can therefore tell when current prices have diverged enough from value for the economy and investors' wealth to be endangered. A sensible discussion of value is therefore extremely important; unfortunately, it is a discussion bedeviled by irrelevant claims which get recycled in popular discussion long after their fatuity has been clearly demonstrated. I often used to discuss with my father, who was an oncologist, whether economics or medicine was most subject to such follies. As health and wealth are among an individual's main concerns in life it is not surprising that medicine and economics are particularly prone to these problems, though my father was able to convince me that medicine suffered more.

Invalid approaches to value typically belong to the world of stockbrokers and investment bankers whose aim is the pursuit of commission rather than the pursuit of truth. The more they achieve their aim the greater is their success at creating confusion rather than helping our understanding. I have already touched on the egregious Fed Model, which purports to value the stock market by comparing its current PE with the yield on bonds. The other most common and ill-considered view is to refer to value by comparing the current PE with its average. The reason why current PEs provide no guide to value is that profits are highly volatile and rotate around their equilibrium level. If profits are at their equilibrium level, and only if they are, then the ratio of the current to average PE will provide a valid estimate of the market's value. Profits can move far from equilibrium and have on occasion been negative, as they were for the US corporate sector as a whole in 1932, and as was also the case for all quoted Japanese companies on several occasions in the 1990s. Those who seek to value the corporate sector, whether quoted or in total, by reference to current profits would therefore have concluded that from time to time the sector was worthless.

It is absurd either to undervalue the stock market simply because current profits are low or zero, or to assume that current PEs give a guide to value when profits are high. Examples of the resulting follies are readily available. Although the whole corporate sector of the US made losses in total in 1932, quoted companies managed to record a small profit. At the end of 1932, the stock market index was at a level at which the resulting PE was 25% above average,[56] but we know with the benefit of hindsight that the stock market was then at or near its cheapest level of all time. We can tell this from the subsequent returns. Investors who purchased shares at the end of 1932 received exceptionally high returns whether they held the shares for a long time or sold them after a year or two. It is surely obvious that a criterion of value which measures a market of exceptional cheapness as being "overpriced" must be useless.[57]

Not all claims to alternative criteria of value are so obviously invalid. One criterion that has been sometimes, though much less commonly, suggested is to compare the divergence of the market from its "trend value". If real equity values, including reinvested income, from a given starting point are plotted on a graph, they will show an upward trend because the values will grow and vary around the long-term average rate. The slope of this trend can be calculated

---

[56] We give the details in Appendix 4, together with evidence to show that low PEs as well as high ones are a poor guide to value.

[57] Current PEs are also no guide to future returns, which is one of the tests which a valid criterion of value must pass. See Harney and Tower, op. cit.

relatively simply.[58] At any time the current level of the stock market will differ from the trend value derived by this method. It is, however, unsound in both theory and practice. It fails the first of the tests set out in Chapter 8 for a valid criterion because the fundamental against which the current price is measured is unstable. In this case the fundamental is the current value that the market would have today if it were at its trend level rather than at its actual price.

It can be readily shown that this trend level is very unstable. This is because the trend changes radically with changes in the level of the stock market. I illustrate this in Chart 20. Using this trend fitting method I have calculated the value of all these markets in 1990, using the data that would then have been available from 1900 to 1990. I have then done the same exercise to produce the value of these markets in 1990, but this time using the additional information which was then available, i.e. the subsequent performance of these markets from 1990 to 2000.

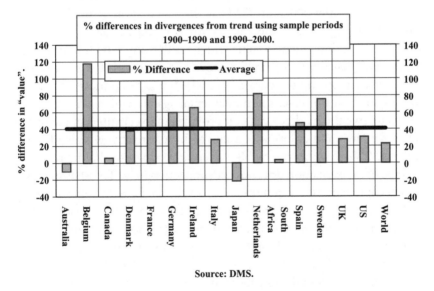

Source: DMS.

Chart 20. Instability of "Value" from Trend Divergence.

[58] The trend will be such that points on it differ as little as possible from the actual points on the graph. As these points will be both above and below the trend, the differences will be both positive and negative. The differences are therefore squared so that they are all positive; the trend is thus derived by "least squares", i.e. the line at which the sum of the squares of the differences with actual points on the graph is less than that of any other possible line.

Table 6. Comparison of Different Stock Market Values Given by Trend Fitting.

	US	World
Misevaluation in 2000 in US $ (1900–2000 trend)	1.78	1.55
Misevaluation in 2000 in Yen (1900–2000 trend)	0.97	0.85
Misevaluation in 2000 in US $ (1900–1990 trend)	2.32	1.90

The difference made by the additional data is startling, as Chart 20 shows. On the basis of data from 1900 to 1990, fair value in 2000 was 40% greater on average for all markets than it was when calculated from the data which subsequently became available.[59] For the US, the difference was 31%.

The instability of values derived from trend divergence is also shown by the differences which arise if the calculations are made in different currencies. As Table 6 shows, the world market appeared to be 15% undervalued in 2000 if the calculation is made in yen and 55% overvalued if the calculation is made in US $.

The large differences in value which result from trend fitting are due to the fact that the trend itself changes so much with the level of the stock market or with the currency in which it is being measured. Since the trend is, in this case, the fundamental against which price is compared to give the market's value, it provides an excellent example of the need for any valid criterion of value to have a relatively stable fundamental. If share prices rise by 50% overnight, it is absurd if the market's degree of misevaluation does not rise proportionately. Trend fitting does not comply with this requirement for a valid measure of value and thus fails to pass the first of the tests set out in Chapter 8. Its fundamental is, for example, wildly unstable compared with those of q and CAPE. Because we measure both of these by comparison with their own averages, they are also affected by subsequent price data, but the effect is small compared with the impact of such changes on trend fitted values.[60]

As explained in Chapter 6, the return to investors over a given period depends on two things: the return made by companies on their net worth and variations in the extent to which share prices

[59] The results are for all countries for which data are available since 1900.
[60] A valid criterion of value must also mean revert, and it can be shown that de-trended cumulative returns will not do so.

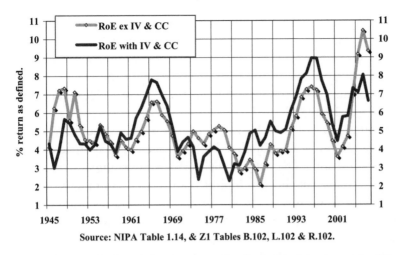

Source: NIPA Table 1.14, & Z1 Tables B.102, L.102 & R.102.

Chart 21. US Return after Tax on Nonfinancial Corporate Net Worth.

are over- or undervalued. A comparison of past returns with their trend, which is the basis of trend fitting, will therefore only provide a good guide to value if the returns that companies earn on their net worth are both mean reverting and extremely stable. Only under these conditions will the fundamental value of the stock market rise steadily and predictably like a time trend.

The first condition is satisfied, but the second is not. Real returns on corporate equity are mean reverting but they are far from stable. We know that long-term returns to shareholders are mean reverting, as illustrated in Charts 11 and 12, which means that the long-term returns on corporate equity must be also. But these returns vary greatly in the short term, as can be seen from Chart 21. For US nonfinancial companies, profits after tax are available on a quarterly basis from 1947 and quarterly net worth figures are available from 1952, so that returns on net worth can be calculated from 1952 onwards.[61]

---

[61] Profit figures are published in the National Income and Profit Accounts (NIPA) Table 1.14 and are shown in two forms. One includes the inventory (IVA) and capital consumption (CC) adjustments and the other excludes them. Of the two, the data excluding the adjustments approximate more closely to the profit figures published by companies. The IVA and CC adjustments are designed to exclude the impact of inflation from profits arising from changes in inventory values and on depreciation. As can be seen from the chart, the instability of profits after tax in the short term is clear whichever measure of profits is used.

While they are consistent with long-term mean reversion, they are
far from stable! For example, they fell by more than 75% from 1966
to 1974 (i.e. from a return on net worth of nearly 8% to one not
much more than 2% on the basis of profits with the inventory and
capital consumption adjustments) and there were 31 years between
the peaks of 1966 and 1997.

Another invalid way of way of seeking to value equities is to try
to derive the cyclically adjusted PE from an assumed trend in real
earnings per share.[62] This naturally depends on the assumption that there
is a stable trend, but this falls foul of both theory and observed data.

A stable trend in the growth of real EPS requires both a stable
return on net worth and a stable payout ratio. There is in theory
an alternative, which is that the return on equities is related to the
payout ratio, so that a high return accompanies a high payout ratio.
This is, however, not only highly unlikely on a priori grounds, but
quite contrary to the data which show that real returns on net
worth are stable over the long term. It follows that a stable growth
in real EPS requires a stable payout ratio and, as Chart 22 shows,
this clearly has not occurred.

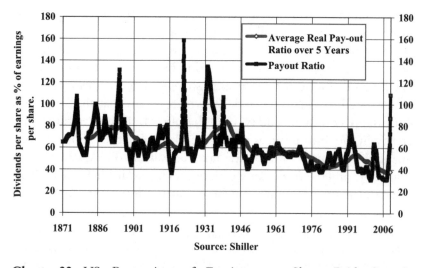

Chart 22. US Proportion of Earnings per Share Paid Out in
Dividends.

[62] An example of this invalid approach is a report by Deutsche Bank, *Fundamental
Credit Special*, 5 November 2008.

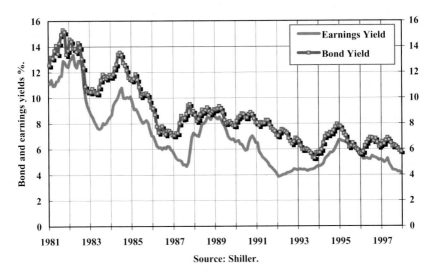

Chart 1. US Bond and Earnings Yields 1981–1997.

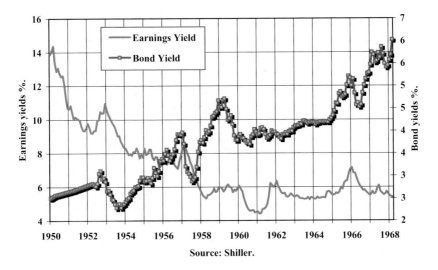

Chart 2. US Bond and Earnings Yields 1950–1968.

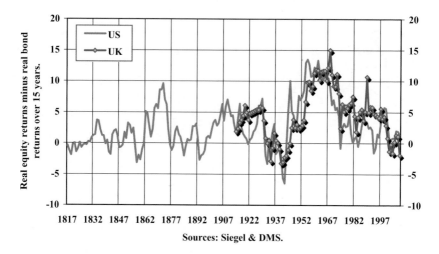

Chart 3. UK & US Real Equity Minus Real Bond Returns.

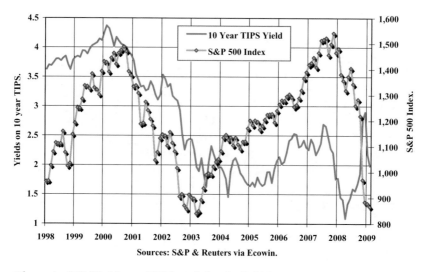

Chart 4. US Yields on TIPS and the S&P 500.

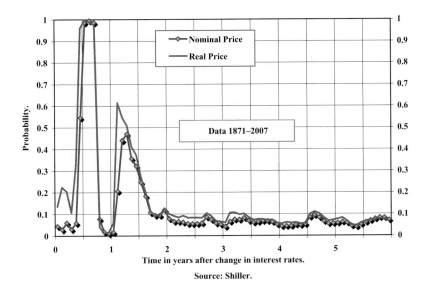

Source: Shiller.

Chart 5. US Probability that Interest Rate Changes Affect Share Price Changes.

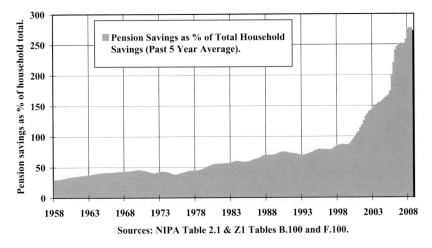

Sources: NIPA Table 2.1 & Z1 Tables B.100 and F.100.

Chart 6. US Pension Savings as % of Total Household Savings.

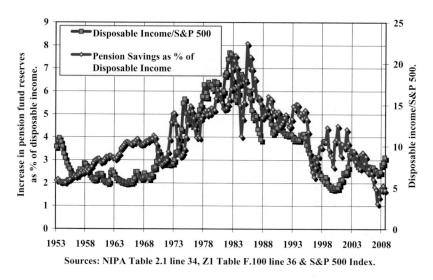

Sources: NIPA Table 2.1 line 34, Z1 Table F.100 line 36 & S&P 500 Index.

Chart 7. US Pension Savings and the Stock Market.

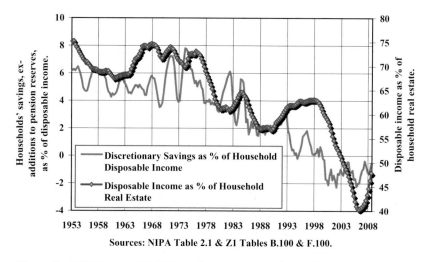

Sources: NIPA Table 2.1 & Z1 Tables B.100 & F.100.

Chart 8. US Household "Discretionary Savings" and the Value of House Property.

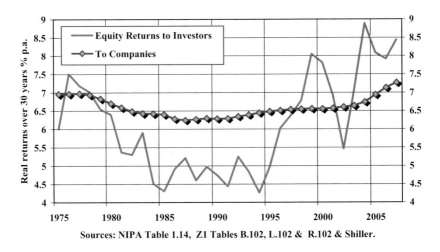

Sources: NIPA Table 1.14, Z1 Tables B.102, L.102 & R.102 & Shiller.

Chart 9. 30 Year Real Returns to Shareholders and on (Nonfinancial) Corporate Net Worth.

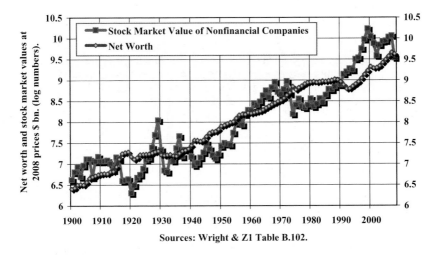

Sources: Wright & Z1 Table B.102.

Chart 10. US Nonfinancial Companies Net Worth and Market Value at Constant Prices.

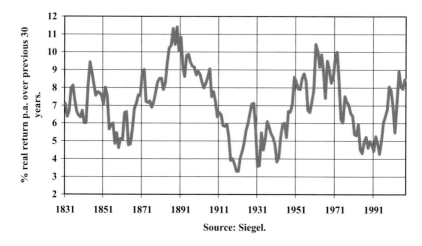

Chart 11. US Real Equity Returns over Previous 30 Years 1831–2007.

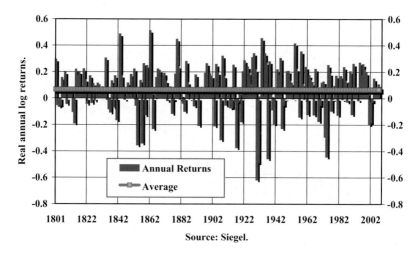

Chart 12. US Annual Real Returns on Equities (1801–2007).

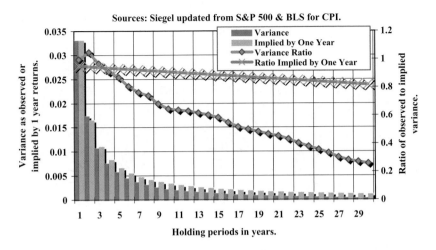

Chart 13. Variance Compression in US Real Equity Returns 1801–2008.

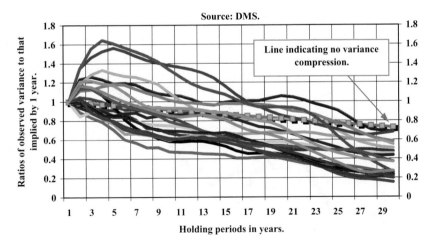

Chart 14. Variance Compression in 17 Markets + World 1900–2007.

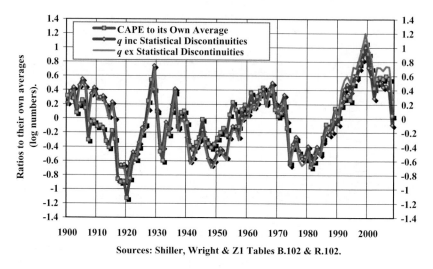

Chart 15. US Stock Market Value at End 2008.

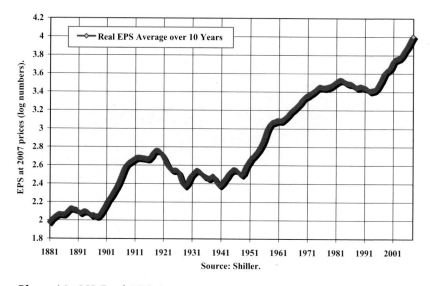

Chart 16. US Real EPS Average over 10 Years.

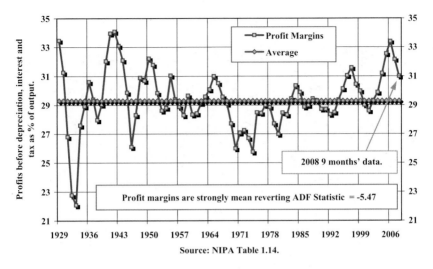

Chart 17. US Corporate Profit Margins Annual Data from 1929.

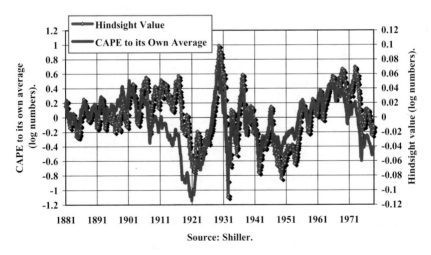

Chart 18. US Stock Market. Comparing CAPE with Hindsight Value.

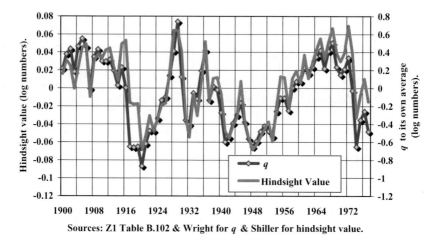

Sources: Z1 Table B.102 & Wright for *q* & Shiller for hindsight value.

Chart 19. US Stock Market. Comparing *q* with Hindsight Value.

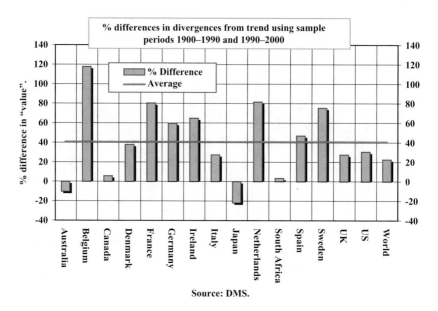

Source: DMS.

Chart 20. Instability of "Value" from Trend Divergence.

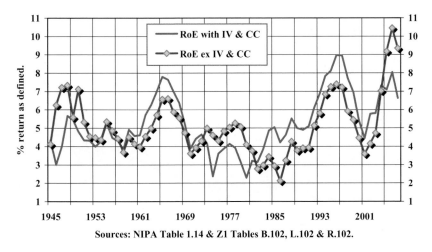

Sources: NIPA Table 1.14 & Z1 Tables B.102, L.102 & R.102.

Chart 21. US Return after Tax on Nonfinancial Corporate Net Worth.

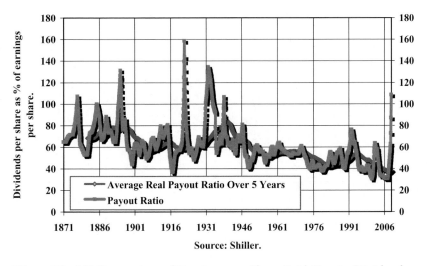

Source: Shiller.

Chart 22. US Proportion of Earnings per Share Paid Out in Dividends.

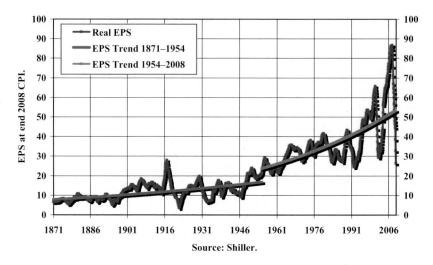

Chart 23. The Instability of US Real EPS Growth.

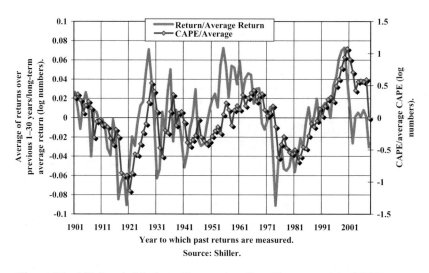

Chart 24. US Stock Market. Comparing Past Returns with CAPE.

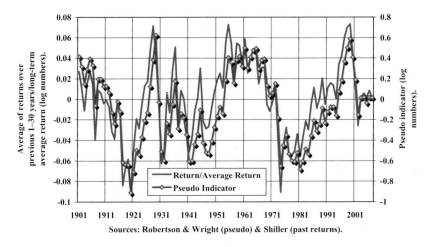

Sources: Robertson & Wright (pseudo) & Shiller (past returns).

Chart 25. US Stock Market. Comparing Past Returns with Pseudo Indicator.

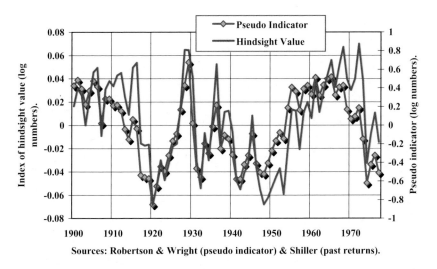

Sources: Robertson & Wright (pseudo indicator) & Shiller (past returns).

Chart 26. US Stock Market. Pseudo Indicator and Hindsight Value.

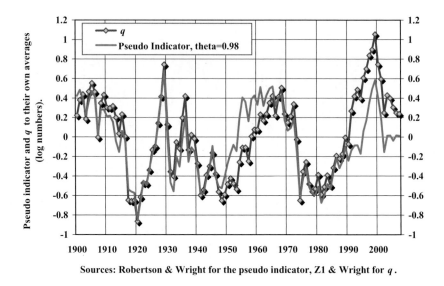

Sources: Robertson & Wright for the pseudo indicator, Z1 & Wright for q.

Chart 27. Comparing q and the Pseudo Indicator.

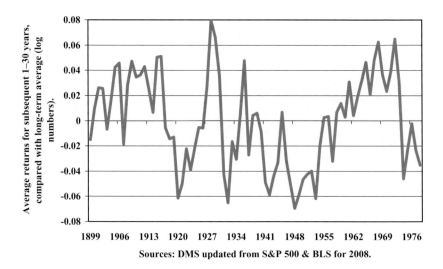

Sources: DMS updated from S&P 500 & BLS for 2008.

Chart 28. US Hindsight Value.

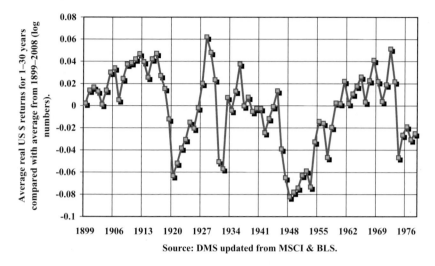

Source: DMS updated from MSCI & BLS.

Chart 29. World Hindsight Value.

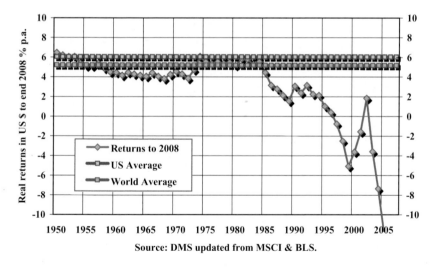

Source: DMS updated from MSCI & BLS.

Chart 30. World Market Returns to End 2008.

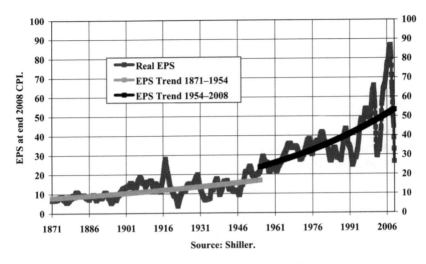

Chart 23. The Instability of US Real EPS Growth.

As the returns on corporate equity are stable and not affected by dividend payout ratios, the equity return can be determined by a variable mix of dividend and dividend growth. If the payout ratio was 50%, so that half the profits are paid out in dividends and half are retained, then a long-term return on equities of 6% could be the result of average dividends of 3% at fair value with 3% additions to net worth each year so that the long-term return was 6% (3% plus 3%); or from a 100% payout ratio so that dividends of 6% of fair value are paid out every year and do not grow in real terms so that the long-term return is also 6% (6% plus 0).

As the real return on equity has been stable, but payout ratios have not, there is unlikely to be a stable trend in real EPS and, as Chart 23 shows, there hasn't been. I have simply split the period for which we have EPS data in half and the trends for the first and second halves are markedly different.

Without a stable trend in EPS, it is not sensible to try to derive the current equilibrium level of EPS by assuming that such a trend exists. Some of those who seek to use this method do not assume that there has been a stable growth in EPS over the long term, but assume such a trend over shorter periods. This has all the advantages and disadvantages of data mining. As the choice of time periods is at the discretion of the user, it has no logical validity and is thus useless for those in pursuit of the truth; on the other hand, the

Table 7. Value of US Stock Market at end 2008, Using Different Measures for PEs and Cyclically Adjusted PEs.

	EPS	PE with S&P 500 @ 903 (31 December 2008)	Average PE	Ratio of current to average PE
EPS for 2008	26.16	34.52	14.10	2.45
CAPE	56.09	16.10	15.50	1.04
Trend PE since 1871	49.33	18.31	14.10	1.30
Trend PE since 1954	53.48	16.89	14.10	1.20

starting date can be chosen to produce any answer desired, which can be helpful to those in pursuit of commission.

Table 7 illustrates some of the ways in which deriving a trend from real EPS can be misused to value the stock market.

At the end of 2008, the S&P 500 was at 903, giving a PE of 34.5 on EPS for 2008, which was 145% above the long-term average. As profits, as published by companies, were depressed, with large write-offs having taken place in Q4 2008, this was an example of current PEs giving a very misleading view of the current value of the stock market. With EPS cyclically adjusted according to the standard CAPE measure, the market was 4% overvalued.[63] However, if the cyclically adjusted PE is derived from the past trend of real EPS, then the stock market is 30% overvalued if the trend is taken from 1871, and 20% overvalued if the trend is taken from 1954. I have no doubt that by using different base dates for the trend other very different estimates could be obtained for the value of the market at end 2008.

If the trend of earnings per share is assessed as a guide to value against the tests set out in Chapter 8, we find that it fails:

1. The fundamental depends on the trend growth of earnings per share which is not stable.
2. It has no basis in economic theory.
3. Due to the instability of the fundamental, its ability to forecast future returns cannot be measured.

---

[63] As CAPE uses an average of the past 10 years' EPS and EPS rise over time, the average PE on this basis is higher than the average of current years.

Valid approaches to valuing the stock market must produce compatible answers. It is therefore important to show that incompatible answers are derived from invalid approaches. I once read in a report from a very large and well known investment bank something along the following lines: "There are sixteen ways to value the market; seven show that it is expensive and nine cheap. We therefore conclude that it is cheap." It is sad that such absurdities can be published by grand organizations and written by highly-paid people.

10

Forecasting Returns without Using Value

One of the purposes of valuing markets is to use the answer as a way of predicting future returns. But the question of prediction can be approached independently of the issue of value. As explained in Chapter 7, stock market returns are not random. Periods of good returns are followed by bad ones and vice versa. To some extent, therefore, it should be possible to predict future returns by comparing returns over, say, the previous 30 years with those over very long periods of 100 years or more. This is a similar approach to the one I used in constructing hindsight value, although instead of looking at the future returns, this involves looking backwards at the average returns over the previous 1 to 30 years.

Chart 24 compares the returns calculated in this way with the values derived by CAPE and it can be seen that the two are very similar.[64]

A mathematically more rigorous approach has been explored by Donald Robertson and Stephen Wright. It is based on the fact that any series, such as the past data on real equity returns, which exhibits negative serial correlation has the interesting characteristic that

---

[64] As with hindsight value the returns are adjusted for inflation and are the averages of all holding periods from 1 to 30 years prior to the year in question. The coefficient of correlation between these returns and CAPE is 0.81.

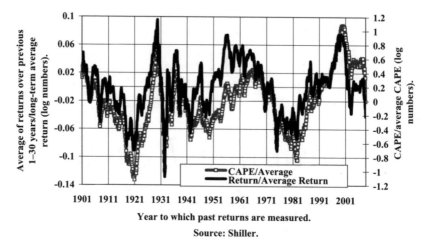

Chart 24. US Stock Market. Comparing Past Returns with CAPE.

the history of those returns contains within it the ability to predict future returns. It is therefore possible to consider the data on past returns set out in Chart 24 in a mathematically more stringent way, by applying different weights to the long- and short-term returns shown by the market and by doing this Robertson and Wright derive a forecast of future returns which they term their "pseudo indicator".[65]

As Chart 25 shows, this pseudo indicator is very similar to the average of past returns.[66] A key point, which is common to both the pseudo indicator and the average of past returns, is that they are not measures of value, because they have no independent measure of the fundamental. On the other hand, they are not derived by trend fitting and hence do not suffer nearly so badly from the problems set out in Chapter 9.

A problem with both the average of past returns and the pseudo indicator is that their results are very sensitive to the long-term return. This raises two different sorts of problem. One arises from the differences in long-term returns that come from different data

[65] See Robertson and Wright (op. cit.).
[66] The coefficient of correlation between the pseudo indicator of Robertson and Wright and the 1 to 30 year average of past returns is 0.84.

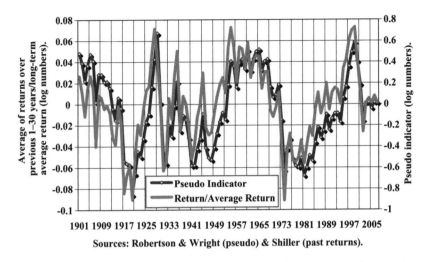

Sources: Robertson & Wright (pseudo) & Shiller (past returns).

Chart 25. US Stock Market. Comparing Past Returns with Pseudo Indicator.

sources. For example, the real return on US equities from the start of 1900 to the start of 2000 was 7% according to the Shiller data, and 6.7% according to that from DMS. Such differences are likely for many reasons, a major one being the difficulty of eliminating "survivor bias".[67] As a result, it is usually the lower return that should be preferred when two otherwise reliable sources disagree. If the errors in valuation were consistent over the whole period, there would be little difference between a series giving a 7% return and one giving a 6.7% return, but if the series are both updated by consistent data or if, as seems likely, survivor bias has been much less evident in the more recent data for both series, the degree of under- or overvaluation given by the pseudo indicator will be significantly different depending on which data set is used for the longer term.

An even more important problem with the pseudo indicator is that the long-term returns differ significantly between different markets. Using all the available data up to the end of 2007, for

---

[67] "Survivor bias" arises from the fact that data on companies which go bankrupt, and thus don't survive, are often difficult to find in the years prior to bankruptcy and, as a result, the data are biased in favour of those companies which we know with hindsight to have been the more successful.

Table 8. US Stock Market Correlations (1901–1977) Between Indicators Derived from Future Returns (Known from Hindsight) and the Pseudo Indicator, q, CAPE and the Indicator Derived from Past Returns.

	Pseudo indicator	CAPE	Past returns	Hindsight	q
Pseudo indicator	1	0.913	0.829	0.802	0.891
CAPE	0.913	1	0.854	0.745	0.843
Past returns	0.829	0.854	1	0.512	0.627
Hindsight	0.802	0.745	0.512	1	0.903
q	0.891	0.843	0.627	0.903	1

example, the long-term real return from the US stock market was 6.9% while that for the UK was 5.6%. It is improbable that investors expected such different returns, so these differences are likely to have arisen from unanticipated events that are unlikely to be repeated. As at the end of 2007, the pseudo indicator for the UK indicated that future returns would be poor and the market needed to be 42% lower for the long-term returns to be matched in the future. At the same time, the pseudo indicator for the US did not indicate the probability of poor returns.

While there are problems with the pseudo indicator, it scores well – at least for the US – when judged by its past ability to forecast future stock returns. If treated as an indicator of value, it has also, for the most part, demonstrated a very similar pattern to those shown by q and CAPE. I illustrate both these qualities in Table 8. As we need 30 years of future data, it is only possible to compare the indicators up to 1977. On this basis, q has the best correlation with hindsight values and thus the best forecasting ability, followed by the pseudo indicator, as shown in Chart 26, and then by CAPE, with the simple use of past returns being significantly less satisfactory than the other indicators.

Valuation and prediction are not, of course, the same. They would only coincide if we could be assured that the stock market would be fairly valued at some point in the future, or at least that we would know what its degree of misevaluation would be. Therefore, the pseudo indicator, q and CAPE are all uncertain indicators of future returns and we cannot necessarily expect their relative success in the past to be reflected in their future successes as forecasters.

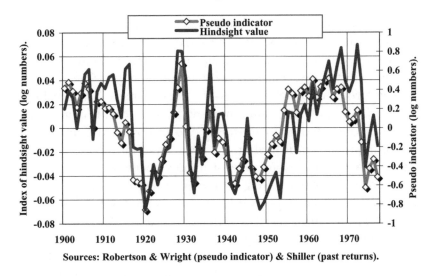

Sources: Robertson & Wright (pseudo indicator) & Shiller (past returns).

Chart 26. US Stock Market. Pseudo Indicator and Hindsight Value.

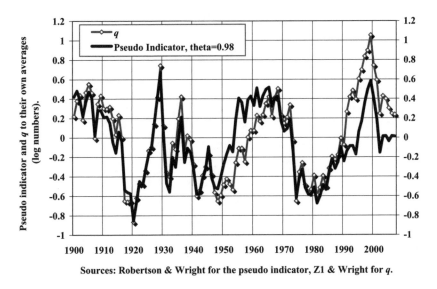

Sources: Robertson & Wright for the pseudo indicator, Z1 & Wright for *q*.

Chart 27. Comparing *q* and the Pseudo Indicator.

As Chart 27 illustrates in the case of *q*, an interesting quality of the pseudo indicator is that it has been very similar to *q* and CAPE, particularly when signaling extreme levels. The pseudo indicator can thus be used as confirming major misevaluations shown by *q* and

CAPE for the US. It has the advantage of being capable of calculation for other markets where the data needed to calculate those
metrics are not available in an adequate and reliable form although,
as I show in the next chapter, there are other ways of overcoming
the data problems of valuing non-US stock markets. The reliability
of the pseudo indicator should improve as more data become available over time, and although this is also true of CAPE and q, the
rate of improvement is likely to be more rapid for the pseudo indicator. This is not only because of improvements in the quality of
the data, but because the long-term market returns are more volatile
than average values of q or CAPE and this volatility falls the longer
the period for which the data series is available.

While the pseudo indicator gives promise for the future, we
must work today on the data which are currently available. In
Chapter 11, I therefore consider how markets outside the US can
be valued, using the data that we already have.

11

Valuing Stock Markets by Hindsight Combined with Subsequent Returns

I have shown that the US stock market can be valued using either q or CAPE and that these two different methods produce very similar results. Unfortunately, reliable long-term data on the net worth of nonfinancial companies, adjusted for inflation (which is needed to calculate q), and on earnings per share (which is needed for CAPE), are not available for any stock market except the US. An alternative approach is therefore needed for other markets and I consider that a combination of hindsight and subsequent returns is the best available.

The method described in Chapter 10 provides one possible solution, but it has the problem that in some markets past returns have suffered badly from defeats in world wars or, as in the case of Spain, by civil war. Dramatic destruction of capital occurred in these defeats. For example, during World War II Japan lost 34% of its domestic industrial plant and equipment and 80% of its shipping, let alone the loss of all the capital it had invested abroad.[68] The result of these, clearly unanticipated, losses is that the long-term real returns to investors from equity and the return on corporate net worth of the unlucky countries were

[68] See Table 10.4 in *The Cambridge History of Japan, Volume 6.*

well below those of the lucky ones. As we have data on these returns from 1900 to 2008, we can compare the average returns in the first half of the period with those in the second, and it can be seen that returns in the second half, which was free from these major catastrophes, were much more similar across countries than in the first half.[69]

The difference between expectations provides, as set out in Chapter 10, a major problem for forecasting returns based solely on past ones. A possible way around this is to use hindsight, which includes the unexpected impact of misfortune, to value markets in the past. I will elaborate on this in more detail later, but in summary it involves using past returns to value markets for which we have enough subsequent data, and from this information find times when they are close to their fair value. From these points the expected returns on markets are likely to have been very similar or, indeed, identical and by comparing the returns that individual markets have achieved since they were at fair value with very long-term averages, their values today can be assessed. Markets which have given high returns since they were last at fair value will be expensive, and those that have given low returns will be cheap.

As explained in Chapter 8, we can measure the value of markets in the past provided we have their subsequent returns over a sufficiently long period, and we term this "hindsight value". This is obtained by taking the returns from any given year over the next 1 to 30 years and averaging them. We then rank each year by the ratio of this average return to the return over the whole period. From hindsight we can find years in which the stock market was very close to fair value. If the market today was also at fair value, the subsequent real return from that date would equal the long-term real equity return and, from the degree to which the actual return differs from this average, we can assess the value of the market today.

11.1 The US Stock Market as a Test Case

To test the validity of this approach we first look at the US market which we know from CAPE and q to have been near fair value at

---

[69] The standard deviation of returns from the 17 countries for which we have data for the whole period was 2.85 for 1899–1954 and 1.61 for 1954–2008. See Appendix 4 for details.

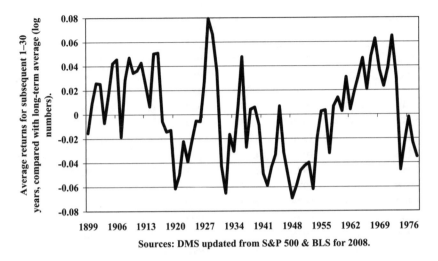

Sources: DMS updated from S&P 500 & BLS for 2008.

Chart 28. US Hindsight Value.

the end of 2008. Chart 28 shows the results for the US stock market from the end of 1899 to the end of 1978, which is the last year for which, at the end of 2008, we have 30-year data. As can be seen from Chart 28, the US market was almost exactly at fair value at the end of 1976, being 0.2% undervalued by hindsight. The return from the end of 1976 to the end of 2008 was 6.1% compared with the return from 1899 to 2008 of 6.02%, as can be seen from Table 9 below.

The return to investors who bought when the market was fair value at the end of 1976 was a little above the US average to the end of 2008, and rather more compared with the world average. Using the US as the appropriate yardstick, the market was 2.4% overpriced at the end of 2008. However, it may reasonably be argued that the long-term return on the US market has been higher than that for the world as a whole and that this to some extent represents good fortune rather than a higher than expected level of return. Since the misfortunes of world wars are more obvious than the good fortune of the US, such an argument would lead to using a long-term average return which was lower than the historic US one, but not as low as that achieved by the world as a whole since 1900. If the world return is used as the appropriate yardstick, the US market was 32.5% overpriced at the end of 2008 and this would seem to be above the range of probable overvaluation.

Table 9. Real Returns on US Equities Starting in 1950 Onwards to 2008.

1950	6.42	1965	4.32	1980	6.29	1995	2.35
1951	6.30	1966	4.74	1981	7.02	1996	1.19
1952	6.19	1967	4.29	1982	6.75	1997	−1.02
1953	6.30	1968	4.17	1983	6.29	1998	−3.03
1954	5.62	1969	4.75	1984	6.60	1999	−5.33
1955	5.29	1970	5.03	1985	5.76	2000	−4.21
1956	5.29	1971	4.80	1986	5.37	2001	−2.99
1957	5.67	1972	4.55	1987	5.73	2002	0.75
1958	5.04	1973	5.55	1988	5.38	2003	−4.14
1959	4.93	1974	7.13	1989	4.51	2004	−7.16
1960	5.04	1975	6.51	1990	5.49	2005	−10.27
1961	4.63	1976	6.10	1991	4.19	2006	−20.01
1962	5.01	1977	6.62	1992	4.08	2007	−36.94
1963	4.72	1978	6.84	1993	3.81		
1964	4.50	1979	6.70	1994	4.28		

Table 10. US Stock Market Value as at 31 December 2008 (S&P 500 = 903).

Valuation method	Over (+) or under (−) valued
CAPE	+4.10%
q including statistical discrepancies	−8.50%
q excluding statistical discrepancies	+30.60%

Using a combination of hindsight value and subsequent returns, the US market at the end of 2008 appears to have been at least 2.4% overvalued and probably rather more so. This fits closely with the value of the US stock market at the end of 2008 derived from *q* and CAPE, which is set out in Table 10.

The similarity of the valuations for the US market at the end of 2008 derived from *q* and CAPE and that derived from a combination of hindsight and the subsequent return is very encouraging. It suggests that reasonably accurate valuations will be provided by using this approach to value markets outside the US, where we have reliable data on their long-term returns but not on their net worth at replacement cost (needed for *q* calculations) or long-term earnings per share data (needed for calculating CAPE).

11.2 The World

Chart 29 shows that, according to hindsight, the world market was
some 0.4% overvalued in 1970 and 0.16% overvalued in 1962. The
real returns since 1950 are illustrated in Chart 30. The returns from
1970 and 1962, when the world market seems, from hindsight, to

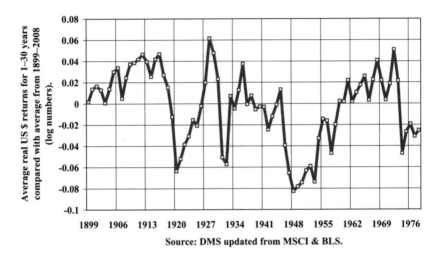

Chart 29. World Hindsight Value.

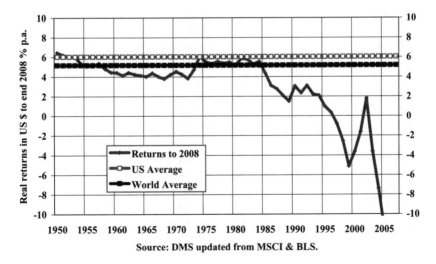

Chart 30. World Market Returns to End 2008.

have been fairly valued have been 4.5% and 4.4% p.a., which is below average even for the world and suggests that markets outside the US were likely to be cheaper than the US itself at the end of 2008.

11.3 Comparative Values of 17 Equity Markets at End 2008

Table 11 gives the returns achieved by investors since the various stock markets were last at fair value, as shown by hindsight, together with the years at which the markets were at fair value. We show these in terms of both the local currency and the US dollar. In terms of the prospective return, the latter is likely to give the better guide for international investors. This is partly because rapidly

Table 11. Real Returns from International Stock Markets Since They Were Last at Fair Value according to Hindsight.

Measured in US $			Measured in home currency		
	Base year	Return		Base year	Return
Switzerland	1963	10.61	Sweden	1972	8.51
South Africa	1973	9.78	South Africa	1964	7.32
Netherlands	1960	9.57	Australia	1975	7.31
Sweden	1972	7.64	Netherlands	1970	6.45
Denmark	1966	7.11	Denmark	1975	6.39
UK	1965	6.13	US	1976	6.10
US	1976	6.10	France	1970	5.92
Norway	1963	5.84	UK	1967	5.41
Australia	1966	5.75	Norway	1970	5.53
Spain	1969	5.46	Canada	1960	5.03
France	1960	5.30	Germany	1972	4.84
Germany	1964	5.27	Switzerland	1967	4.65
Ireland	1965	5.25	World (US $)	1962	4.41
Canada	1960	5.03	Spain	1968	4.20
World	1962	4.41	Ireland	1965	4.11
Belgium	1963	4.36	Belgium	1965	3.80
Italy	1975	4.19	Italy	1975	3.57
Japan	1973	2.88	Japan	1969	2.23

Data source: DMS.

growing economies naturally have currencies that appreciate in real terms, according to both theory and practice, and their equilibrium returns, measured in the home currency, are lower than those in mature ones. But the equilibrium returns are the same everywhere when measured, for example, in dollars.

Where economies have had similar growth rates over the past 30 years, large differences between returns in dollars and home currencies point to misvalued exchange rates. Future returns from these markets are thus likely to be higher when measured in their home currencies than when measured in dollars.

The following conclusions follow from the data set out in Table 11:

1. The world market was around 27% below fair value at the end of 2008.[70]
2. Among major markets the US is probably the most expensive, but France, Germany and the UK are more likely to be fairly valued than cheap, with Germany likely to be slightly cheaper than the other major European markets.
3. The overpriced markets were South Africa, the Netherlands, Sweden, Denmark and Australia, which are all relatively small and thus have little influence on world returns as a whole.
4. Japan appears to have been outstandingly cheap.

It will be interesting and informative to see, looking back 20 years from now, whether these conclusions will appear to have been justified.

---

[70] This is the difference between the value of the world market at the end of 2008, based on its return of 4.5% since 1970 and the value that it would have had had the return been its 5.17% long-term average.

12

House Prices

I have so far concentrated on the value of the stock market, but I have remarked that this is only one of the three key asset prices with which central bankers need to be concerned. The others are house prices and the price of liquidity. I look at house prices in this chapter and liquidity in Chapter 13.

My interpretation of our current financial tribulations is that they are largely the result of mistakes by central banks, with the Federal Reserve being the most culpable. The original error was not to adjust policy to moderate the degree of overvaluation of the equity market in the last few years of the 20th century. This failure seriously impaired the Federal Reserve's ability to influence the real economy thereafter. The US economy recovered after the recession of 2001, but it required an unusually large degree of monetary stimulus for it to do so, despite the help given by the tax cuts announced in late 2000 by the incoming Republican administration. It could be argued that the degree of monetary stimulus was more than was needed to achieve recovery or, indeed, that the Federal Reserve was led to excessive stimulus in order to justify its earlier indifference to asset prices. What might have happened had economic policies been different cannot, of course, be known. What is clear is that monetary ease was marked after the 2001 recession and that it was accompanied by large increases in the prices of shares and houses and a large fall in the return to investors when sacrificing liquidity, which I have termed the "price of liquidity". These are the three asset prices which I claimed in Chapter 5 to be the ones that central bankers should watch most closely because of their impact on the real economy.

With the monetary stimulus that occurred after 2001, there were some new excesses in the stock market which recovered strongly. Although market levels at the two peaks were almost identical in nominal terms, the peak in 2007 was lower in terms of the market's overvaluation, due to the rise in the real value of capital from retained profits and to the increase in nominal value due to inflation, as Chart 17 shows. It was in house prices and other symptoms of low risk aversion, shown notably in the price of liquidity, that excessive asset prices were most marked in the second round of their responses to the follies of the Federal Reserve. Had the US central bank adjusted its policy and succeeded in avoiding the excesses of the 2000 stock market bubble, the subsequent bubbles in house prices and many financial assets would probably not have happened. But bubbles outside the stock market may arise independently of share prices and it follows that central banks also need to be able to judge whether house prices and risk aversion had moved to dangerous levels.

A considerable effort has been made by economists to address the question of house prices. Indeed, it seems to me that this has occupied the attention of economists rather more than the misvaluation of stock markets. What seems clear from this work is that the cost of constructing houses has not had much influence on prices during the post-war period. Although it is difficult to disentangle the improvement in housing quality from house prices, it is likely that construction costs have moved more or less in line with inflation as the improvement in productivity in house building has not been very different from that for the economy as a whole. What prevents house prices from rising in line with inflation is the importance of land prices. It is worth noting that if land prices are a large constituent of corporate net worth, as they have been on occasions in Japan and Hong Kong, then it would not be possible to use q as an indication of share values, unless land prices were themselves mean reverting. This seems a long way from being the case.

As land prices are so important, the value of houses cannot be related to their construction costs. But this does not mean that there is no practical limit to the price of houses, since demand for them

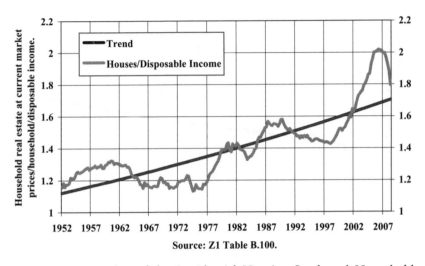

Chart 31. US Value of the Residential Housing Stock and Household Disposable Income.

must decline as they become less easily affordable. But houses are not only an expense, they are also an asset; as their prices rise, owners are pleased, and those who don't own them are increasingly anxious to do so. This dual character of houses, which are both forms of consumption and very important capital assets, makes it likely that they will respond to two different forces. In the short run, expectations regarding future house prices will, as appears to happen in share markets, often rise when prices rise, making them volatile in the short to medium term. Over the longer run, however, such expectations will ebb and flow and house prices will be related to incomes. While shares fluctuate around their fair value, house prices are likely to fluctuate around their affordability. As Chart 31 (for the US) and Chart 32 (for the UK) show, this model whereby house prices rotate around some level of affordability fits with their observed behaviour. The level of affordability may constitute a rising or even a falling proportion of available incomes, as the wish to spend income on houses may change relative to other forms of consumption as incomes rise, and the relationship between disposable incomes and affordability may also vary with changes in taxation and interest rates. The charts suggest that in the post-war period at least, households in the UK and US have been happy to spend a higher proportion of their disposable incomes on housing.

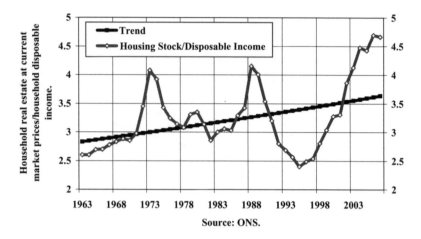

Source: ONS.

Chart 32. UK Housing Affordability.

In the case of the UK, this has happened despite tax changes which have made ownership more expensive by first reducing and then eliminating the deductibility of mortgage interest from income.

Even if we allow for the trend rise in the ratio of house values to incomes, it is clear from the charts that houses had become extremely expensive well before they actually peaked in 2007. In the US, for example, the ratio of the value of the housing stock to disposable incomes had risen to its previous peak, relative to its trend, by the middle of 2003. The danger presented by this was widely recognized, but did not result in action being taken by central banks. If the Federal Reserve and the Bank of England had been concerned with asset prices, as this book argues they should, then they had plenty of evidence that house prices had risen to dangerous levels.

13

The Price of Liquidity — The Return for Holding Illiquid Assets

Shares and houses share a common characteristic in that they are both titles to the ownership of real assets. Excesses in financial markets, with their propensity to cause subsequent grief in the real economy, are not, however, limited to real assets. Financial assets, with only a limited connection to real ones, are also capable of becoming seriously mispriced and, as with shares and houses, can then pose a danger to the economy. Central banks therefore need the capability to measure this danger and in this chapter I seek to show how this can be done.

From time to time, banks and other financial institutions have become insufficiently risk averse. In such circumstances, loans become too readily available and credit expands at a dangerous speed. When conditions change, the value of the loans made in the boom time falls. As banks have total assets which can be 30 times or more than the value of their equity,[71] even small changes in the

---

[71] This was the average ratio for large UK banks according to the Bank of England's financial stability review published in November 2008. One large bank had assets equal to 60 times its equity.

value of their assets have a dramatic impact on the value of their equity. For example, a fall equal to 3.3% of the book value of its assets would completely wipe out the equity capital of a bank with assets equal to 30 times its equity. Excessive ease in credit markets is therefore extremely dangerous. As we have seen recently, when the reaction comes, the result is very tight credit, as banks struggle to reduce the size of their balance sheets to match the reduction in their equity capital. Central banks therefore need to be alert to credit conditions and should seek to restrain them if they become excessively easy. Measuring credit conditions and identifying times of excess are thus key requirements.

One sign that debt is becoming a problem is simply its scale relative to GDP. Chart 33 shows that this has been growing rapidly and with barely any setback over the post-war period. In recent years, however, it has been argued that the US economy has become less volatile than it used to be and this expansion of debt levels did not represent any significant rise in risk. While this claim, often called the "great moderation", no longer has many adherents, it could also be argued that the rate of growth of debt provided no cause for alarm. As Chart 34 shows, changes in the rate of debt growth do not seem to have formed a pattern from which periods of excess can readily be judged.

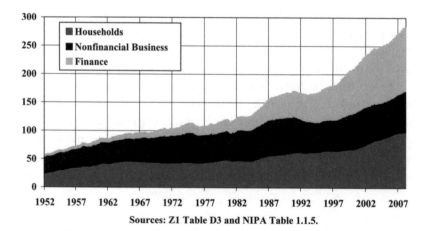

Sources: Z1 Table D3 and NIPA Table 1.1.5.

Chart 33. US Private Sector Debt as % of GDP.

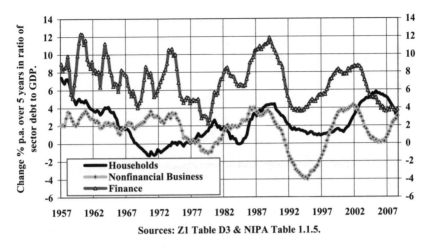

Sources: Z1 Table D3 & NIPA Table 1.1.5.

Chart 34. Growth of US Private Sector Debt.

There are also problems in measuring debt levels and, therefore, their growth. In the world economy as a whole there is no net debt, since there is an asset equal to every liability. Measures of debt are therefore measures of the gross level and may involve double counting. If, for example, a bank borrows 100 from its depositors and then lends the proceeds to a company, both the bank and company have gross debts amounting in total to 200, whereas if the depositors had lent directly to the company the total debt would only have been 100.

Credit conditions can, however, be judged without reference to either the level or the growth of debt, through an analysis of the spreads between different types of debt. Although the actual risk of default is unknown, its expected level can be calculated by the use of option theory and details of how this can be done have been published by the Bank of England.[72] The analysis enables the spread between different types of private sector debt and government debt

---

[72] See "Decomposing Corporate Bond Spreads" by Lewis Webber and Rohan Churm, *Bank of England Quarterly Bulletin*, 2007 Q4, page 233, and "Decomposing Credit Spreads" by Rohan Churm and Nikolaos Panigirtzoglou, published in Bank of England Working Paper No. 253.

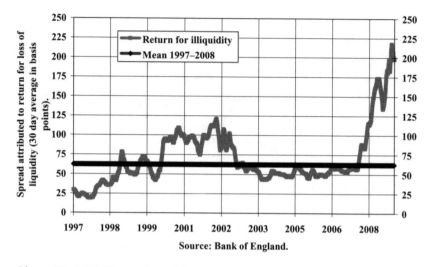

Source: Bank of England.

Chart 35. US$-Denominated Investment-Grade Corporate Bond Spreads. Estimated Return Attributed to Loss of Liquidity.

of the same maturity – for which there is no risk of default – to be separated into different parts. One is the risk of default and another is the uncertainty about this risk, which can also be isolated. This leaves a residual which is reasonably assumed to mainly represent the reward that investors receive from being prepared to buy an illiquid asset in preference to one which can be readily realized at any time (for example, if there is a sudden need for cash as typically arises in credit squeezes). This is the aspect I have termed the price of liquidity.

Chart 35 compares the return which can be attributed to the loss of liquidity to investors on US investment grade corporate bonds from 1997 to 2008 with their average level. On this measure, credit conditions would appear to have been too lax from 1997 to 2000 and from 2003 to 2007. The first period coincided with the stock market bubble (Chart 15), and the second with both an overvalued and rising stock market and with house prices which were above and moving further above their trend level (Chart 31).

Another possible measure of excess in credit conditions may be provided by money supply measures. The European Central Bank (ECB) watches the broad measure of money supply and, in theory at least, could raise interest rates if it considered that this was growing too rapidly. This does not seem in practice to have

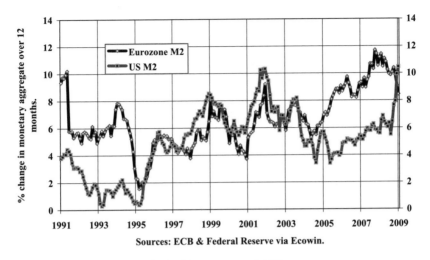

Chart 36. Money Supply in Eurozone and US.

happened, despite the extremely rapid growth in the Eurozone money supply illustrated in Chart 36. The opposite problem with using money supply is illustrated by the US data also in Chart 36. The price of liquidity indicated that there was a dangerously low level of risk aversion from 1997 to 2000 and from 2003 to 2007, as shown in Chart 35. Monetary data did not, however, give helpful signals. While the pick-up in growth from 1997 to 1999 fits with the indications given by the price of liquidity, the opposite signal was been given by the slowing of monetary growth from 2003 to 2007. While I think that money supply is important and should not be ignored by central banks, the evidence points to the price of liquidity being a more useful indicator of insufficient risk aversion and dangerously eased credit conditions.

I have remarked that the three asset prices which should receive particular attention from central banks are shares, houses and debt assets, measured in terms of the reward offered for loss of liquidity. Each of these is important, but particularly so when they move together, as they did during both the stock market bubble at the end of the 20th century and the more recent bubble which covered house prices as well. This is clearly helpful for central bank policy, which I will discuss later. First of all, however, I give further attention to aspects of the returns from equities, which have been largely overlooked and, as a result, led to widespread misunderstandings.

14

The Return on Equities and the Return on Equity Portfolios

The Equity Risk Premium (ERP) – which is a central issue in this chapter – has, I believe, been the source of a great deal of misunderstanding. I may have been unlucky in my reading of the financial press, but I am yet to encounter a reference to the ERP by a journalist which did not strike me as unsound in fact or inference.

The ERP is the difference between the returns that investors receive from equities and that which is available on less risky assets such as government bonds or bank deposits. In practice, it has proved to be unstable and therefore cannot be sensibly used to value equities, as I showed in Chapter 3, or other risky assets such as houses. It is nonetheless common to find attempts to do so, not only in the financial press but in academic papers. One of the common criticisms about economists is that they often remain attached to their theories despite contrary evidence. In an old joke, an economist is held to observe that "It may be alright in practice, but it would never work in theory". I mentioned in Chapter 1 that this criticism can be readily applied to practitioners in other disciplines and its sociological description by T. S. Kuhn, in terms of the problems of paradigm shifts, has general application to science, not

Table 12. The US Equity Risk Premium, 1800–2000.

	1800–2000	1800–1900	1900–2000
US real equity returns % p.a.	7.0	7.5	6.5
US real bond returns % p.a.	3.4	5.0	1.8
ERP (ex-post) % p.a.	3.6	2.5	4.7
ERP (ex-post) deducting 0.5% p.a. for higher equity costs	3.1	2.0	4.2

just to economics. But unjustified attachment to the concept of a stable ERP represents an important element, I think, in the resistance to a new paradigm in financial economics and deserves therefore to receive considerable attention.

As Table 12 shows, the ERP (ex-post – i.e. defined in terms of the outturn rather than in terms of expectations) was almost twice as large during the 20th century as it had been in the 19th. As the comparison is made between returns before expenses – and the cost of running an equity portfolio is significantly greater than that of owning government bonds – it is probably better to show the result after deducting an additional 0.5% p.a. from the equity return, which I do in the bottom row of the table. Given that the management of equity portfolios was probably higher in the 19th than the 20th century, an even higher deduction might be appropriate for returns from 1800 to 1900.

As explained in Chapter 3, it is likely that a major cause for the fall in the ex-post bond return between the two centuries has been that inflation was unexpectedly high in the 20th century, and it follows that the ex-ante ERP (i.e. the expected premium) may well have been around 2% p.a. in both centuries. Nevertheless, for long-term investors this is a handsome reward, particularly as the risks of inflation fall more heavily on bond than on equity holders. This is because the long-term stability of real equity returns means that equity returns are largely unaffected by changes in inflation whereas bond holders will either benefit or lose depending on whether inflation is above or below expectations. On the usual assumption that an increase in wealth does not produce an increase in welfare which matches the pain induced by an equal decline in wealth, the additional risks borne by bond holders appear to deserve additional reward.

It is thus reasonable to ask why the ERP, however measured, has not been narrowed by investors borrowing money to invest in equities.

As the long-term real return on equities has averaged around 6% or more and the cost of risk-free debt has seldom been above 4%, it appears at first sight that large profits are available to those who are willing to leverage an equity portfolio. If this were actually available, this opportunity for profit would surely be exploited to the point where the ERP shrinks, as equity returns fall in response to the increased demand for equities and real interest rates rise with the increased supply of new debt. In practice, however, while it is generally considered sensible for long-term investors to hold equities rather than bonds, it is not standard practice to encourage them to invest in a leveraged portfolio of equities. The issue can therefore be seen as whether this conventional wisdom is in practice correct, or simply an ill-considered shibboleth that has impeded the efficient working of financial markets. As might reasonably be expected, it is one of those examples where conventional wisdom can be shown to be justified. Investors have not in fact been persistently foolish over the past two centuries. The reason why conventional wisdom is justified in this instance is that the intuitive assumption usually made about the possible profits only applies if share prices follow a random walk. Once the negative serial correlation of equity returns is understood and the consequences applied, the returns from leverage are less and the risks greater.

The underlying misconception lies in the assumption that if debt can be borrowed at, say, 4% and invested in an asset yielding 6%, then − in addition to the 6% return made on the unleveraged investment in equities − a further 2% p.a. will be available if an equal amount of debt as the original investment is borrowed and invested. The total return will thus be 8% on the original investment, compared with 6% which would be available from an investment in equities without the benefit of leverage. The implicit and usually unnoticed assumption which this involves is that the impact of leverage works in a stable way; in mathematical terms it is linear, which means that the improvement in return and the deterioration in risk rise proportionately with the amount of leverage. But in practice, due to the impact of negative serial correlation, the returns rise less rapidly and the risks more.

It is quite simple to see how things turn out differently from such expectations, by comparing the impact of leverage under two different assumptions about the behaviour of the stock market. One assumption is that share prices follow a random walk, and the other assumes that returns exhibit negative serial correlation (Chapter 3). Under the

assumption that prices follow a random walk, the prospective return
to investors will not be affected by the past behaviour of share prices.
After a period of good or bad returns, average returns will still be
the most likely returns in the future. Under this assumption, the
returns on investors' equity portfolios will not be affected by the
incidence of cash withdrawals needed to pay interest on the debt
which has been borrowed to leverage the equity portfolio. When
returns exhibit negative serial correlation, however, the situation is
very different. The interest payments that must be made are fixed by
the terms of the debt and they do not rise and fall with the value
of the portfolio. Thus, when share prices are low and prospective
returns are high, the payments are high in proportion to the value of
the portfolio and vice versa. The result is that proportionately large
withdrawals are made when prospective returns are high and relatively
small ones when the likely future returns are low.[73] Although the
"return on equities" is unaffected by the withdrawals, the return on
equity portfolios financed partly by debt is heavily affected, and the
same applies to equity portfolios from which withdrawals are made
for purposes other than the payment of interest.[74]

The standard and eminently reasonable convention for measuring
the "return on equities" is to assume that all income is reinvested and
that there are no cash withdrawals from the portfolio. This is not,
however, the general experience of investors and it is not in aggregate
possible. If all income from equities were reinvested in the corporate
sector, it would have to grow at the rate of return on equities, rather
than in line with the growth of the economy as a whole which, for
mature economies at least, is around half the rate of real return on
equities. Even investors who have something approaching an infinite
time horizon, such as universities and foundations, need to spend

---

[73] It might, of course, be possible to raise debt on the basis that payments on the
debt would fluctuate with the stock market. However, such lenders would be
accepting an equity risk and would demand equivalent returns on the debt, thus
making leverage pointless.

[74] For those who are familiar with discussions about the measurement of the performance of investment portfolios, the difference is analogous to the distinction
between money-weighted and time-weighted performance. The time-weighted
performance will be unaffected by the timing of the withdrawals, but the money-
weighted performance, which determines the return actually achieved on the
money invested, will be heavily influenced.

income. Such long-term investors can sensibly invest their endowments in equities, but they may easily find themselves in financial difficulties unless they can vary their expenditure to take account of year-to-year changes in the value of their endowment or are able to increase their resources by gifts or increased fees.

There are investors, such as those saving for retirement, for whom it is sensible and practical to reinvest all their dividend income. Uniquely for this class of investors, the return on equities over a given period, as conventionally calculated, will be the same as the return on a portfolio of equities. For other investors, the realized returns will vary with the amounts and timing of any withdrawals. If these are low when the market is cheap and high when it's expensive, the portfolios will produce higher returns than the "return on equities" as conventionally measured, but lower if the withdrawals are unfavourably timed. If the amounts and timing of withdrawals are random, then the most likely return will be the same as the "return on equities", but the likely spread of returns will be wider. When dividend income is spent, the withdrawals over the long term will tend to vary with the value of the portfolio and there should thus be little adverse impact arising from negative serial correlation of returns. But if only dividend income is spent, the real income available from an equity portfolio is highly unstable as dividends, measured in real terms, have in the past fallen over periods of many years.

Chart 37 shows how unstable real dividends per share have been in the US. An investor seeking to live on his dividend income from 1931 to 1935 would have found it falling in real terms by 40% and again by 25% from 1966 to 1976.

Negative serial correlation, which is a key characteristic of equity returns, thus has widespread implications. It not only has a profound impact on the risks and returns of leverage equity portfolios, it applies to investors generally. The "return on equity" will only be the return on an equity portfolio for those investors who automatically reinvest their dividend income and make no income or capital withdrawals from equity portfolios. Other investors, including those who wish to use the return on equities to finance consumption, will not receive the same return.[75]

---

[75] The consumption asset pricing model which has been used to assert that the Equity Risk Premium is "too large" requires, naturally enough, that the return

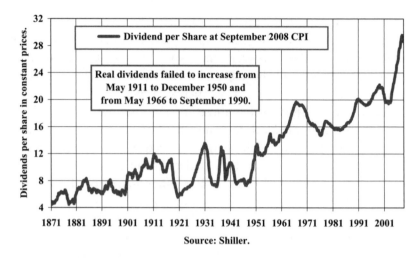

Chart 37. US Stock Market Real Dividends per Share 1871–2008.

Investors saving for retirement and reinvesting their dividends will thus be the class of investors for whom the risk-adjusted returns on equities are most favourable. Other types of investors will often prefer to hold equities in preference to other assets and, provided they can afford to do this after allowing for their spending needs and have a long enough time horizon, they will usually have made a sound decision. But it is wrong to assume, as is commonly done, that the risk-adjusted returns derived from the conventionally calculated "return on equities" will be available to investors who are not always able to reinvest their dividend income. For other types of investor, returns will often be worse and will certainly be more risky.

---

from equities should be used to finance consumption. But if this is done, the return on equity portfolios will not be the same as "the return on equities" which requires dividends to be reinvested. However, the ERP, which has then been claimed to be too large, is the difference between the "return on equities" and, typically, the return on short dated bonds. But I suggest that these assumptions are incompatible. If the return from an equity portfolio is used to finance consumption, it should not be assumed that the return on equities can be used to calculate the Equity Risk Premium. See, for example, "The Equity Premium: A Puzzle?" by Rajnish Mehra and Edward Prescott, *Journal of Monetary Economics*, Vol. 15 (1985). Combining a consumption-based model with an ERP which depends on income being reinvested assumes that investors can have their cake and eat it.

15

The General Undesirability of Leveraging Equity Portfolios

If the ERP was really as large as it is assumed to be, investing in equities with borrowed money would resemble a "free lunch" which, as Milton Friedman has memorably pointed out, is not to be found in a competitive economy.

The difference between the likely return to a class of investors and the "return on equities" derives from the negative serial correlation exhibited by equities. This general principle has a particular application in the case of leveraged portfolios and explains how the risks involved are such that the ERP is not reduced by investors habitually choosing to employ leverage to finance their equity portfolios.

If investors wish to borrow to invest in equities, they will not be able to do so unless the lender has very limited risks. For example, the assets which act as security for the loan will normally have to have a value very much larger than the loan itself. If debt is incurred to buy equities, a fall in the value of the equities will mean that sales have to be made so that debt can be repaid and the "cover" for the debt maintained at its required level. If, for example, the minimum required cover is 50%, then every time the market falls by that amount from the date on which the loan is taken out, the borrower will face a total loss. If the loan is long dated, the situation will be even worse, as the value of the loan will often rise with falls in interest rates, at the same time as the value of the equity portfolio has fallen. When equities have to be sold to maintain cover, the investor will be unable to benefit fully from any subsequent rebound in the stock market. Leveraged portfolios can result in a total loss of the original investment. Even if the long-term "returns on equities" are excellent, a poor period in the intervening years can force shares to be sold and as these sales will be made at times when the market is low, they are made when returns on equities are prospectively high.

It follows that for most investors taking out a long dated loan to invest in equities is too risky to be sensible. There are, however, investors who are so rich in terms of their total assets that they can afford to take such risks to a very small degree. But even for these privileged investors there has in the past been no advantage to be gained from doing so.

Chart 38 illustrates the difference in the returns for investors who are 100% invested in US equities over periods of 20 years from

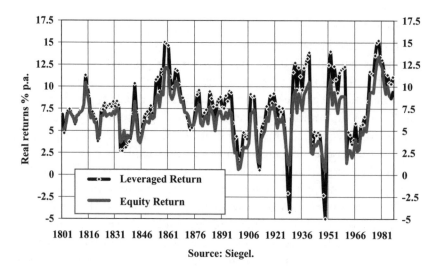

Chart 38. US Real Equity Returns over 20 Years from 1801 with and without Bond Financed Leverage.

1801, and compares their returns with investors who bought equities but leveraged their position with bonds to finance a total equity portfolio twice the size of that held by the unleveraged investors. I have assumed that the costs of managing the equity portfolios amount to 0.5% p.a. − i.e. that the return after management costs is 0.5% less than the return on equities if no costs are involved − and that the cost of borrowing is the government bond rate plus 1% − i.e. that the borrower has to pay 1% more than the risk-free rate at which the government can borrow. The returns from the leveraged portfolio have averaged more than those from the unleveraged one, but the risks have increased hugely. While there was no 20-year period over which the unleveraged portfolio failed to give a positive real return, large losses of up to 5% p.a. were recorded on the leveraged portfolio, with the result that investors would have lost over 60% of their money when they became due to repay the debt.

Leverage thus has the effect of increasing the returns at the cost of much higher risk. The combined effect of these can be measured by the Sharpe Ratio[76] and the results are shown in Table 13. This shows that the effect of leverage is to reduce the risk-adjusted return, as the Sharpe Ratio for the unleveraged equity portfolio is greater than that of the leveraged one. The table also shows that leverage would have been satisfactory had the impact of leverage been linear, as in that case the Sharpe Ratio would have been the same as that of the unleveraged portfolio.

Table 13. Comparison of Leveraged and Unleveraged Equity Portfolio Returns Over 20 years from 1801 using Bonds.

	Unleveraged equities	Bonds	Linear leveraged equities	Actual leveraged equities
Return	6.45	3.24	9.55	7.47
Sharpe Ratio	1.33	n/a	1.33	1.32

Source: Siegel.

[76] This standard measure of risk adjusted returns is calculated by dividing the actual return minus the risk-free return by the standard deviation of the return.

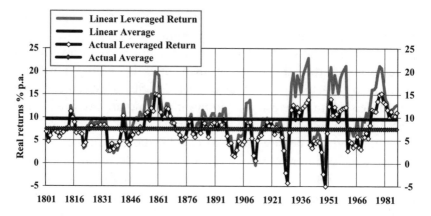

Chart 39. US Leveraged Equity Returns. Comparing Actual Results with "Linear" Leverage.

The impact of negative serial correlation is illustrated in Chart 39. This compares the returns from the actual leveraged portfolios to those which would have been available if the impact of leverage had been linear, i.e. if equity returns did not exhibit negative serial correlation and share prices followed a random walk. Not only are the returns in practice two percentage points p.a. worse than they would have been had share prices followed a random walk, but the effect is to lower all the returns, including both the peaks and the troughs, so that negative results are far more likely.

When equity portfolios are leveraged with debt, it is not only the long-term return which affects the actual result but the pattern of returns and the level of the interest payments. This can be illustrated by an extreme example. Had an equity portfolio been bought with debt costing 5% just before the stock market fell by 90%, then 50% of the portfolio would have had to be sold to pay the interest at the end of the first year. If there had been no recovery in the next year, the rest of the portfolio would then have had to be sold. If the market then recovered in year 3 to 120% of its original value, a profit would have been made, had the financing been made with a zero coupon bond, on which the interest would only have been payable at the end of the period. Equally, had the market risen steadily each year to 120% by the end of year 3, a profit would have been made, even with interest being deducted each year. The "return on equities" over the three years would have been the same in each case.

But borrowing on a long-term fixed basis is not the only way by which investors might seek to leverage an equity portfolio with short-term debt. If they choose the latter route, they will have the advantage, over the long term, of paying out less interest than if they had elected to borrow on a long-term basis. The lenders will, however, require that their risks are constrained. They will therefore require that the value of the portfolio held as security for their loan should always exceed the value of the debt. As the equity market has in the past fallen by as much as 89% over three years, this requirement will mean that investors who do not have other proportionately large sources of wealth will have to sell part of their portfolios when share prices fall. The ratio of the total value of the assets to the debt provides the "cover" for the lender. The greater the cover, the less will be the risk incurred by the lender and the less the margin that the lender will require above the "risk free" rate available on short-term deposits.

Equity portfolios can be leveraged with short-term debt, and they can also be deleveraged by investing less than 100% in equities and having the rest invested in cash on deposit. The interest on both the debt and the invested cash will vary with short-term interest rates and is thus known as being on a "floating rate" basis. On average, the interest on deposits is lower than the return on equities, so portfolios partly invested in cash seem likely to have lower returns than those invested only in equities and returns are likely to be increased further by the addition of leverage. While in practice this expectation is generally realized, it is substantially modified by the destabilizing effect not only of the interest payments, but through the purchases and sales of equities which are needed to maintain stable cover for the debt and by the stabilizing effect which occurs when the portfolios are partly invested in cash. Where leverage is used, a fall in the stock market requires shares to be sold, as otherwise the cover will fall below the required level and, where cash is part of the portfolio, the opposite effect is seen as shares are purchased when prices fall as this increases the liquidity ratio.

To see how, in practice, these forces offset one another, I have constructed a series of portfolios based on historic data, which range from 100% cash up to 100% in equities and then to 200% equities (i.e. having debt equal to the amount of the investors' own resources). As the stock market fluctuates, equities will need to be regularly bought and sold to preserve these ratios. Without adjusting the portfolio frequently, it will be impossible for most investors to borrow at anywhere near the risk-free rate and if the benefits of leverage are calculated on the assumption that risky debt can be borrowed at a risk-free rate, they will obviously produce misleading answers. In practice, the cost of the debt will rise as the cover falls, but I have made no allowance for this as the requirements will no doubt change over time, and even without such adjustments the reason why investors do not leverage is readily apparent. While the results of this exercise therefore tend to overstate the benefits of leverage, these benefits are still inadequate to make leverage generally worthwhile.

I have assumed that debt can be borrowed, or cash deposited, at the three months commercial paper (CP) rate and the portfolio is adjusted to maintain various cash or debt levels at each monthly valuation. Since the stock market has not yet fallen by over 50% in one month, it is reasonable to assume that, even at the highest of these debt levels, the risk to the lender would not rise to a point at which borrowing would cost significantly more than the CP rate.[77]

There are additional advantages in this approach; not only does it make a significant level of leverage a practical possibility, which would not otherwise be the case, but the timing decision about when to leverage becomes random. This is necessary if we are to distinguish between the impact of leverage which does not seek to benefit from market timing and from attempts to use leverage to exploit fluctuations in the price of shares away from their fair or fundamental value. The returns from these portfolios which are frequently adjusted to preserve a stable level of leverage are therefore a proper guide to those that can be achieved by investors who are not seeking to benefit from market timing.

---

[77] On these terms, borrowing will in practice cost more than the risk-free rate to provide a return and cover the costs of management, but it should not need to include any significant additional spread to cover the default risk.

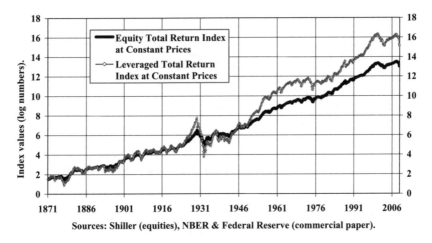

Sources: Shiller (equities), NBER & Federal Reserve (commercial paper).

Chart 40. US Stock Market Performance of Leveraged and Unleveraged Equity Portfolios 1871–2008.

I have taken 25 years as a suitable time horizon for long-term investors, on the grounds that those saving for retirement, as explained in Chapter 12, have the best risk-adjusted returns from investing in equities. If, on average, they start work at 20 and retire at 65, they will work for 45 years, and if they save evenly over their working lives, the average life of their investments will be 22.5 years. The results are very different from those that would occur if the stock market was fully efficient and did not fluctuate around its value creating the observed negative serial correlation of returns.

Chart 40 compares the value, in constant prices, of an unleveraged equity portfolio starting in 1871 with that of a portfolio which is leveraged to the extent that 50% is debt financed. Although the leveraged portfolio has given a higher return than the unleveraged one over the whole period, it is interesting to observe that for the first 80 years up to 1951, the returns on the two portfolios were the same. It has only been since World War II, when inflation rose to unanticipated levels, that leverage paid. It is thus doubtful whether there would have been any benefit in terms of added return if inflationary expectations had been met.

Chart 40 compares only the returns and not the risks and does so only for two portfolios, the unleveraged and the fully leveraged. In Chart 41 I show the way in which both risks and returns vary for the full range of the portfolios from 100% cash to 100%

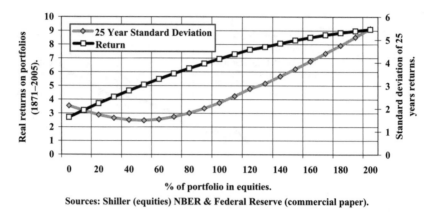

Sources: Shiller (equities) NBER & Federal Reserve (commercial paper).

Chart 41. Long-term Volatility and Real Returns from US Portfolios from 100% Cash to 100% Leveraged.

leveraged.[78] The returns rise quickly as the proportion of the portfolio invested in equities rises but, once leverage is introduced, the impact weakens to the point where little extra benefit is gained. The volatility of the returns, which measures their degree of risk, actually falls as the portfolio moves from being 100% invested in cash to having a higher proportion of equities. This changes once the equity proportion rises to about 60% and then the volatility rises at an increasing rate, first as the portfolio becomes 100% invested in equities and then as it becomes increasingly leveraged.

In Chart 42 I show the risk-adjusted returns for the different portfolios via their Sharpe Ratios. This shows that leverage of this sort doesn't pay. The most efficient portfolio in terms of its risk-adjusted return doesn't use any leverage at all but is 80% equities and 20% cash.

The result is that the best long-term portfolio from the viewpoint of optimizing the balance between risk and return is one that is less than 100% invested in equities. Some economists[79] have sought

[78] The returns are annual measured at constant price and the risks are measured by the standard deviation of those returns.
[79] For example "Junior Can't Borrow: A New Perspective on the Equity Premium Puzzle", by Constantinides, Donaldson and Mehra. *Quarterly Journal of Economics,* 2001.

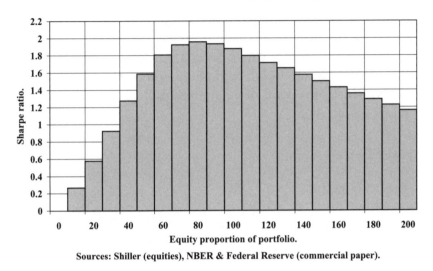

Sources: Shiller (equities), NBER & Federal Reserve (commercial paper).

Chart 42. The Sharpe Ratio.

explanations as to why the observed ERP has not been lowered by the arbitrage effect of leverage. But the apparent paradox disappears if their implicit assumption, which is that share prices follow a random walk, is dropped in favour of the observed negatively serial correlation of returns. The assumption that this was due to the fact that "Junior" (i.e. investors with a long-term investment horizon) couldn't borrow can be seen to be unnecessary. Juniors appear to be smarter than they were thought to be. The reason they don't borrow is not because they can't, but because they are wise enough not to do so. Far from the optimal portfolio being leveraged, it benefits from being less than fully invested in equities. A portfolio which maintains a steady ratio of cash to equities will benefit from "dollar averaging" and achieve a better balance between risk and return than one which is 100% invested in equities.

It can be argued that, while the above observations are valid if the Sharpe Ratio accurately represents the desired risk posture of the average investor, this is not necessarily the case. Investors may be more or less willing to accept risk for the sake of higher returns than the Sharpe Ratio implies. It is, however, possible to adapt the ratio in a number of different ways to allow for those who are more or less eager to take risk. One way is to increase the perceived benefit of holding risky assets by lowering the assumed risk-free return, but if this is done the optimal cash ratio is virtually unchanged.[80]

The results shown in Charts 38 to 42 are not surprising in terms of theory, as they are in line with those expected as a result of the negative serial correlation of equity returns.[81]

[80] This calculation has an additional benefit, as I have assumed that the risk-free rate is the same as the 3-month return on commercial paper. The risk-free rate will in practice be a bit less than this as, if investors want a truly risk-free return, they must have the right to withdraw their deposits on demand without penalty. The calculations show that lowering the risk-free rate does not affect the conclusions regarding the impact of leverage on risk and return.

[81] See Appendix 4 for an algebraic demonstration that negative serial correlation can make the leverage of an equity portfolio unattractive.

16

A Rare Exception to the Rule Against Leverage

If markets were perfectly efficient, it could never pay to leverage an equity portfolio. It would either pay to do so always or never and, if always, then arbitrage would rapidly destroy the benefit. But if markets are only moderately efficient, rare opportunities to benefit from leverage may arise and, I think, have recently done so.

In the previous chapter, I showed that leverage is not, as a general rule, a sensible policy for even long-term equity investors. The key to this is that equity returns exhibit negative serial correlation. But this quality also means that these returns are, to some extent, capable of being forecast. It follows that while leverage is generally foolish, it may not be always. I emphasized in Chapter 8 that the ability to forecast returns must be only moderate, or it would be exploited by arbitrage until it ceased to exist. Nonetheless, even that moderate ability becomes quite useful if the time horizon is long enough. Provided that the stock market is not too overpriced, there is a strong likelihood that it will give a return reasonably close to its very long-term average to investors who plan to stay invested for 30 or 40 years. If, at the same time, it is possible to borrow at very low cost, there may be times when it is possible

Table 14. UK and US Government Bond Yields as at 3 May 2008.

	Nominal	Index-linked
UK	4.57[1]	0.83[2]
US	4.56[3]	2.00[4]

Source: Financial Times [1]4.25% 2036. [2]2% 2035. [3]4.38% 2038.
Source: Ecowin [4]3.375% 2032.

to benefit from leverage, by borrowing long-term and investing in the stock market.

In such circumstances long-term debt has one marked advantage over borrowing on a floating rate basis: the cost is known and does not change during its life. Thus, if investors are going to attempt to time their use of leverage, it is likely that the ideal method will be to use long dated debt and the ideal time will be when bond yields are low.

In May 2008, bond yields became very low and this was particularly the case for UK index-linked bonds, which are those where the coupon and the principle are linked to the retail price index and the investors are thus protected against the adverse impact of inflation and can be assured of the return that they will receive in constant prices. Similar bonds issued in the US are called Treasury Inflation Protected (TIPS).

Table 14 shows the levels to which bond yields had fallen in May 2008. In Table 2 I showed that real bond returns had averaged 3.32% in the US over the past 207 years, and since this seems to have been reduced by unanticipated inflation in the 20th century, the expected real return on long dated bonds has probably been significantly higher. It thus seemed clear that the index-linked bond yields were very low, particularly in the UK, and that given any likely assumptions about inflation, this was also true − though less obvious − of the nominal yields as well.

The possibility of benefiting from these very unusual conditions was therefore raised at a meeting of the Investment Committee of Clare College, Cambridge, of which I am a member, and which manages the College's endowments. It was decided that the matter deserved careful study and Stephen Wright and I were asked to prepare a report in which we would assess the risks and potential rewards for raising long-term debt to invest in the stock market. We were also asked, if this did appear a good idea, whether the debt

Table 15. Historic Real Returns on UK and US Equities.

UK (1900–2007)	US (1801–2007)
5.6%	6.8%

should be in traditional fixed-interest terms with a fixed nominal coupon, or in index-linked terms.

For such leverage to be sensible, the first condition was that the equity risk premium must be highly unstable. A stable ERP would mean that the level cost of borrowing would probably be matched by a low return on equities. Our first step was therefore to show, as I have in Chapter 3, that low bond yields did not imply anything about future equity returns. If this had not been the case, it would either always be sensible to borrow and invest or never, as the probable return on equity investment would rise and fall with the cost of borrowing.

The second condition was that either the cost of borrowing was exceptionally low or the prospective returns on equity were exceptionally high. Provided that the College, as well as the UK government, could borrow at a very low current cost, then the gap between average long-term equity returns, as shown in Table 15, and the costs of borrowing was clearly much greater than usual. This opened up the possibility, but by no means the probability, that the conditions were sufficiently unusual to make a leveraged investment in equities sensible.

As the borrowing cost was exceptionally low, the key issues were the likely returns on equities and the associated risks. Although the instability of the ERP meant that equity returns were independent of bond yields, this did not mean that equity returns might not be below average. This was indeed the Investment Committee's view. We had sold approximately one-third of the College's share holdings in 1999 when we thought (it now seems with hindsight correctly) that world equity markets had become ludicrously overpriced. We had retained the cash in the expectation of being able to buy later on more favourable terms, and had so far decided that markets had not yet fallen enough to justify reinvestment. In the meantime, the fall in the stock market had had the effect of greatly increasing our liquidity ratio.

In our report we advised Clare College to proceed with the borrowing but to delay purchasing shares. We strongly advised that the money should be borrowed on an index-linked (inflation protected) basis. The market conditions were particularly favourable for this type of borrowing. UK pension fund advisers had become so nervous of the risks involved in meeting their obligations, which were linked to inflation, that they appeared to be willing to pay an exceptionally – and indeed in our view excessively – high premium for being insured against this risk. This consideration was, however, only one reason for our preference. An exceedingly important part lay in the much lower level of interest payments involved compared with raising debt on the traditional basis of a higher nominal interest rate. As I explained in Chapter 15, the impact of negative serial correlation is to cause returns to be high when the stock market is depressed and to be low when it has boomed. It therefore follows that interest payments, which are proportional to the initial amount borrowed, will be high relative to the current value of the invested portfolio when the stock market is depressed, thus giving above-average prospective returns and vice versa. A key advantage of index-linked borrowing was that initial interest payments would be about one-fifth of the amount needed had the debt been in nominal terms.

I have subsequently received many questions about the College's decision. It is clear that interaction between the level of interest payments and the negative serial correlation of equity returns is the issue least often considered by those who have contemplated raising debt to invest in a similar way and, in general, is the least understood feature of stock markets.

In our report we had not only considered the likely returns from equities, but also the risks that actual results would diverge substantially from our central forecast. We concluded that, while the likely range of returns was quite wide, it was significantly reduced over our 40-year time horizon by the compressed volatility of the market over these long periods. Even if returns were well below our central forecast, this was high enough – provided that shares were not purchased when the stock market was overpriced – to reduce the risk of loss to an acceptably low level.

As things turned out, the negotiations over the borrowing proved to be quite protracted and bond yields fell even further from the levels that had seemed so attractive in May 2008. To make matters even more helpful, the stock market had fallen sharply. By October, the deal was finalised. The College had managed to borrow money for 40 years at a real cost of just over 1% p.a., and had the opportunity to buy shares at much lower prices than those we had considered in May and at levels which then appeared to represent reasonable values. The real return over the next 40 years from equities purchased towards the end of 2008 was therefore unlikely to differ greatly from its long-term average.

When the arrangements were finally completed, they received considerable publicity, notably in an article in the *Financial Times*. This produced a response in the form of two letters to the paper critical of Clare College's decision. I was interested to observe that, while there were risks involved which could reasonably have been the cause of objections, neither of the letters seemed to me to be soundly based. Both of them assumed, implicitly and I thought therefore almost certainly without the authors' realizing that they had made these assumptions, that financial markets were perfectly efficient. The College would not have proceeded with the transaction had the evidence against the EMH not been so strong. But the fact that the letters both assumed that it held and did not refer to the fact that they had made this assumption, showed how pervasive and pernicious the idea has become. Few assumptions are more destructive of sound reasoning than those which are both incorrect and frequently used without the users being aware that they are doing so.

17

Profits are Overstated

The return that investors have received over the long term provides very important information about the economy. It is, however, information that has largely been neglected. There are probably two main reasons for this. The first is that, when looking at long-term economic developments, the attention of economists has been concentrated on data from the national accounts. Secondly, as already mentioned, stock markets have been seen as being not quite respectable by many economists and thus not worthy of the attention that they truly deserve. As a result of this neglect very little attention has been given to important identities which provide the connection between information about the economy and stock market data.

It is both correct and generally understood that if a bond is issued at a given yield this will, over its life, also be the cost to the issuer and the return to the holder. As I have explained, the same equivalent identity exists in the case of equities, but is less generally appreciated, probably because it is obscured by the fact that shares do not have a preset life span. The same identities between yield, cost and return apply to shares, but investors are even less likely to hold shares than they are to hold bonds over their respective life spans. The total return on shares for all investors will be the same whether we look just at the dividends they pay and the rate at which these dividends change, or whether we average the returns that accrue to all investors, after allowing for the capital gains and losses that are made when they buy and sell them. But as most investors hold shares over relatively limited periods, returns on shares are usually considered in terms of a return, in which changes in capital value between purchase and sale are a key and often the dominant part.

But as shares cannot be sold by one investor without being bought by another, the capital gains and losses must even out over time, unless supported by the prospect of future increases in the dividends. For investors, what matters is the income from shares, not just what has been paid in the past but what will rationally be expected to be paid in the future. It follows that over the long term and in equilibrium, the return on equities to investors, the cost of equity finance to companies, and the prospective yield, allowing for future increases in dividends, must all be the same. If equities have a stable long-term return, as we have shown they have had, then this will be the same as their long-term average earnings yield, calculated by dividing the current share prices by earnings per share over the next 12 months, and this can be readily shown to be the same as the average dividend yield plus the rate at which this dividend will grow in the future.[82] Earnings are either paid out in dividends, or are reinvested in the companies to expand their net worth per share, either by additions to the companies' capital stock or through buying back a proportion of the companies' equity. If long-term equity returns are stable, the growth in dividends per share will depend on the proportion of profits which is paid out in dividends. But the return will not be affected by this payout ratio, although it will determine the proportion of the total return which comes from the dividend yield and the proportion which comes from the growth of dividends per share. For example, a long-term real return on equities of 7% could be achieved by a payout ratio averaging 50%, or one averaging 100%, provided that profits are correctly calculated. In the former case, the average dividend yield would be 3.5% and the long-term growth in real dividends also 3.5%, while in the latter the average dividend yield would be 7% and there would be no growth in dividends per share.

It follows that in equilibrium and over the long term, though not the short, there are four identities:

1. The return on equity to investors.
2. The average earnings yield.

---

[82] This is known after its authors as the Miller–Modigliani theorem.

Table 16. US Payout Ratios, Comparing the Implied Rise in Real
Dividends with the Observed Rise.

Long-term average payout ratio	59.5%
Long-term average earnings yield	7.4%
Implied long-term ploughback per share and thus implied rise in dividends per share	3.00%
Long-term observed rise in real dividends per share	1.2%

Source: Shiller, 1871–2006.

3. The return on corporate net worth, adjusted for inflation.
4. The average dividend yield plus the growth in dividends per share.

As I mentioned, these identities depend on profits being correctly measured. This proviso is extremely important as we can see by comparing average dividend yields and the growth of dividends per share with long-term returns to investors. When this is done, it becomes clear that profits as announced by companies have been consistently overstated in the past and, although this does not necessarily apply to profits as stated in the national accounts, other evidence points to this also being the case.

According to Professor Shiller's compilation of data for the US stock market from 1871 (Table 16), the average dividend yield has been 4.3% and the increase in real dividends per share 1.2% p.a.[83] As these sum to 5.5%, they point to a real return on corporate capital which is well below the average earnings yield, on the next 12 months earnings, of 7.4%.

A likely explanation of this discrepancy is that profits have been persistently overstated. This assumption is also the most likely explanation for another oddity, which is that dividends have grown much more slowly than the data on profits suggest that they should have done.

Subject to one possible complication, we know that if profits had been correctly calculated and the real return on equity has been stable over time, then the rise in real dividends should have been

---

[83] The DMS data published in *Triumph of the Optimists* by Dimson, Marsh and Staunton show the average US dividend yield as being a bit less over the 20th century and the growth of real dividends per share as being only 1% p.a.

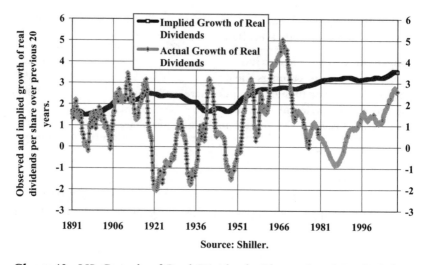

Chart 43. US Growth of Real Dividends Observed and Implied from Payout Ratios.

proportionate to the level of retentions. As Table 16 shows, from 1871 to 2006 the level of retentions implies that real dividends should have risen at 3% p.a. in real terms. However, as the table also shows, the observed rate was less than half that.

A complication arises from the fact that the dividend payout ratio has not been stable. If the payout ratio falls steadily and fast enough, this could explain the apparent discrepancy between the implied and observed rates of dividend growth shown in Table 16. The payout ratio, which is the proportion of earnings paid out in dividends, has tended to fall over time and this will have accounted for part of the observed discrepancy between the ploughback and dividend growth.

But Chart 43 shows that the fall in the payout ratio is not sufficient to account for the whole discrepancy, because the observed growth in dividends has only briefly, and on rare occasions, matched or exceeded the rate implied by ploughback. It is therefore clear that the rise in the payout ratio is not a sufficient explanation of the slow rise in the real dividend per share.[84] In addition, the real

---

[84] The observed growth in real dividends per share is simply the rate of growth over the past 20 years, while the implied rate is calculated from the average retention of real earnings over the past 20 years, i.e. the proportion of EPS that is not

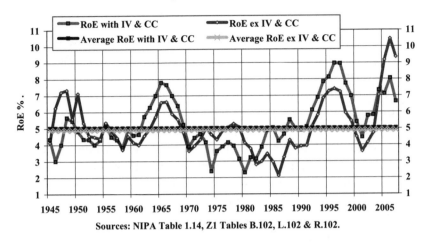

Chart 44. US Nonfinancial Companies Return on Domestic Net Worth 1945–2007.

ploughback must have been much less than the published level. As with the discrepancy between the real return on equity to investors, the most likely explanation is that profits have been persistently overstated.

A similar problem arises if the return on corporate equity is compared with the return to investors. We have annual data for the US from 1947 and the return on corporate equity which it reveals has averaged 5% p.a., as Chart 44 illustrates.[85] Again, the simplest explanation for this is to assume that profits have been habitually overstated. As the taxes and dividends paid are unaffected, a reduction in profits has a markedly greater impact on the retained profits. As the calculations of corporate net worth in the Flow of Funds Accounts of the United States (Z1) are derived from the past accumulations of retained profits, the result of assuming that profits have been overstated is that net worth will have been overstated to an even greater extent.

If profits had been correctly calculated, the long-term equilibrium between the value of the corporate sector as shown by the

---

paid out in dividends, and the long-term real rate of return on equities which was 6.1% from 1871 to 2008. Thus a retention rate of 33% implied that dividend growth will be one-third of 6.1% p.a., i.e. 2.03% p.a.

[85] The calculations for Chart 44 are the same as those for Chart 9, which are explained in detail in footnote 34.

stock market and its value in terms of corporate net worth would have averaged 1. If net worth has been overstated, because of overstated profits, then this average q ratio will be, as it is observed to be, less than 1.

The evidence that profits have been habitually overstated is thus strong because:

1. From 1871 to 2008, the long-term average earnings yield has been 7.4%. This is 15% higher than the long-term real return on equities to investors of 6.5% over the same period, and 10% above the return from 1871 to 2007.
2. The growth of dividends has been too slow in relation to the recorded level of retained profits.
3. The average return on corporate equity since 1945, as shown in Chart 43, has been 4.9%, which is 20% below the long-term real return to investors.
4. The average level of q is 0.64 rather than 1.

Overstated profits cause retained profits to be overstated by an even larger proportion, as the deductions for tax and dividends are unchanged. I do not have data on tax rates paid by listed companies from 1871, so I can only show an example of how profit overstatement affects retained profits and thus net worth, rather than a detailed estimate. Table 17 shows that if profits are consistently overstated by 10%, the rate of corporation tax averages 30% and the payout ratio is 50%, then the "real" net worth of companies will, on average, be only 71% of the official figure as estimated in the Flow of Funds Accounts. This is a bit higher than that suggested by

Table 17. Example to Illustrate Impact of Overstated Profits on Net Worth.

	Published	Adjusted
Profits before tax	100	90
Tax	30	30
Dividend	35	35
Retained profit	35	25
Adjusted retained profit as % of published		71.43
Adjusted net worth as % of published		71.43

the average q ratio, and indicates that profits are likely to have been overstated by between 10% and 20%, which fits well with the difference between the long-term earnings yield and the long-term real return to investors.

Data from other countries indicate that the overstatement of profits is not restricted to the US but seems to be universal. From 1900 to 2000, real dividends per share are reported to have fallen in nine out of 15 countries for whose markets adequate data appear to be available. For the level of profits in these countries to have been correctly recorded, they would have had to have shown a persistent overdistribution of profits.

18

Intangibles

The evidence, set out in Chapter 17, that profits have been habitually over- rather than understated becomes of great importance when considering the question of intangibles. When teaching a course on the valuation of equity markets, I find that the question about whether intangibles have value in aggregate is frequently raised by the students. It is clear that individual companies can make substantial profits from their intangible assets and it is natural, therefore, to assume that such assets have some aggregate value. However, CAPE measures the aggregate value of companies solely through their profits and q measures them purely through their tangible assets' values; these two separate metrics are highly correlated and agree in the measure of the aggregate value of the market, as shown in Chapter 8.

There are three possible conclusions about the total value of intangibles which follow from this.

The first is that intangibles in aggregate have no value. This does not mean that individual cases of valuable intangible assets cannot exist, so that such companies will be more valuable than their tangible net worth, but that these will be balanced by companies whose total value is below their tangible net worth. The former will have a "goodwill" value which will be shown by the fact that such companies have an above average return on their tangible net worth, while the latter group will have "illwill" as they will have a below average return on their tangible net worth. As accountants will be willing to acknowledge the existence of goodwill but not illwill, this underlying reality will not be readily seen from company balance sheets which will, under these conditions, show an aggregate value for intangibles. This explanation would be adequate if the only reason why companies had above or below average returns was luck, and as this is often true it represents a partial, but by no means full, account of the difference between individual and aggregate goodwill. Good and bad luck can arise in many ways. For example, companies in different industries will frequently make poor forecasts about the growth of demand for certain products, and where demand turns out to be below forecast the resulting over capacity will lead to below average returns for the industry as a whole. Equally, unexpectedly strong demand for a product will lead to high returns.

The second possibility is that the aggregate amount of investment made into creating intangible assets has a constant ratio to the amount of investment made into tangible assets. There can then be real value in aggregate which can be ascribed to the goodwill arising from investment in, for example, research or advertising. But while the ratio of goodwill to tangible assets may differ from company to company, the aggregate value of intangibles will have a constant ratio to the aggregate value of tangible assets. In this case, the value of companies in aggregate would always be proportionate to the total value of their tangible capital and the average value of q would then be just as stable as if only tangible capital is included in the calculation.

Finally, there is the possibility that, while the amount of investment in intangibles may vary, the benefits from it will vary inversely with the amount invested. The value of intangibles could then have a stable relationship with tangible assets even though the relative amounts invested in each vary over time.

The first of these possible solutions clearly has its place in understanding the way in which the sum of individual companies' goodwill and the aggregate total differ. The second does not seem to apply as it appears from research sponsored by the Federal Reserve that investment in research and advertising has risen relative to tangible investment.[86] The evidence therefore points to the third

[86] See *Intangible Capital and Economic Growth* by Carol Corrado, Charles Hulten and Daniel Sichel, published by the Federal Reserve in their Finance and Economic Discussion series 2006-24.

solution in which the relative returns from intangible investment fall as the amount rises. To show how this happens it is necessary to consider the conventions under which national and corporate accounts are constructed.

It is clear that without the growth of knowledge and the investment in human capital that allows technological progress to be applied to economic output, real wages could not rise. The resulting "advancement of learning" would not occur without a great deal of spending on education and research, which can thus reasonably be considered to be investment, but which is not categorized as such in national accounts. There is therefore a reasonable case that national accounts would provide a better reflection of reality if two changes were made. First, expenditure on education should be considered as investment rather than consumption and, second, intangible investment by corporations should be reclassified as a final rather than an intermediate output.

From the viewpoint of investors, only the second of these possible changes is relevant. Under the current convention only physical investment is included as such in the national accounts. If this was changed to include investment in research, and possibly in other forms of intangible investments such as advertising, the result would be to increase GDP and gross corporate profit before depreciation. We know, however, that the return on corporate equity must, over the long term, equal the return on equity investment to shareholders. As this will not be altered by a change in the convention for recording gross profits, before depreciation, we know that any increase in them must be matched by an equal rise in depreciation.

Investment in intangibles, such as research or advertising, can result, if successful, in improved profits for individual companies, but will not increase profits in aggregate. This is because such investment will either result in a rise in market share or improved productivity. Both will be a zero sum game in aggregate, because the improvement that will result from the profits of an individual company will be matched by the reduced profits of others. Improved market share is possible for one company, but not for all. Improved productivity increases real wages and depreciation is a function of the speed at which real wages rise. Any advance in productivity will benefit the company that leads the way, but will have a matching negative impact on all the others. Changing the convention under which national accounts are drawn up could therefore result in a rise in gross profits before depreciation, but not in any change in post-depreciation profits, provided depreciation is correctly accounted.

Improved living standards depend on increased knowledge. As a result of savings and investment, the quantity of tangible capital such as plant and machinery grows steadily over time. Parallel with this growth in the stock of capital, there has been a steady increase in real wages. But this can only occur if technology is steadily improving as knowledge advances. If wages per employee rise in real terms without a matching rise in productivity, then the return on capital will fall steadily, as the output per person employed would not change but the cost of employing each person would rise. As continuing falls in the return on capital cannot be sustained, real wages can only rise as technology improves. The rise in output, which cannot be explained by increased supplies of labour or capital, is termed total factor productivity and is usually treated by economists as if it fell like manna from heaven – or, in economists' language, it is "exogenous". It seems probable that knowledge advances, to some extent at least, because resources are invested in it. But these resources are not identified in national accounts as these are currently presented. There is therefore a reasonable case that investment, as defined in national accounts, is seriously understated.

While this view seems eminently reasonable, what does not follow are a series of propositions which are often assumed to do so.

1. That what is not measured can be measured.
2. That if it could be measured, there would be any practical benefit from doing so.
3. That economic growth is understated by the failure to record investment in the advancement of learning.
4. That corporate profits and asset values would be increased if investment in intangibles were measured and included in national data.

National accounts, including such figures as GDP and broadly defined profits, are produced on the basis of certain agreed conventions. If these conventions are changed, the resulting figures must also change. It would be easy to change these conventions to include some of the unrecorded investment made in the advancement of learning. Reasonable changes could be made that would increase the current level of GDP and its past rate of growth. These changes would, obviously enough, neither increase our current material welfare nor the rate at which it has advanced. As I will seek to explain, the reason for this apparent dichotomy is that material welfare is not measured by GDP but rather, if the correct adjustments are made, by net domestic product (NDP). This is because only consumption, current or prospective, affects welfare. An increase in investment which did not result in future consumption being greater than it would otherwise have been has no value at all; it is simply wasted. For the capital stock to grow, gross investment has to be larger than depreciation. The difference, which is the level of net investment, therefore has to be positive. The current level of material welfare is current consumption, plus the present value of future increases and this is the sum of current consumption plus net investment. This equals NDP in a closed economy.[87]

The difference between GDP and NDP lies in capital consumption. Broadly speaking, this is the fall in the value of the existing stock of capital which accompanies growth and is its inescapable consequence.[88] If gross output is increased by a change in the conventions used to measure it, but our material welfare has not changed, it follows that the changes in the conventions must involve

---

[87] For a formal equivalence between NDP and aggregate welfare, net investment should be deflated using a price index of consumption. This is not current practice in the national accounts. NDP, with net investment appropriately deflated, has been shown to provide a measure of aggregate welfare under various assumptions, including non-constant interest rates, thereby allowing net investment to be non-zero. See "The Concept of Income in a General Equilibrium" by J. A. Sefton and M. R. Weale, *Review of Economic Studies*, 2006, for a formal demonstration.

[88] Once allowance is made for the consumption of raw materials, the situation is even worse. Rising living standards depend on improved technology, they cannot rise without it, but with sufficient improvement raw material supplies will not prevent growth. This is why economic models, in which technology advances, involve changes in the stock of labour and capital, but do not need to make any allowance for the exhaustion of raw material supplies. These models effectively assume that there are no limits to knowledge. Claims that there are limits to economic growth assume, usually without realising that the assumption is being made, that there are limits to knowledge. So far, the optimistic view that there are no limits to knowledge appears to have been justified, but we cannot be sure that it will be in the future and it is not a subject on which economics can shed light. However, for a non-economist's optimistic view of these issues see "On 'The Effecting of All Things Possible'" by P. B. Medawar, published in *Hope of Progress* by Methuen & Co., 1972.

an equal and balancing change in the measurement of NDP and thus in the measurement of capital consumption. But while the change in the system of measurement cannot increase material welfare, it may provide a better assessment of it than the previous convention. A key issue therefore is whether there exists a way whereby NDP can be measured directly, without needing assumptions to be made about capital consumption. The answer to this is yes, provided that a long time period is used.

NDP can be divided into income from labour and income from capital. As capital consumption applies by definition only to capital, if we can find a measure of income from it after depreciation, then this figure plus labour incomes must provide us with a measure of NDP, which does not require any assumptions to be made about the level of depreciation. Furthermore, we will then know the level of depreciation. This will be the difference between NDP, as measured by our alternative approach which I describe below, and GDP, measured on either of the different conventions that are under consideration. If, therefore, the conventions used for the calculation of GDP are changed, then there must be compensating changes made in the calculation of depreciation. The way in which we can measure the level of capital incomes after depreciation comes from the identity that must exist between the return on equity to investors and to companies. But this identity will only be shown over the long term.

As shown in Charts 11 and 12, the long-term real return on equity has been stable. This average return must be equal to the average return that companies have obtained on their net worth, after depreciation. We therefore know that a change in the conventions used for the calculation of GDP cannot result in a rise in NDP, and must therefore produce an equal rise in depreciation, if that is correctly calculated in accordance with the change in the convention for calculating GDP.

A change in the calculation of GDP will not therefore necessarily lead to a change in the calculation of NDP. It should only do so if the change will produce an improved figure for NDP. If the calculation of GDP is increased by a new convention, depreciation must rise by enough to leave NDP unchanged, unless it was previously misstated.

We know, however, from the analysis set out in Chapter 17 that profits have been over- rather than understated. As NDP is the sum of profits after depreciation and labour incomes, we know that it is unlikely to have been overstated, as it is extremely improbable that wages and salaries have been very different from the figures shown in the national accounts. We can therefore be confident that a change in the conventions used to measure GDP must involve at least an equal rise in depreciation, provided we are looking at sufficiently long-term data. This does not necessarily apply over shorter time periods. A change in the convention which had no long-term consequences for NDP, but pointed to different short-term data, might represent an improvement in its calculation. The long-term evidence of returns to investors cannot be used in a short-term context, as returns to investors are highly volatile in the short term.

The current convention for the measurement of GDP defines all final output as being either consumption or investment in tangible assets. The production of other goods and services is considered to be intermediate, i.e. things necessary for the production of a final product. For example, steel output is not usually included as a final output, but appears in the data for output through the use of steel in such things as automobiles and chemical plant. Depreciation is then deducted from the combined final output arrived at by this convention. The conventional way to estimate depreciation is to assume that it is exogenous and to derive estimates for it on the assumption that different types of physical capital have set working lives, which are independent of the growth of the economy. But depreciation is not exogenous. It largely represents the decline in the value of capital equipment that arises from increases in real wages. There are severe limits to the extent to which productivity can be improved without additional investment in up-to-date plant. Without such investment, the output per person employed will be more or less static, so that the profits from the existing equipment will fall as real wages rise. It follows that the faster real wages rise, the faster depreciation will be if properly measured. The correct level of depreciation can therefore only be known when many other details about the growth of the economy are known, and involve much more complex calculations than are currently involved in its estimation.[89]

---

[89] The information needed for total accuracy is unlikely to be available for many years after the event and it would also depend on the conventions used. For example, the rate of depreciation depends on the cost of servicing non-depreciating capital, which in turn depends, inter alia, on the cost of capital and the value of land.

The current approach to estimating depreciation has consider-able practical justification, but has also given rise to some problems which have probably been aggravated by the fact that, in recent years, economists have largely ignored the important issues that arise once the endogenous nature of depreciation is accepted.

1. It has led to the understatement of corporate depreciation and thus to the overstatement of profits and to the even greater overstatement of net worth, which was explained in Chapter 17.
2. It has been accompanied by widespread misunderstanding of the cause and nature of depreciation, which is illustrated in a common confusion between depreciation and maintenance.[90]

It is clearly possible to produce national accounts which are based on different conventions. For example, net investment could be measured by the rise in the market value of the capital stock. If these market values could be readily measured and were always correct, this should provide a very accurate answer. The resulting figures for NDP would presumably be those which believers in the Efficient Market Hypothesis would consider to be "correct". If this convention were possible and followed, it would be the equivalent for the national accounts that "mark to market" accounting is for companies' accounts. Net output would simply be defined as the sum of goods and services consumed, plus the rise in value of the capital stock. This sum would give the value of NDP and some assumed level of depreciation would then have to be added to produce the figures for GDP if it were thought that these were needed.[91] I will show in the next chapter that the extreme volatility of the GDP figures that would result would render them incredible and largely useless for practical purposes. It is not surprising that

[90] Sadly, this confusion is not confined to non-economists, as I realized when I found an undergraduate textbook on sale in Cambridge which claimed that depreciation was maintenance.

[91] It is not easy to see why they should be required; NDP data would be available and are a better guide than GDP for economic growth and welfare. For example, a rise in GDP which is not matched by a rise in NDP has no value in terms of economic welfare. No one is better off unless NDP rises.

national accountants have been sensible enough to ignore the EMH when producing their data.

Another way in which the conventions used for the production of national accounts could be changed would be to classify corporate investment in intangibles such as advertising and research as final rather than intermediate outputs, on the grounds that they are not needed for the current production of either consumer goods and services or tangible investment. Such a change in the conventions would neither increase past consumption nor the historic return that investors have received on their investments. NDP would remain unchanged and the increase in GDP, which would be revealed by the new calculations, would thus have to be matched by an equal rise in depreciation.

The current convention treats investment in intangibles as an intermediate rather than a final output. If this were changed and such investment were treated as a final output, then GDP would rise. NDP and profits would also rise unless either the depreciation attributable to intangibles was 100% or, if a lower rate is used, a faster rate of depreciation is applied to tangible investment. A paper published under the auspices of the Federal Reserve,[92] estimates that investment in intangibles by non-farm business has risen from around 3% of output in 1950 to around 13% in 2003, with the rise being a steady one over the long term rather than represented by a sudden jump in recent years.

If, as the paper in question proposes, this intangible investment is (i) included as a final output, (ii) not written off fully in year 1 and (iii) no increase is made in the depreciation of tangible assets, then not only would GDP be increased, but there would be a significant increase also in profits and corporate net worth. We know, however, that if the real return on equity investment is stable over the long term, then profits under the current convention are already overstated. A change in the convention which produces even higher profits must therefore be wrong.

It is clear that the paper's proposals cannot be correct unless either the evidence for the mean reversion of investor returns is ignored, or the Federal Reserve's data on intangible investment are

---

[92] *Intangible Capital and Economic Growth*, op. cit.

assumed to be wrong. As I see no justification for either view, this leaves various other possibilities:

1. The current convention is correct in theory, as investment in intangibles should be treated as an intermediate rather than a final output; i.e. there should be no change in output or profits in the national accounts.
2. The convention is correct in practice if not in theory, because 100% of investment in intangibles should be written off in the year in which it is incurred; i.e. GDP should be increased, but not NDP, or profits, or corporate net worth.
3. The convention is correct in practice if not in theory, because an increase in intangible investment causes a proportionate rise in the rate at which tangible capital should be depreciated.

From the viewpoint of calculating aggregate profits after depreciation or the NDP, it is irrelevant which of these solutions is preferred.

Two of the possibilities put forward accepted the idea that treating investment in intangibles as an addition to final output was justified, but that any such increase left NDP and net profits unchanged because it had to be matched by an equal rise in depreciation. This rise in depreciation could be applied to tangible as well as intangible assets. If an individual company increases its investment in intangibles, then the expenditure may produce no return whatever; but, as already mentioned, if successful it will either increase the market share of the company or its productivity, with the latter taking either the form of producing the same goods with lower labour input, or of producing a superior good, e.g. a new pharmaceutical. It can readily be seen that either result, while beneficial for the individual firm, amounts to a zero sum game in aggregate.

This is probably most obvious in terms of market share, but it applies equally to improved productivity. If one company increases its labour productivity, this will increase its profits at the same level of output. But increases in productivity also raise the level of real wages and, as Chart 17 in Chapter 8 showed, profit margins are strongly mean reverting, so that real wages rise in line with changes in productivity. This means that when one company improves its productivity the resulting increase in its profit is matched by a fall in the profits of other companies, though the individual amount suffered by any one company will be tiny when spread across the corporate sector in total. It follows that, while investment in intangibles makes sense for individual companies and makes a vital contribution to economic growth if it improves total factor productivity, it produces no aggregate improvement in profits.[93]

The results from individual expenditures on intangibles cannot be forecast but, if they match aggregate expectations, then the return on them will match the cost of capital. If the return on these investments accrues immediately, then they will have no capital cost and the appropriate rate of depreciation will be 100% immediately. If, however, some of the return will accrue in the future, then they will have value after the end of the period in which they have been incurred. This does not, however, mean that a rise in the proportion of intangible to tangible investment will increase aggregate profits or net worth. If the rise in intangible investment takes the form of advertising then, if the outturn matches expectations, everyone will invest enough to preserve their market shares. Investment in advertising will take place up to the point where the immediate return on it is zero and there will be no future value. Advertising will be as much a defensive as an offensive investment, designed to prevent a loss of market share as much as to create a hoped-for gain. It will not necessarily appear as such if, as seems likely, most companies' plans involve the assumption that they will increase market share.

Investment in research will have a similar result. If all companies engage in it and all are equally successful, then productivity will rise equally and so will the increase in labour rates. The correct rate of depreciation on such research expenditure will be 100%. If investment in research is limited, then those companies that engage in it will suffer from the expense but gain from a relative rise in productivity. Companies will logically engage in research to the point where they consider that further investment will yield no return. With imperfect foresight, results for individual companies will

---

[93] The impact of research expenditure, even on the profits of individual firms, is far from clear. "R&D spending frenzy may be a waste of money, says study" was the headline of an article in the *Financial Times* of 13 November 2006, reporting on a study by Booz Allen Hamilton.

sometimes be positive and sometimes negative but, in aggregate, the result will always be zero, as an improvement in productivity by any individual company raises labour costs. The faster productivity rises, the faster will be the correct level of depreciation on the tangible assets owned. Changes in the level of intangible investment relative to the level of tangible investment will thus have no impact on aggregate profits or net worth.

If it appears odd that the present value of companies in aggregate is not increased if they increase their investment in intangibles, it is worth noting that this applies also to investment in tangibles. The present value of a company or of companies in general is not changed by the proportion of profits that is invested or returned to shareholders as cash. The evidence points to the long-term real return on equity as being stable and substantially greater, in the absence of catastrophes, than the growth rate of mature economies. According to the Miller–Modigliani theorem, the return is independent of the payout ratio. If we compare two economies with the same increase in labour productivity, which have different growth rates in terms of labour supply, the return to equity will be the same in both, but the level of ploughback and the growth of the capital stock will be greater in the country with the faster growth in labour supply. The level of tangible investment and the return on equity will be independent of one another.

It should not therefore cause surprise if the same thing applies to investment in intangibles. Investment in them will not depress equity returns, nor will it increase them. The benefit from increased and successful investment in either tangible assets or research should be a faster rate of growth for the economy and for real wages, but it will be a zero sum game for the corporate sector and investors in it.

National accountants seek to measure the amount spent on physical investment, but not that spent on the advancement of knowledge or on the human capital which allows new knowledge to be used to improve productivity. The measurement of GDP could be changed to allow for this lacuna. A new convention would be needed and it would perforce be somewhat arbitrary. It would be relatively easy to treat money spent on education as an investment rather than a form of consumption and to include companies' expenditure on research as an investment rather than an intermediary output. It would not, however, be sensible to try to estimate the amount of investment that parents make in the upbringing of their children in ways that do not involve monetary transactions. If what could be done were done, GDP would change in two ways: expenditure previously classed as consumption would become classified as investment and GDP would rise by the reclassification of intermediate output as final.

If the expenditure on education were depreciated, to allow for the fact that the educated do not work or live for ever, NDP would presumably be reduced. As we may be allowed to consider our current welfare to include the education of our children, this would seem to create at least as many problems as it solves. If the amount of consumption were left unchanged, then GDP would rise by the extent to which intermediate output had been reclassified as final. However, NDP would be unchanged, as the reclassification would have increased depreciation by the same amount. This would properly reflect the fact that people were neither "better nor worse off" than before.[94]

Including investment in intangibles, and then increasing the amount of depreciation by the same amount, might have the advantage of making it clear that the change has no impact on profits. The convention under which the change was introduced would necessarily be an arbitrary one. Should all expenditure which is made with the intention of improving future profits be called investment? If not, why not and, if so, should this include advertising as well as research and share options and bonuses which are designed to motivate management to do better in the future? Whatever answers the reader may choose to give to these questions, the key point about intangibles is that the current accounting conventions, which put no aggregate value on them, do not lead to an understatement of profits or net worth.

---

[94] "... as well-off should be considered to mean that the present discounted value of current and future utility should be unchanged over the interval considered." From "The Concept of Income in a General Equilibrium" by J. A. Sefton and M. R. Weale, *Review of Economic Studies*, 2006.

19

Accounting Issues

In the previous chapter I referred to the possibility that national accounts might be produced as if the EMH was correct. In such circumstances, the value ascribed by the stock market to corporate net worth would be the "correct" value in place of that currently used by the national accounting convention, which is based on original cost, subject to depreciation and inflation. Profits, if correctly calculated, are the sum of dividends and changes in net worth, before the impact of additions or depletions to net worth arising from the issue of new equity or its negative equivalent through buybacks.[95]

Due to the increasing use of market prices, the differences between profits in corporate and national accounts are widening. If market prices were used in national accounts, the results would be derided. As Chart 45 illustrates, swings in GDP over one year of 20% plus and minus would have been common.[96] Over the period

---

[95] This principle is named "Hicksian Equivalence" after Sir John Hicks, who is also reputed to have remarked that it is sometimes difficult to tell the difference between capital and income. In response, Sir Dennis Robertson pointed out that the jails were full of those who had failed to draw the distinction.

[96] To calculate profits from the change in the stock market, I have taken the change in the value of US companies from Z1 Table L.213 line 20, and added the cash distributed to shareholders other than via dividends from Z1 Table F.102 line 39 (for nonfinancials) and F.213 lines 5 & 17 (for commercial banks), adding dividends from NIPA Table 1.14 line 14; this constitutes Hicksian profits using stock market values. I have then adjusted nominal GDP (NIPA Table 1.1.5 line 1)

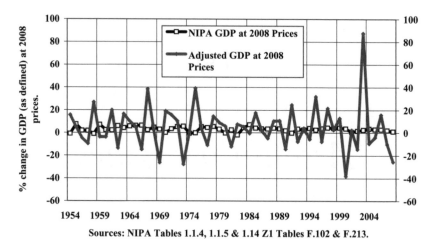

Chart 45. Annual Changes in US GDP as Published and Adjusted for Stock Market Prices.

(1952–2008 Q3) the growth of GDP at constant prices as measured by the national accounts or using stock market prices is reasonably close, being 3.2% and 2.8% p.a. respectively, but the changes are much more volatile when stock market prices are used and the difference in volatility has been particularly marked in recent years. As such volatility would be seen as both improbable and uninformative, it is not surprising that the national accountants seem never to have been tempted to produce their data in a form consistent with the underlying assumption of the EHM.

Until about 20 years ago, the published accounts of companies followed a similar convention to that used by the national accountants. Assets were generally valued at book cost less depreciation. As the understatement of depreciation had less impact than inflation, this led to the assets of companies, as shown in company accounts,

---

for the difference between the adjusted profits and those published (NIPA Table 1.14 line 13). These two nominal GDP series are then adjusted to constant (2008) prices from NIPA Table 1.1.4. As Z1 data for Q4 2008 were not available when I made these calculations, I have adjusted the value of companies by the change in the S&P 500 from end Q3 to end Q4 2008, and otherwise used 9 months' data annualized. As Q4 is likely to show a decline in buybacks by companies the fall in GDP, adjusted for changes in share prices, is likely to be greater than this estimate.

being under- rather than overstated. But the opposite impact occurred in the national accounts, however, where allowance was made for inflation in the valuation of corporate assets. On balance, profits in the national accounts and the net worth of companies derived from them has been habitually overstated, as I explained in Chapter 17.

Over the past two decades there has been a marked change in the presentation of company accounts which now strive to value assets at market rather than book prices. If this practice were universally applied, which is not practical or likely in the absence of market prices for many corporate assets, company accounts would become as volatile as the stock market. Plant and equipment is usually specific to individual industries and often to individual companies and, as few transactions in them take place, no market prices for these assets are available. However, companies have been buying and selling subsidiaries and smaller operating units for many years and these transactions have become increasingly common, to the extent that they seem to take a larger part of senior managements' attention than actually running their businesses. When such sales occur they set an arm's length price for the assets involved and when the stock market flourishes they usually take place at above the underlying asset values, adjusted for inflation. Not only is a profit usually recorded by the seller, but the transaction will boost its net worth above the value that it would have even if the original cost was adjusted for inflation. In terms of the national accounts, however, the transaction has had no impact on the underlying value of assets in the economy. This boost in the value of the sellers' net worth needs therefore to be matched by a similar reduction in the net worth of the buyer. This is, of course, not what happens, at least in terms of the published accounts of companies. No loss at the time of the acquisition is recorded by the buyer, even if the "goodwill" which arises from the seller's profit is subsequently amortized.

So long as business is generally flourishing and intercompany transactions are growing, the net result will be to boost aggregate corporate profits as recorded in the company accounts. But the transfer of assets between companies clearly makes no difference to the aggregate level of corporate profits in any real way nor, indeed, in terms of the national accounts. The increase in these types of transactions, combined with the change in corporate accounting practices, thus has the effect of producing a growing disparity between the aggregate value of profits shown in company accounts and the total value of the corporate sector's profits shown in the national accounts.

In the long run, this discrepancy should be corrected. The excess value created by the sale of assets at more than their inflation-adjusted cost is unlikely to be sustainable in bad times. As these assets fail to produce the level of profits that was expected when the transactions occurred, the inflated values of those assets, which were justified to the accountants on the grounds that they would produce the expected level of profits, will become suspect. In time, probably with the arrival of new management, the assets will be written down. New managements tend to arrive when times are tough, and their predecessors are blamed for past mistakes. The more heavily assets are written down, the worse the past appears to be and the better the future. This process means that assets tend to be written up to some extent with the stock market in good times and to be written down again in the tough ones. Buying and selling companies thus tends to boost the asset values of the companies involved in the transactions, compared with those where no deals have taken place. But competition between both types of companies will mean that similar assets will give similar returns, independently of their assumed book values. Over time, therefore, the value of all these assets will have to reflect their underlying rather than their book value.

Where plant and equipment continue in the ownership of the original corporate investor, contemporary accounting techniques continue, at least in general, to value these assets as before. However, the valuation of financial assets is readily changed to market prices, and when market prices are not readily available the dubious prac-tice of valuing these assets at "model prices" has become common. The difference between national and corporate profits has thus tended to increase, not only with the increasing use of current price accounting, but also with the rise in the importance of financial assets in the balance sheets of nonfinancial companies. These have grown from being equal to 30% of tangible assets and net worth in 1952 to between 80% and 90% today. The problem is aggravated by the growth of "off-balance sheet" debt. Although accountants are aware that obligations to pay rent can, for example, be substituted for obligations to pay interest, they have not yet generally succeeded in getting such obligations placed on company balance sheets. A full picture of corporate leverage would therefore require the addition of off- to on-balance sheet debt. This is not, however, readily available. If, for example, an airline sells its aeroplanes to a leasing company, the debt will move from the nonfinancial to the financial corporate sector. It is, however, far from clear how large a proportion of total financial debt can be attributed to the off-balance sheet financing of the nonfinancial sector. What we do know is that the growth of financial debt has been explosive and has risen, relative to GDP, by 85% over the past decade.

In practice, modern accounting is moving to a sort of half-way house in which the volatility of profits as published by companies is growing relative to their volatility in national account terms, but is still well short of the level that would be found if profits were assessed on the assumption that the EMH held. Neither fluctuations in intercompany transactions, nor the change in accounting to its new mark-to-market basis will produce, over the long term, a rise in reported profits relative to those in the national accounts, but they are likely to make them more volatile and these variations are likely to rise and fall with the stock market.

The growing difference between aggregate profits as published and aggregate profits as recorded in national accounts is also reflected in a growing disparity between corporate balance sheets derived from the two sources. The official treatment of this has been different in the UK, where the data on corporate balance sheets are produced by the Office of National Statistics (ONS) than in the US, where they are produced by the Federal Reserve.

As Chart 46 illustrates, the official data show that UK non-financial companies were twice as heavily leveraged as US[97] ones at the end of 2007, and that debt ratios have been rising rapidly in the UK. If we are to believe these data, today's comparatively high leverage is a dramatic change from 1989, when UK companies had more conservative balance sheets than those in the US.

This is not the common perception which, until recently at least, has been that balance sheets on both sides of the Atlantic are

---

[97] The US data used are drawn from lines 1 to 32 of B.102 which is "with tangible assets stated at either market value or replacement cost".

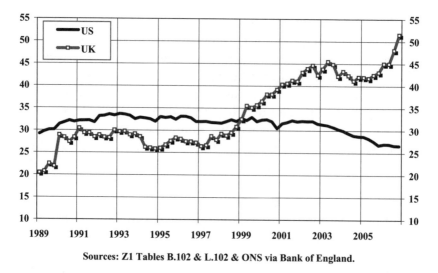

Sources: Z1 Tables B.102 & L.102 & ONS via Bank of England.

Chart 46. UK & US: Private Nonfinancial Companies' Net Debt as % of Assets at Replacement Cost.

similarly "in good shape".[98] It seems, for example, that stockbrokers' data assembled from the balance sheets of UK-quoted nonfinancial companies show that net debt as a proportion of net worth has barely changed over the past five years.

Following discussions via email with staff members at the ONS and the Federal Reserve, my analysis suggests that the reason for the apparent disparity between the two sources of data lies in the fact that the ONS derive their balance sheet data from their own national account flow data on corporate profits, whereas the Federal Reserve adjust the balance sheet data that they derive from the Bureau of Economic Analysis (BEA) national account flow data to the aggregate data that they obtain on company balance sheets. These adjustments take two main forms, illustrated in Chart 47. The first allows for the changing value of company-owned real estate, which is not normally included in national account profits, and the

[98] Examples of this general perception are found in "Parallel Worlds" (*Financial Times* 17.08.07) where Chris Giles, Gillian Tett and Paul J. Davies write "... corporate debt in aggregate has been falling and balance sheets growing ever more healthy." And again, in John Plender's column on 19.08.07: "... corporate balance sheets are in good shape ... we need more than a rate cut ...".

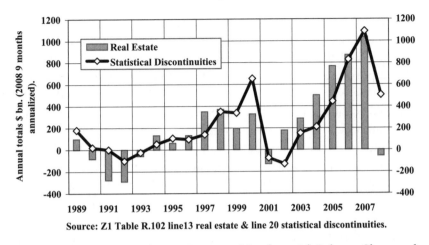

Source: Z1 Table R.102 line13 real estate & line 20 statistical discontinuities.

Chart 47. US Reconciliation Between Nonfinancial Balance Sheet and Flow Data.

second is for the changing values of other assets which are included in company but not in national account profits. These latter adjustments are called "statistical discontinuities" and, as the chart shows, ran at over $1 trillion a year in 2007, approximately the same as the total value of profits after tax of nonfinancial companies as shown in the national accounts. It is therefore obvious that the validity or otherwise of these adjustments is of great importance for our understanding of the true level of profits in the US economy.

Another accounting issue which affects the measurement of net worth arises from the massive rise in corporate "buybacks" of various kinds. If companies purchase shares, either their own or those of another company, their net worth will be affected by the price they pay relative to the shares' underlying net worth. If the price and net worth are equal, there will be no impact on net worth, but if the shares are purchased above that level there will be a reduction in net worth and vice versa.

According to the principle of Hicksian equivalence, this change in net worth should be reflected in profits. In practice, however, it is almost certain not to be included in the profits that are declared by companies, and may or may not be in the national accounts. There will, of course, be no change in GDP as a result of share transactions, as output is unaffected, but any loss made by the corporate sector when shares are bought at prices above their net worth will be reflected in a profit to the seller, which will typically be the household sector. Only if this profit is reflected in household incomes will this transfer of wealth affect the profits of companies. When purchases are made by companies to offset the issue of shares, usually by way of options, they will probably be included in the national accounts, but not in the profits declared by companies. But in other circumstances, any reductions or increases in net worth resulting from the share transactions of companies are likely to be ignored in both national and company accounts.

In recent years, buybacks have been taking place when shares have been generally overvalued, so that they will have tended to reduce corporate net worth, but without this being recognized in either the NIPA data on profits or the Flow of Funds data on company balance sheets. There is an additional complication due to the fact that the net worth of corporations is significantly overstated in the US Flow of Funds accounts.[99] If we had sufficient information to adjust the profits of the corporate sector for the impact of buybacks, we would almost certainly find that, in the 1980s, profits would have been better than those published and balance sheets would have improved by more than the amount shown because buybacks were generally made at prices below the underlying net worth of companies. More recently, the reverse has occurred on a massive scale, through the purchase of shares at more than their inherent net worth. It is not possible to know by how much this leads profits to be overstated in the national accounts, because buybacks do not necessarily occur at the average level of overvaluation and estimates of overvaluation are naturally uncertain.[100]

The change in company accounting practice and the way that the ONS and Federal Reserve have, in their different ways, responded to it, have had at least two important consequences.

---

[99] As explained in Chapter 17, the overstatement of net worth is the result of the overstatement of profits.

[100] Data on the real return to investors from equity investment assume that dividends are reinvested in the market. In times of overvaluation, this destroys value and vice versa. If companies buy back shares, the value destruction in times of overvaluation is undertaken by them rather than by investors. The agent is different but the effect is the same. But these activities have no impact on output and should therefore be excluded from calculations of GDP; when they occur, they represent transfers of value between individuals and companies with no net impact on output.

1. Comparing company balance sheets today with those of 10 to 20 years ago, either individually or in aggregate, makes the mistake of comparing today's apples with yesterday's pears.
2. While corporate net worth, as shown for the UK by the ONS data, is produced on a similar basis to that ruling in the past, there has been a significant change in the data produced by the Federal Reserve in the US.

There still seems to be a widespread view that corporate balance sheets are less highly leveraged than they were 10 to 15 years ago. Although it seems likely that this will change under the impact of the recession and its associated profit disappointments, it is important to understand whether this view has been justified or was a myth which arose from the change in accounting practice. If corporate balance sheets are in much worse shape than is generally understood, this will make the economic recovery even more difficult than would otherwise be the case.

Leverage can be expressed in terms of "asset cover" defined as assets valued at replacement cost, or at market, or as some hybrid of the two, as data derived from corporate accounts tend to do. The hybrid is the least informative as the extent to which market values and replacement cost are being used varies over time. As a result, those considering the data derived from corporate accounts have no reliable basis for comparing the leverage for one period with another.

Leverage can also be defined in terms of "interest cover" as well as asset cover and this is usually done by lenders. The high volatility of profits means, however, that this measure is unsatisfactory if the lender wishes to judge the safety of the loan over time. The same criticism applies to leverage compared with market values and, increasingly over time, with leverage based on modern corporate accounts. We therefore need alternative approaches to the measurement of leverage which can be used to circumvent the problem. One way is to remove from corporate net worth the "statistical discontinuities" and thereby produce leverage ratios which are consistent with the national accounts definition of profits, thus putting the US data on to the same footing as that for the UK. Another way is to compare debt to output.

In Charts 48, 49 and 50, I compare the leverage of US nonfinancial companies on different bases.

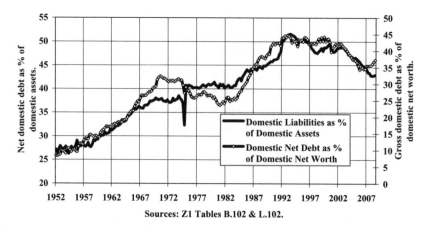

Chart 48. US Nonfinancial Corporate Leverage without Adjusting for Changes in Accounting Practice.

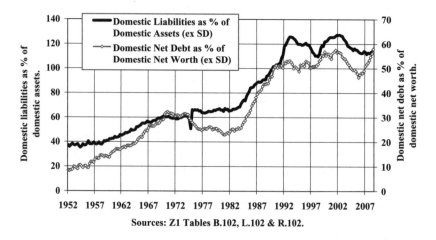

Chart 49. US Nonfinancial Corporate Leverage Adjusted for Changes in Accounting Practice.

Chart 48 is basically derived from company accounts and appears to show that leverage has improved since 1993. Chart 49, derived from national accounts' flow data by excluding the "statistical discontinuities", shows that leverage is at a record high level and Chart 50 below, comparing debt with output, tells the same story.

The widespread belief that nonfinancial company accounts were, at the end of 2007, "in good shape" is, in my view, likely to be

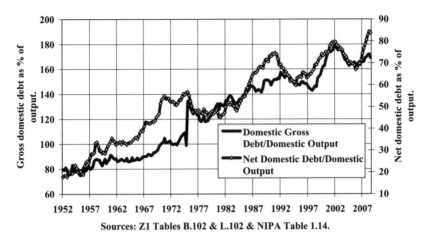

Sources: Z1 Tables B.102 & L.102 & NIPA Table 1.14.

Chart 50. US Nonfinancial Corporate Domestic Leverage as % of Domestic Output.

found to be a major piece of misinformation. It has been rightly remarked that no one's judgement is better than their information and judgements based on misinformation are likely to prove to have been very poor. One major threat to the US economy as I write is that bank lending to nonfinancial corporations will, in retrospect, appear to have been as ill-considered as mortgage lending and the need for a satisfactory resolution of the latter is only a part of the challenge currently faced by the US banking industry and therefore by the US Treasury and the Federal Reserve. The same problem is likely to be found in the UK and the Eurozone.

20

The Impact on q

In Chapter 19 I pointed out the different approaches pursued by the ONS and the Federal Reserve with regard to the growing divergence between corporate balance sheets derived from corporate and national accounting. This meant that, while the current national UK data could reasonably be compared with those for earlier years, those for the US could not. It is, however, easy to adjust the US data on to the same basis as that for the UK, as the Flow of Funds Accounts (Z1) published by the Fed include a table (R.102) which shows the amounts by which flow data have been adjusted to conform to the balance sheet data published by corporations. There are two types of adjustment. One is for changes in the value of property, which have not yet been included in company accounts, and the second is for adjustments for other disparities known as "statistical discontinuities".

The logical, if impractical, extension of marking-to-market would be such that the net worth of companies would always equal their market capitalization. The result would be that the q ratio would always be 1 and thus useless as a guide to the valuation of markets. Even with the current halfway house of partly marking assets and sometimes liabilities to market, the value of the data has been impaired. It is therefore sensible to adjust the net worth data published by the US for the changes in the statistical discontinuities though not for the changes in land prices, since there is no evidence that the latter are mean reverting and may thus represent a permanent change in corporate values. Once this is done, the data on nonfinancial corporate leverage for both the US and the UK are on the same basis.

It is unfortunate that the published series for these UK data are only available from 1987, though earlier data going back to 1920 can be found. Quarterly data for the US are published by the Fed from 1952 onwards and reasonable data have been compiled by economists going back to 1900.[101] As a result, consistent data over a long period up to today are not available from either source. It would therefore have been much better, at least in my view, if the Federal Reserve had followed the ONS's example and published the aggregate data for nonfinancial corporate balance sheets without adjusting them to fit the data published by companies.

However, as noted, the Federal Reserve publishes the adjustments that it makes. This makes it possible to readjust the corporate net worth data on to a similar basis as that provided by the ONS for the UK, and thus one which is consistent with national account data. In Chart 15 in Chapter 8, I show the value of the US stock market according to CAPE and to q, using two net worth figures, one that includes the statistical discontinuities and the other which excludes them.

As Chart 51 shows, it is only in recent years that the two series have diverged to any significant extent. This fits with my understanding that the main cause is the change in corporate accounting and the increased use of marking-to-market in corporate accounts, while those in the national accounts have been left largely unchanged.[102] Chart 51 also shows there is now a significant difference in the value of the US stock market depending on whether the inclusion or exclusion of the statistical discontinuities is

---

[101] James Tobin sent me a considerable amount of these data which had been compiled by several people and Stephen Wright has since assembled them in a consistent form from these and other sources. His results are available on his website and from "Measures of Stock Market Value for the US Non-financial Corporate Sector", published in *Review of Income and Wealth*, December 2004.

[102] The figure for net worth including the statistical discontinuities is taken from Z1 Table B.102 line 32. To derive the figure excluding these oddities I have accumulated the quarterly figures for the statistical discrepancies shown in Table R.102 line 21 and deducted these, which are sometimes negative, from the net worth figure in B.102 line 32.

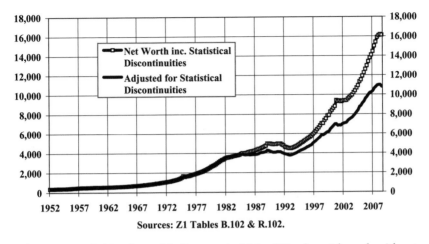

Sources: Z1 Tables B.102 & R.102.

Chart 51. US Nonfinancial Companies' Net Worth, with and without Statistical Discontinuities.

preferred. As Table 9 in Chapter 11 shows, at the end of 2008 the US nonfinancials were 8.5% undervalued if statistical discontinuities are included and 30.6% overvalued if they are excluded. I think that the series which excludes these oddities should be preferred to that which includes them.

21

Problems with Valuing the Markets of Developing Economies

There is a widespread belief that the return on capital and, by extension, some definition of "the rate of interest" is determined by the rate of growth of the economy. While this might be true for the world as a whole, it is clearly not the case for individual countries. In the 1960s two economists, Bela Balassa and Paul Samuelson working independently, came to the conclusion that rapidly growing economies naturally have an appreciating real exchange rate, provided that the rapid growth is the result, as it has invariably been in recent years, of a sharp rise in labour productivity rather than in population. This Balassa-Samuelson effect is due to the fact that changes in labour productivity are spread unevenly through the economy, with the major advances taking place in traded goods such as steel, chemicals and automobiles, while many services, such as hairdressers or restaurants, show little change. As the goods where productivity grows rapidly are the main constituent of international trade, the cost of producing such goods in rapidly growing economies falls relative to those produced in mature economies and there would be growing trade imbalances if real exchange rates were stable.

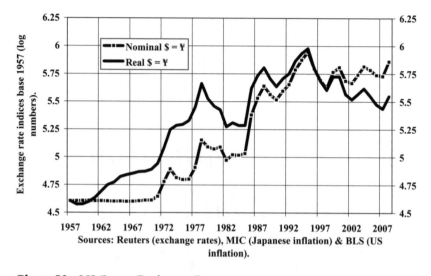

Chart 52. US/Japan Exchange Rate.

The Balassa-Samuelson effect is an example of an economic theory which seems to work in practice. It would be pleasing, not least for economists, if economic theories always proved to be so helpful and correct. Currencies have indeed risen in real terms in response to rapid growth in productivity, or when constrained have resulted in large and growing trade imbalances. The post-war strength of the yen and the rapid growth of the Japanese economy have been marked examples of the first and the growing trade surpluses of China in response to the pegging of the renminbi is an example of the second.

Chart 52 illustrates how, from 1957 to 2008, the yen appreciated at 2.4% p.a. against the dollar in nominal terms and at 1.9% p.a. in real terms – i.e. after adjusting for the differences in inflation which averaged 3.4% for Japan and 4.1% for the US.

If an exchange rate appreciates in real terms, then the equilibrium level of real interest rates will be lower in that country. Otherwise investors would be assured of a higher return by holding the investments in that country since they would receive the same real rate of interest plus the benefit of the appreciation in the exchange rate. Thus, far from the real rate of interest being higher in rapidly growing economies, as is often assumed, it is naturally lower. For example, the real short-term interest rate in Japan from 1957 to

2008 would have needed to have been 3.1% below the US to compensate for the rise in the value of the yen compared with the US dollar.

This difference will not only apply to short-term real rates of interest but to all other returns, including long bond yields and the return on equities. Thus, if profits are correctly calculated, the PE ratios on shares in rapidly growing economies will, in equilibrium, be higher than those in mature ones. This is often assumed to be the case; not, however, because of the arguments set out above, but as the result of some fundamental misunderstandings. It seems, for example, to be commonly thought that as rapidly growing companies deserve higher PEs than slow growing ones, the same should apply to countries. But rapidly growing companies will only deserve high PEs if they have some temporary monopoly that allows them to have an above average return on capital, i.e. a return that is higher than the average return for companies in mature economies. While this advantage lasts they will be able to achieve rapid growth from internally generated financial resources, but the rate at which this growth should be discounted will not be their own high return but the lower one that is general for the economy as a whole. In the case of an individual company, which generates returns on capital that are above the average for that country, the growth is rapid but the discount rate at which future profits should be valued is the same as that for companies with lower returns on capital. Almost the exact opposite reasoning applies to the PEs of rapidly growing economies. In these instances, as a result of the Balassa-Samuelson effect the cost of capital will be depressed compared with the cost in mature economies. Thus the reason that individual growth companies in mature economies deserve high PEs is that they have an above-average return on equity, and the reason that companies in general in rapidly growing economies deserve high PEs is that they have the common characteristic of low cost of capital, which should include equity.

Companies based in rapidly growing economies are, on average, justified in having high PEs when their profits and their returns on equity are at equilibrium levels, provided that their profits are no more miscalculated than the profits of companies based in mature economies. Unfortunately, this condition is probably not met, at least as a general rule. The main reason for the habitual overstatement of corporate profits in mature economies is probably the understatement of depreciation. It seems likely that the understatement of depreciation in rapidly growing economies is even greater. This is because depreciation is a function of the rate of growth of real wages, which is very quick in rapidly growing economies, and because the connection between the rate of growth of real wages and the rate of depreciation seems to be largely ignored by accountants, probably because they are completely ignorant of the existence of the relationship.

The faster real wages rise, the faster will any given piece of plant become uneconomic and need to be replaced by a new, more labour efficient one, and thus the faster will depreciation be, if correctly calculated. As rapid increases in real GDP and real wages go together, depreciation rates in rapidly growing economies need to be much greater than those in mature economies and it seems unlikely that sufficient allowance for this is usually made.

It is therefore difficult to know the correct equilibrium PE for a rapidly growing economy. Rapid growth has often been accompanied by volatility as the investment fluctuates more than consumption. This leads to greater volatility of total output in rapidly growing economies which cannot grow rapidly unless they have a high ratio of investment to GDP. The estimation of the equilibrium level of output tends therefore to be more difficult than it is in mature economies and this adds to the uncertainties involved in trying to value developing economies by comparing their PEs at equilibrium profit levels with their average PEs. The uncertainty extends to nearly every variable. The measure of profits is even less certain than it is in mature economies. The equilibrium level of profits would also be more uncertain, even if those profits were reliably measured. In addition, the rate of growth of these economies tends to slow as they become more mature, so the average PE, even if the earnings on which it is based were correctly calculated, would not be a good guide to the cyclically adjusted PE at fair value.

Another problem in valuing markets is the importance of land prices. In principle, this applies generally and in practice has been particularly important in Japan and Hong Kong, which have for much of the post-war era been rapidly growing rather than mature economies. While the equilibrium value of plant and equipment should in the long run equate to their construction costs, this very obviously does not apply to land. In most countries, land is not a very important element in corporate net worth, but it can be and, in the case of Japan and Hong Kong, has been.[103] If land is a large proportion of net worth then large, and possibly ephemeral, changes in net worth will occur as land prices fluctuate and this greatly reduces its usefulness of q as a guide to value. The first condition, set out in Chapter 8, which has to be met by a valid criterion of value is that the fundamental should be reasonably stable. This condition will not be met if land represents a large proportion of net worth and the price of land is highly volatile.

In Chapter 11 I set out an approach to the value of non-US stock markets which did not depend on any of the uncertainties outlined above. Neither the measurement of profits nor net worth were involved. Furthermore, both hindsight value and future returns were measured in both domestic currency and US dollars and this circumvents the problem of a rising real exchange rate affecting the equilibrium return as it only applies when the return is measured in the domestic currency. When measured in a common currency, such as US dollars, the equilibrium return should be unaffected by the growth rate of the economy, because the lower domestic return natural to rapidly growing economies should be matched by the rise in the real exchange rate. Nonetheless, it should be recognized that the exchange rates are not always at their equilibrium values, so that the measurement of value based on hindsight plus subsequent returns is more likely to err if the economy in question has been a rapidly growing rather than a mature one.

---

[103] We do not have data on Japanese balance sheets at replacement cost. However, one-third of Japanese nonfinancial companies' net worth was represented by land at book cost, in Q3 2008, and had been over 50% in 2002. In the US, at book cost real estate, less value of structures, was only 9% of net worth.

22

Central Banks' Response to Asset Prices

It is a central thesis of this book that central bankers should be concerned when equities or other asset prices become excessive. While high precision about the extent of any overvaluation would be welcome, it is not essential for the purpose of forming a reasonable judgement as to whether the stock market is moving into dangerous territory. On the basis of the evidence from q and CAPE, it is relatively easy to form such a judgement; the stock market has only become 50% or more overpriced, using either q or CAPE as the metric, on the five occasions which ended with the peaks of 1906, 1929, 1936, 1968 and 2000. On all these occasions, both metrics showed that there was cause for concern and in each case the subsequent market fall was accompanied, or shortly followed, by a recession.

Central bankers will need to exercise judgement when deciding whether the stock market is approaching a dangerous level, but the evidence suggests that this is a much less difficult exercise than another which is generally accepted as being crucial to decisions about whether or not to raise interest rates. It is generally agreed that, in the absence of swings in inflationary expectations and the impact of changes in international prices, inflation will tend to fall if an economy is operating with a positive "output gap". At any time, economies have an ability to operate up to this level without generating inflation. If they are operating below that level then there is a positive output gap, and if above it, there is a negative output gap. At this level, inflation will tend to pick up. Judging whether at the current level of output there is a positive or negative gap is thus extremely important for central banks, but it has also been shown to be extremely difficult.[104]

Central bankers have been effectively claiming that it is not possible to form a reasonable judgement about the level of the stock market but that it is possible to make such a claim with regard to the output gap. I hope that this book will convince the reader that, on the evidence available, this claim is unjustified. Central banks should respond if asset prices become too high and I show how, in mature economies at least, they can know if share prices have reached excessive levels. I have also claimed two other things. First, that it is similarly possible to judge excesses in house prices or those of risky debt assets, in the latter case through the price of liquidity. Second, that shares, houses and liquidity are the three groups of asset prices which central banks need to consider, in addition to their expectations about consumer prices, when deciding on changes in monetary policy. This obviously leaves open two questions: At what level of asset mispricing should central banks take action, and what action should they take?

If central banks have only one policy instrument, namely short-term interest rates, the only possible response is to "lean against the wind", as suggested by Sushil Wadhwani[105] among others. Had this been the policy of the Fed during the bubble that developed in the late 20th century, it seems likely that the stock market would not have risen to the heights it did. The Federal Reserve would not then have needed to reduce interest rates as much as it did in order for the US economy to recover from the 2001 recession that fol-lowed the sharp fall in the stock market. The subsequent recovery would then have been of a more traditional and orderly kind and

---

[104] The difficulty of this decision is well set out in a paper by Orphanides and van Norden on "The Unreliability of Output Gap Estimates in Real Time", CIRANO November 2001 and subsequently in 2002 in the *Review of Economics and Statistics*, Vol 84, pp. 569–583.
[105] See footnote 13.

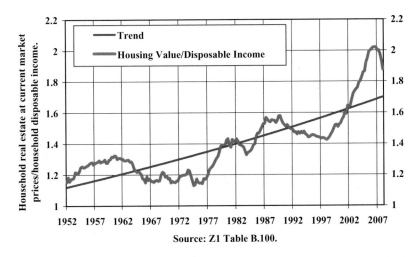

Source: Z1 Table B.100.

Chart 31. US Value of the Residential Housing Stock and Household Disposable Income.

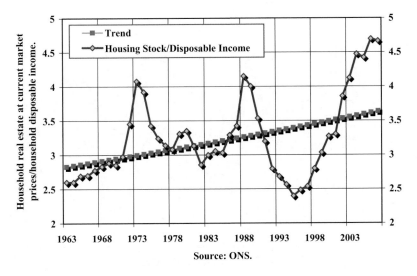

Source: ONS.

Chart 32. UK Housing Affordability.

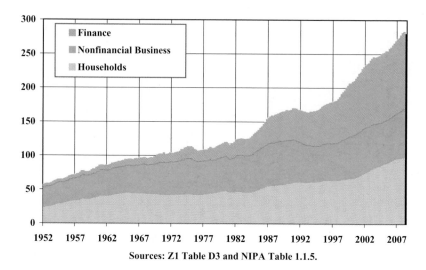

Sources: Z1 Table D3 and NIPA Table 1.1.5.

Chart 33. US Private Sector Debt as % of GDP.

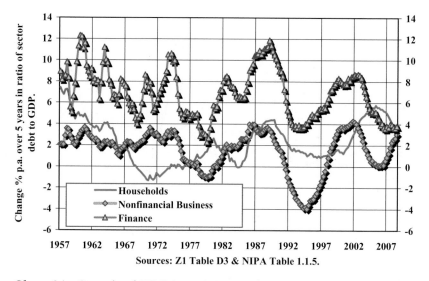

Sources: Z1 Table D3 & NIPA Table 1.1.5.

Chart 34. Growth of US Private Sector Debt.

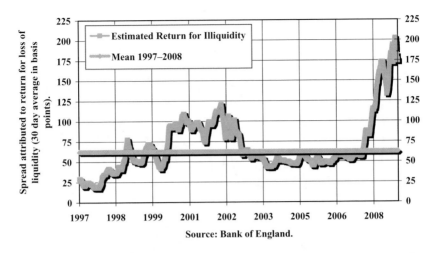

Source: Bank of England.

Chart 35. US$-Denominated Investment-Grade Corporate Bond Spreads. Estimated Return Attributed to Loss of Liquidity.

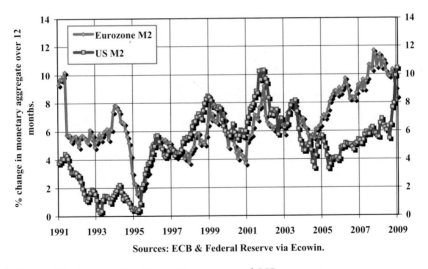

Sources: ECB & Federal Reserve via Ecowin.

Chart 36. Money Supply in Eurozone and US.

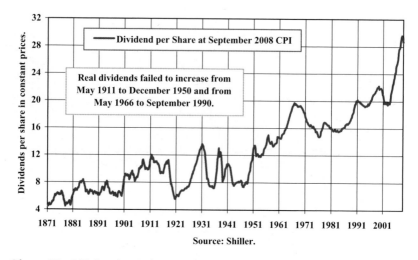

Source: Shiller.

Chart 37. US Stock Market Real Dividends per Share 1871–2008.

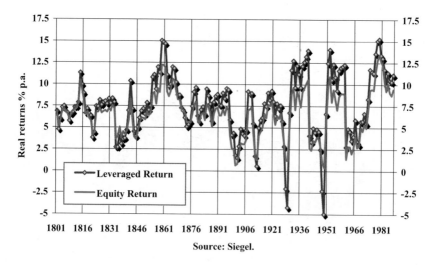

Source: Siegel.

Chart 38. US Real Equity Returns over 20 Years from 1801 with and without Bond Financed Leverage.

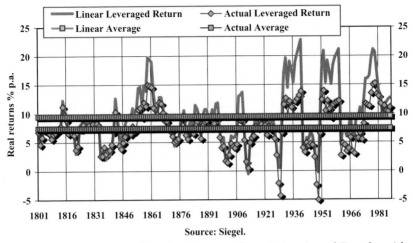

Source: Siegel.

Chart 39. US Leveraged Equity Returns. Comparing Actual Results with "Linear" Leverage.

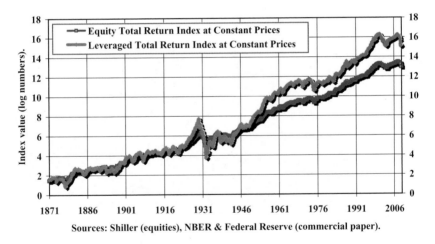

Sources: Shiller (equities), NBER & Federal Reserve (commercial paper).

Chart 40. US Stock Market Performance of Leveraged and Unleveraged Equity Portfolios 1871–2008.

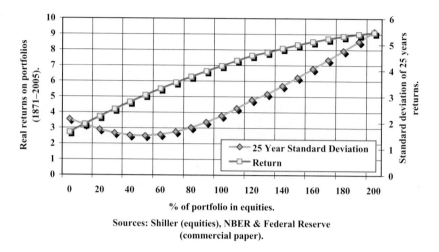

Sources: Shiller (equities), NBER & Federal Reserve
(commercial paper).

Chart 41. Long-term Volatility and Real Returns from US Portfolios from 100% Cash to 100% Leveraged.

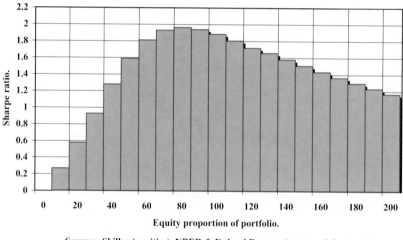

Sources: Shiller (equities), NBER & Federal Reserve (commercial paper).

Chart 42. The Sharpe Ratio.

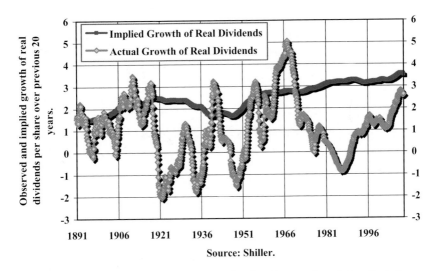

Source: Shiller.

Chart 43. US Growth of Real Dividends Observed and Implied from Payout Ratios.

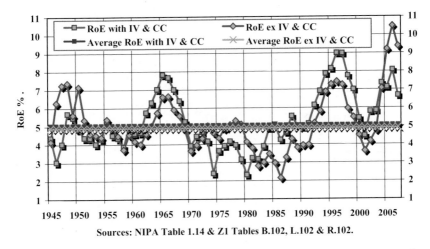

Sources: NIPA Table 1.14 & Z1 Tables B.102, L.102 & R.102.

Chart 44. US Nonfinancial Companies Return on Domestic Net Worth 1945–2007.

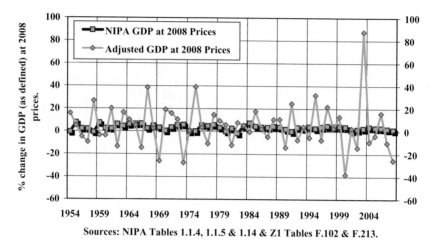

Sources: NIPA Tables 1.1.4, 1.1.5 & 1.14 & Z1 Tables F.102 & F.213.

Chart 45. Annual Changes in US GDP As Published and Adjusted for Stock Market Prices.

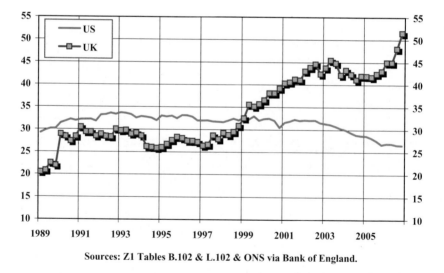

Sources: Z1 Tables B.102 & L.102 & ONS via Bank of England.

Chart 46 UK & US Private Nonfinancial Companies' Net Debt as % of Assets at Replacement Cost.

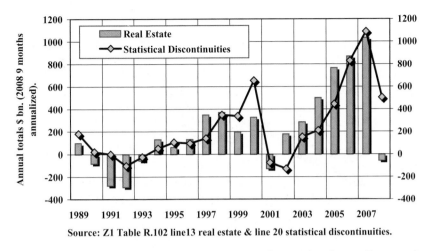

Source: Z1 Table R.102 line13 real estate & line 20 statistical discontinuities.

Chart 47. US Reconciliation Between Nonfinancial Balance Sheet and Flow Data.

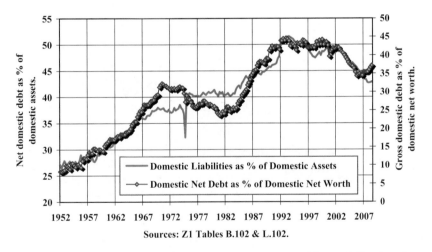

Sources: Z1 Tables B.102 & L.102.

Chart 48. US Nonfinancial Corporate Leverage without Adjusting for Changes in Accounting Practice.

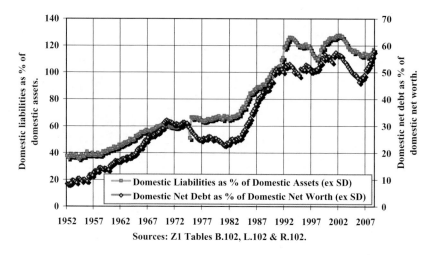

Chart 49. US Nonfinancial Corporate Leverage Adjusted for Changes in Accounting Practice.

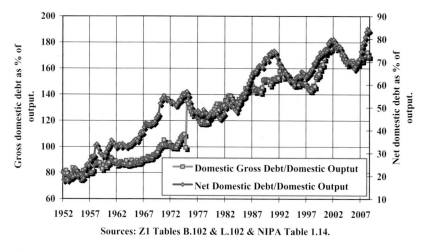

Chart 50. US Nonfinancial Corporate Domestic Leverage as % of Domestic Output.

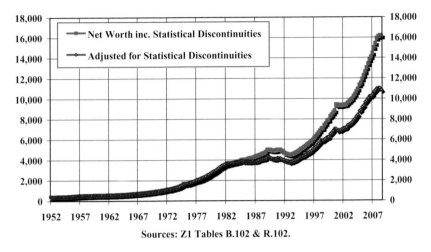

Sources: Z1 Tables B.102 & R.102.

Chart 51. US Nonfinancial Companies' Net Worth, with and without Statistical Discontinuities.

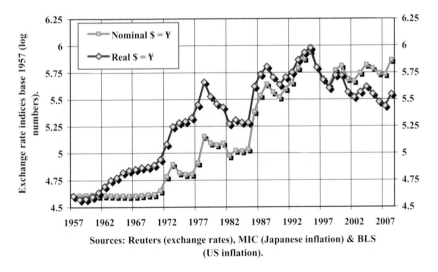

Sources: Reuters (exchange rates), MIC (Japanese inflation) & BLS (US inflation).

Chart 52. US/Japan Exchange Rate.

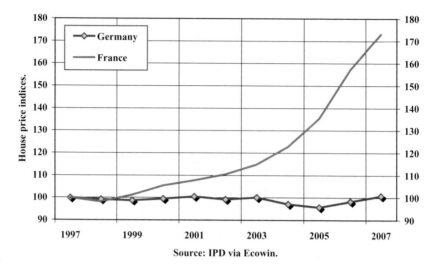

Source: IPD via Ecowin.

Chart 53. France & Germany House Prices.

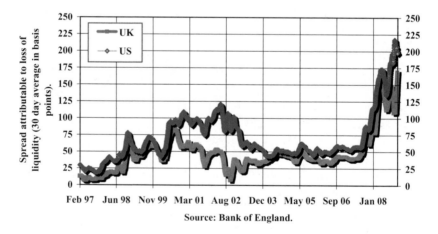

Source: Bank of England.

Chart 54. UK & US. Investment Grade Corporate Bonds. Spreads Attributable to Reward for Reduced Liquidity.

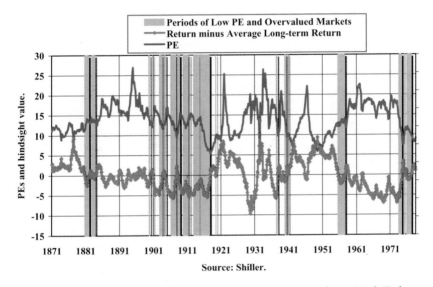

Chart A1. Showing Periods When Overvalued Markets Had Below Average PEs.

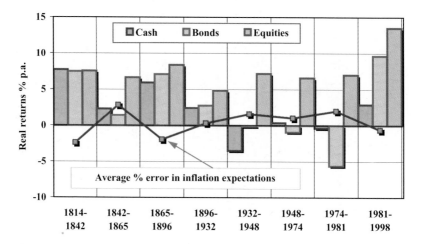

Chart A2. Returns on Equities, Bonds and Cash between Stock Market Troughs.

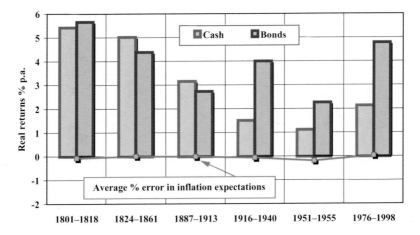

Chart A3. Returns on Bonds and Cash When Inflation Expectations Were (Roughly) Correct.

the second round bubbles which broke in 2007 would not have occurred. As I pointed out earlier, these assumptions seem reasonable, but in the nature of things we cannot prove what might have been. Whether or not leaning against the wind would have produced a better outcome for the economy must therefore be a matter of judgement. What can be said, unequivocally, is that the actual outturn of events, which followed very different policies by the Federal Reserve, has been of a kind that we will wish to avoid if possible in the future.

If it were agreed that a response to the stock market bubble of the late 20th century would have been desirable, the first question is at what level should this have taken place. Chart 15 provides a good guide to this, if share prices are considered in isolation from other asset prices. Once the value of the stock market had risen to 0.4 in natural logs, which is 50% above average, it would have matched the previous peaks of 1906, 1936 and 1968. Only the peak of 1929, and subsequently that of 2000, were significantly higher than these. Although these earlier peaks were followed by difficult times for the economy, they were not subject to the outstanding problems of the 1930s or of today. It would probably have been sensible for the Federal Reserve to have taken some action to dampen the stock market in advance of each of these peaks, but certainly not to have ignored the signals given by the stock market from 1927 and 1997 onwards.

If share or house prices rise too much they should become danger signals on which central banks should act. The case for action is reinforced if both support each other or are supported by the price of liquidity (Chart 35). The level of the stock market and the price of liquidity have, since 1997 when the Bank of England's data series start, confirmed each other's signals. House prices, however, as Chart 31 for the US and Chart 32 for the UK show, did not confirm the danger signals from 1997 to 2000, but did so from 2003 onwards. Helped as we are by hindsight, it seems reasonable to conclude that share prices alone were signaling sufficient danger that action by central banks would have been sensible from 1997 onwards, and that even by 2003 the coincidence of excesses in all three asset prices indicated the need for action.

Given that asset prices would have produced sensible signals as to when central bank action would be desirable, the next question is what action should then have been taken. Leaning against the wind involves raising interest rates before such an action would have appeared desirable given the outlook for consumer prices. This is the only action that is currently available to central bankers and it has been attacked on the grounds that, if it had been taken, it would have resulted in an unnecessary recession. Even if it is accepted that a recession would have resulted, it is reasonable to think that mild recessions are preferable to the costs of avoiding them if that cost is, as subsequent events suggest, very high in terms of subsequent large losses in output, financial turmoil and large increases in fiscal deficits and government debt levels. Until recently, such ideas ran completely contrary to the attitudes of the remarkably confident and optimistic era which has ended so suddenly. This involved statements which even at the time struck me and others as being rash. For example, Alan Blinder, former vice-chairman of the Federal Reserve, claimed that: "For the economy to go into a significant recession, never mind a depression, important policy makers would have to take leave of their senses." Stephen Wright and I wrote then that "Time will tell whether Professor Blinder's confidence proves to be admirable or foolhardy".[106] Time has since spoken.

With the evidence that has been provided by our current troubles, central bankers are likely to take a more cautious view of their ability to control economies and to have a greater concern with the consequences of asset bubbles. But if they are to do this, it would help if they had a policy instrument other than interest rates. In terms of simple logic, there is a clear case that if there are two targets, in this case asset as well as consumer prices, it makes sense for central banks to have two different policy instruments that they can use. Ideally, these policy instruments would each be effective in controlling one of the two objectives without affecting the other. It would be ideal if there was an instrument whose change would depress asset prices without affecting the outlook for consumer inflation. In practice, such an ideal is unlikely, but it would still be helpful if one of the two policy instruments had its primary impact on asset prices, thus leaving interest rates to be mainly used for targeting consumer inflation. Interest rate policy would not then have to be used to dampen rises in asset prices.

[106] "The Economic Consequences of Alan Greenspan" (op. cit.).

I mentioned in Chapter 2 that one suggested new policy instrument appeals to me as a possible answer to the widely recognized need for central bankers to be able to address asset price problems other than by raising interest rates. This is the ability to vary banks' minimum capital ratios. This has been proposed as a way of offsetting the tendency of banks to exaggerate cycles,[107] but as this problem is associated with the rise and fall of asset prices, there is no conflict in using it also as a way to dampen asset prices. The two objectives are in particular harmony when one of the asset prices under consideration is the liquidity price, as this indicates when lenders have become (by past standards) insufficiently risk averse. It is in just these conditions that a constraint on excessive ease in bank lending is clearly desirable.

In the recent debates about how to avoid a recurrence of the current banking crisis, most of the attention has been on the microeconomic aspects of the problem and in particular the regulation of banks. It is often implicitly assumed that if banks were better regulated they would be less likely to find that they were suddenly suffering from large losses, and that the restricted level of their equity capital made it desirable for them to restrict their lending. As restrictions in bank lending aggravate recessions, this process increases the loss that the banks suffer and creates a vicious circle. This behaviour of banks is termed pro-cyclical, as it tends to exaggerate rather than modify economic cycles. While improved banking regulation is desirable for several reasons – including that of reducing the risk of loss to tax payers that is a necessary consequence of protecting the banking system – it is unlikely that it will prevent bank crises. These have been a regular feature of economies since banks were invented and therefore cannot sensibly be ascribed to either the failure of the current regulatory system or to a change in the behaviour of bankers. As I have already remarked, bankers will always hang us if they are given enough rope and the major cause of the current crisis was the huge amount of rope provided by the Federal Reserve and other central banks. It was not a change in the behaviour of bankers which caused the excesses. Given the

---

[107] See "The Fundamental Principles of Financial Regulation" by Markus Brunnermeier, Andrew Crocket, Charles Goodhart, Avinash Persaud and Hyun Shin (op. cit.).

scope provided by loose monetary policy, bankers' behaviour would have had to alter for the current crisis to have been avoided. While the invention of new and complex financial instruments, and the incentive to managements' folly given by their absurd bonuses and remuneration, may have added zest to the flames, the fuel on which the fire relied was the excessive liquidity provided by central banks and the asymmetric management of interest rates. This was described as the "Greenspan Put" as the Federal Reserve's behaviour had, justifiably I think, given the impression that it would reduce interest rates in response to falls in asset prices while remaining indifferent to any rises.

The proposal that central banks should be able to alter banks' minimum capital ratios is a completely different approach to the problem compared with proposals to change bank regulations. The supervision of individual banks can be carried out by central banks or by an independent body, such as the FSA in the UK or the FDIC in the US. Even if this role is undertaken by the central bank, it would need to be managed by a unit which was totally separate from that concerned with the control of inflation, including both consumer and asset prices. However, the committee of the central bank charged with the responsibility for interest rates would also need to be the body with the responsibility for regulating banks' minimum capital requirements. This would be essential because of the overlap in the impact on the economy of both policy instruments. This overlap means that the decisions about variations in minimum capital ratios need to be taken by each central bank with regard to is own currency; it would not be an appropriate matter for international agreement on a world-wide scale even if such an utopian idea could work in practice.

This would leave the Bank of International Settlements (BIS) as the appropriate body for regulating banks on an international scale. It would continue, for example, to decide on the risk asset weighting of different types of assets in bank balance sheets and thus how much equity should be held to back a bank's corporate loan or mortgage portfolio. But these minimum internationally required ratios could readily be altered proportionately by any central bank, which could also introduce additional capital requirements.

The responsibility of the FSA and the FDIC for the financial stability of individual banks does not absolve these central banks

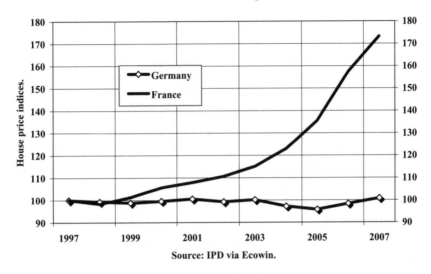

Chart 53. France & Germany House Prices.

from the responsibility for ensuring financial stability in terms of the economy as a whole.

The independence of national asset markets, and thus the need for national responses to their signals, is only obvious in the case of house prices. They seem to move in one country completely independently of their behaviour in another, as can be seen by comparing the way in which they have diverged even between France and Germany, as I illustrate in Chart 53. It would probably have been very beneficial if national central banks, which still exist in the Eurozone, had been able to take action to restrain house price inflation within their own national borders. Had the Irish and Spanish central banks, for example, been able and willing to increase the minimum capital requirements of banks within their jurisdiction, perhaps solely with regard to mortgages, then the current problems of collapsing house prices in these countries could have been greatly mitigated. It might be argued that this would simply have transferred the business to foreign banks, but it should be possible to discourage this (subject to agreement within the Eurozone) by limiting the ability of banks which were not operating through domestic subsidiaries to foreclose on mortgage loans. The announcement of an increase in minimum capital requirements is also likely to have some moderating impact on banks' willingness to lend, provided that the central banks take further action if asset prices continue to rise.

The independence of house prices between different countries and regions is not, however, found in the other two key asset prices: those of shares and that represented by liquidity. Share prices in international markets move together and the tendency has grown in recent years. In addition, it seems that changes in the US stock market dominate, so that other markets respond to changes on Wall Street.[108] This clearly puts a higher responsibility on the Federal Reserve, above all other central banks, to adjust policy to dampen stock market bubbles, and therefore to act in exactly the opposite way that it did when it created the impression that the "Greenspan Put" existed. Over time, as the relative economic importance of the US economy recedes, this may change but at the moment the prime responsibility to prevent a recurrence of the late 20th century stock market craze must lie with the Federal Reserve.

The problem with liquidity has a similar international element. Chart 54 shows that the returns attributable to the loss of liquidity to buyers of investment grade corporate bonds have moved closely together in the UK and US.[109] But this does not mean that the

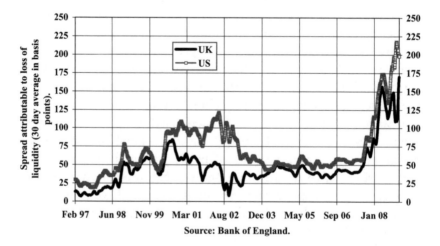

Source: Bank of England.

Chart 54. UK & US. Investment Grade Corporate Bonds. Spreads Attributable to Reward for Reduced Liquidity.

---

[108] Details are set out in Appendix 8.
[109] The correlation coefficient between the UK and US is 0.863.

Bank of England cannot, for example, tighten domestic credit while the Federal Reserve continues a policy of unchanged ease. A rise in the sterling risk free rate of interest will raise the cost of private sector borrowing even if the return attributed to a loss of liquidity remains unchanged. The strong correlation between the liquidity element in private sector debt does, however, mean that changing the minimum capital requirements of banks may not be an effective response if the liquidity price falls to a level which causes concern to the Bank of England and if this concern is not shared by the Federal Reserve.

It cannot be surprising that the increase in international trade and capital flows makes it increasingly difficult for central banks to control their own economies. It is therefore likely that smaller central banks will be able to respond more effectively to changes in house prices than to changes in stock markets and the price of liquidity. International cooperation is a necessary condition for a well-managed world economy and its importance grows with the increase in trade and capital flows.

If banks need to have higher equity ratios to support any given level of lending, then they will have to increase their lending margins to achieve the same return on equity. Changing the minimum capital requirements of banks and the short-term risk free interest rate will both increase the cost of borrowing and both are therefore likely to have a depressing impact on total demand. Their impacts will differ, however, because the change in minimum capital requirements will raise the cost of bank intermediated debt relative to the cost of raising funds directly from savers via bond and equity markets. This should increase the relative supply of bonds and equities, which should help depress their prices as intended. The impact of lowering the risk free rate of interest while increasing the minimum capital requirements of banks provides a way of considering the different ways in which the two changes operate. In combination they could leave the total level of demand unchanged, but by increasing the relative cost of bank debt, the changes should switch corporate financing away from banks towards the stock market and help dampen its rise.

In this chapter I have suggested practical ways in which central banks could adjust their policy when asset prices become excessive and to consider the practical problems which might arise. These suggestions are, of course, far from being the only ways in which central banks might adjust their policy to mitigate the threats posed by errant moves in asset prices. When asset prices fall from excessive levels, they have a strongly negative impact on demand which can be greater than the positive impact on the economy that comes from falls in risk free interest rates. Central banks then lose control of their economies, as credit is restricted not by their actions but by those of commercial banks. In order to recover from the subsequent recession, fiscal deficits are likely to be needed both to refinance the banks and to stimulate demand. At the same time, central banks seek to inject large amounts of liquidity into their economies by purchasing government bonds or even private sector debt assets. When the recovery comes, the deficits need to be reduced sharply and the liquidity withdrawn quickly.

If this is not done, there is a great danger that inflationary expectations as well as inflation will rise. This creates problems which are often overlooked by those who see inflation as a way of resolving excess debt. When inflationary expectations rise, interest rates have to be raised very sharply to bring them down again, as was seen in the late 1970s and early 1980s. If this is not done, inflation and inflationary expectations continue to rise, even if the economy is operating with significant spare capacity and the unpleasant combination of low output and high inflation, known as stagflation, results.

The initial risk when asset prices fall is that the economy will have falling consumer prices, but the policy response needed to avoid a severe recession raises the risk that inflation will pick up rapidly when the economy recovers. Asset bubbles thus raise the risks of both deflation and inflation. The sound management of an economy requires that both these risks should be avoided.

It is therefore surely clear that central banks should seek to prevent asset prices rising to excessive heights. This has been resisted by many central bankers: first, on the grounds that they cannot judge when asset prices have become too high; and second, because it is easier to adjust policy to meet any subsequent problems that may come with the falls than to adjust policy to prevent the rises. The evidence of the world economy today makes the second argument absurd and I hope that I will have convinced readers that the first is equally without merit.

23

The Response to Asset Prices from Investors, Fund Managers and Pension Consultants

Asset prices are of great importance to many other people in addition to central bankers. In Chapter 8, I showed that it was only on rare occasions that it was clearly sensible for long-term investors, who were natural holders of equities, to sell. Indeed, the clear case for doing so appears to have occurred only twice in modern times, when the market had risen to about twice fair value, which occurred in the run ups to the peaks of 1929 and 2000. Those investors who did so would have been well rewarded, but they would have had a difficult time in choosing when to reinvest. Had the investors of 1929 waited until the market was fair value, they would have reinvested in 1931; this would have seemed far too early as they would have lost around 50% of their investment before the market bottomed in March 1933. While this would have been preferable to losing 89% of their wealth, as happened to those who suffered the full loss from the peak of the market to its trough, few investors would have been happy with the result. Equally, those who sold in

2000 would have had to wait until November 2008 before reinvesting and would have had to have strong nerves and an indifference to taunts at cocktail parties.

While value is an indispensable piece of information for investors, it provides little guide to action in most circumstances. The type of investor who benefits most from the long-term real return that can usually be expected from equities is, as I have pointed out, those who are saving for their retirement and have time horizons of 20 years or more. Understanding value is of particular benefit to these investors in three ways:

1. It will guide them to sell in the rare, but wealth-destroying times, when markets become seriously overvalued.
2. It should help them keep their nerve and discourage them from selling when stock markets offer, as they do as I write, the prospect of good long-term real returns. This is important as these times are often, as they are today, times when the pressure to sell in the light of bad economic news is strong.
3. It is extremely useful as these long-term investors move towards their retirement. As the investors' time horizon shortens, value can be used to assess the way in which the risks and potential returns are changing. The nearer investors are to retirement, the more attention they need to give to value. Even moderately overvalued markets should be sold as the time horizon shortens.

It is very important that pension trustees and those who advise them should understand the issues involved in valuing stock markets. The most probable return over any time horizon can be calculated by combining the long-term expected return at fair value with the current level of the market. At the very least, this would have avoided an error common in recent years, which has been to assume that the stock market was likely to give its long-term average return when it was near its peak. As a result, pension funds were encouraged to remain in equities, while employers were reducing their contributions. This has led to serious problems for many pension funds and great distress for some unfortunate beneficiaries.

In many ways the issue of value is most difficult for fund managers. When stock markets are very overpriced they are faced with a conflict between the risks to their clients' wealth and the risks to their own business. At the peak of the stock market in 2000, it had, on reasonable assumptions, around a 70% chance of falling over the next year. Fund managers who understood this would have been in a very difficult position. It was in the interests of their clients that they should go liquid but, if they did, there was a 30% chance that the market would not fall and that they would underperform the competition over a year. This would have been bad for their business and they would still have a significant risk that the market would rise again in the following year.

24

International Imbalances

The current crisis is the result of poor decisions by central bankers. They allowed asset prices to reach absurd levels, which would not have been possible without very lax monetary policies whose excessive ease was demonstrated by the low level of risk aversion, shown by the price of liquidity, and the exceptionally high prices of shares and houses. This account is not in conflict with another which is sometimes seen as an alternative, namely that our troubles are due to an excess of intended savings on a worldwide basis. It is argued that it was necessary to offset the high savings of Asia and in oil exporting countries by depressing savings elsewhere, as without such action there would have been a recession. If this argument is accepted, then the easy money policy which drove up asset prices and depressed household savings was a necessary condition for a stable and growing world economy. The result, however, was large current account imbalances between major economies, as excess intended savings in some countries could only be absorbed by deficiencies elsewhere.

I find this account of events very reasonable. It connects the imbalances in savings flows with those in asset markets. My quarrel is with the assumption that central banks in Europe and America had to follow policies of excessive monetary ease so that domestic savings fell to offset the high levels of intended savings elsewhere. Accommodating the policies of China and others, which involved the export of their excess savings, was not sustainable and was not therefore sensible unless it was accompanied by international negotiations which would have allowed it to be very short lived. I do not doubt that a less expansive monetary policy by the Federal Reserve, the Bank of England and other central banks might well have produced an earlier recession than the one we have today, but this might not have occurred and, if it had, it would almost certainly have been less deep, easier to solve and raised far less unpleasant long-term problems.

The current recession – to the surprise of many who thought that developing economies, particularly in Asia, would be more or less immune – has hit the exporting economies as much – and possibly more than – the Anglo-Saxon ones, which are most directly exposed to the downturn in financial services. They are responding by fiscal and monetary stimuli designed to encourage an increase in the importance of domestic consumption as a proportion of total demand. This is an essential part of the rebalancing of the world economy. The national savings rates of the UK and US must rise to bring their economies back towards a more sustainable equilibrium. This rise in savings will have to be matched either by a rise in world investment or a fall in the national savings rates of the economies such as China, Germany, Japan and OPEC, which have large current account surpluses. The easy money policies pursued by the Federal Reserve have had the effect of postponing this necessary adjustment and, while doing so, made the scale of the necessary adjustment much larger and more difficult.

Underlying this policy error was the erroneous belief that avoiding recessions should be a major objective for central banks. I think their objective should be to avoid major recessions. Periodic minor recessions may well be a necessary condition for achieving this, as these mild shocks provide a necessary reminder to lenders and investors of the risks they run and help to restrain excesses.

25

Summing Up

Financial markets are not perfectly efficient. Neither are they irrational casinos. They are imperfectly efficient, with prices rotating around fair value, which is the level at which they would be priced if markets were perfectly efficient. This hypothesis is testable, unlike the EMH, and is robust under testing. We can therefore measure the extent to which asset prices move away from fair value. The claim that this is not possible is without merit and has been a major cause of central banks' failure to address the problems that come from exorbitant asset prices. Together with its associated claim, that central banks could readily deal with any problems for the real economy which resulted from falling asset prices, this led to monetary policy ignoring excess asset prices.

Changes in interest rates have an ephemeral impact on asset prices, which have in turn an important impact on the real economy via their impact on household savings rates. But there is no long-term relationship between interest rates and asset prices. If the latter rise too much they will fall independently of changes in interest rates and, as a result, monetary policy in its usual form ceases to be effective. We are currently suffering from this.

It follows that central banks should monitor asset prices and adjust their policies if they become too high. It would be helpful if another policy instrument could be introduced that central banks could use in response to excessive increases in asset prices, thus leaving interest rates to respond to consumer prices. This might improve the management of the economy, but it remains likely that minor recessions will be necessary from time to time to prevent excesses in asset prices and to avoid major recessions.

While few economists still believe that financial markets approach perfect efficiency, the legacy of the Efficient Market Hypothesis hinders the progress of financial economics. We need a paradigm shift. An implicit and unacknowledged acceptance of the EMH occurs frequently in discussion about financial markets, leading to confusion. This often takes the form of an assumption about the stability of the equity risk premium, which runs contrary to the evidence. The impact of negative serial correlation on leveraged equity portfolios is another important example of the problems arising from the legacy of the EMH.

We are able to value financial markets and we will greatly improve our ability to manage the economy well if we acknowledge this and apply valid criteria to the process of valuation. This meets obstruction not only from economists influenced by the damaging legacy of the EMH, but also from investment bankers in pursuit of commission and the financial press who read their reports without a sufficiently critical appraisal. I have therefore sought to explain how not to value the stock market as well as how to do it.

Appendix 1

Sources and Obligations

In terms of people, these fall into three main groups.

First are those past collaborators with whom I have written papers, the conclusions of which are incorporated in the text, most notably James Mitchell, Daniel Murray, Derry Pickford, Martin Weale and Stephen Wright. In particular, I would like to thank:

- James Mitchell for his work on the relationship between changes in interest rates and share prices which is set out in Chapter 4 and Appendix 3;
- Stephen Wright for many helpful comments on early drafts which have resulted in significant changes; for too many things in this book to be mentioned separately and without which it could not have been written; and in particular his analysis of expected real bond rates set out in Appendix 6, for which he insists on giving me some credit;
- Martin Weale for much helpful research and advice that the effect of leverage is nonlinear due to the impact of negative serial correlation on equity returns.

I am indebted to Daniel Murray for his help in demonstrating the folly of the "Fed Model" and to Derry Pickford for many helpful discussions on q.

Others from whom I have received helpful comments include Sam Brittan, Charles Goodhart, Seppo Honkapohja, Andrew Large and David Miles. I mention in the text that, together with Stephen

Wright, I have been teaching fund managers and others about stock market value as part of a course called A Practical History of Financial Markets. This was originally financed by the Stewart Ivory Foundation and its continuing success has been heavily dependent on the hard work and enthusiasm of Russell Napier.

A second group to whom debts are owed are those who have undertaken invaluable and unglamorous research into compiling reliable data on the stock markets. I would like to thank in particular:

- Jeremy Siegel who had produced data on US stock market, bank deposits and bond returns from 1800 onwards and who kindly sent me his data (data source shown on charts and in the text as "Siegel");
- Elroy Dimson, Paul Marsh and Mike Staunton, who have produced data on 17 markets from 1900 onwards (data source as "DMS");
- Robert Shiller whose website is regularly updated on an invaluable pro bono basis and which shows data, including earnings and dividends per share, for the US stock market since 1871 (data source as "Shiller")
- Stephen Wright who has compiled the data used for q calculations prior to 1947, when series published in the Federal Reserve Flow of Funds Accounts for the United States ("Z1") starts (data source as "Wright");
- Lewis Webber who provided me with the data on decomposed corporate bond and loan spreads used in Chapter 13.

The third group is those economists who have, unfashionably as I mention in the text, engaged in research into stock markets and published invaluable books and papers. Those whose work I have found particularly helpful include John Campbell, Andrew Lo, Craig Mackinlay and Robert Shiller.

The official data sources which I have used extensively are the US National Income and Product Accounts (NIPA) published by the Bureau of Economic Analysis, the Flow of Funds Accounts of the United States (Z1) published by the Federal Reserve, and the CPI data published by the Bureau of Labour Statistics. In addition to the DMS, Siegel and Shiller data, particularly when updating the series to bring them to the end of 2008, I have used the S&P 500, the FT All Share Index and Morgan Stanley Capital International (MSCI) indices. UK data are largely derived from the Office of National Statistics and from the Bank of England. Data sources for charts and tables are given in the text, and I have explained in footnotes the methods I have used for the less straightforward calculations involved.

Appendix 2

Glossary of Terms

Basis points   Used to measure small changes in interest rates. 20 basis points is the same as a change of 0.2 percentage points. The use of the term is helpful as it avoids the confusion that can arise between percentage changes and changes in percentage points.

Bond and credit spreads   These are the gaps, which vary from borrower to borrower, that private sector borrowers pay in excess of the rate of interest paid by the government for debts of similar maturity.

Capital consumption (depreciation)   The loss in the value of plant and equipment which comes from the rise in real wages. Often misinterpreted as the cost of maintaining the plant.

Capital consumption adjustment (CC)   Company profits habitually use historic cost for calculating depreciation. But in real terms depreciation will be affected by inflation and this adjustment seeks to remove the resulting distortion from the national accounts.

Cash flow dividend yield   The cash paid out to shareholders in any year × 100 divided by the price. The cash is the dividend plus buybacks and takeovers financed by cash or debt less new issues of equity.

Correlation coefficient   A measure used to assess the strength of any underlying relationship between two variables.

Cyclically Adjusted PE (CAPE)   Calculated by dividing the current value of a stock market with the average eps for the past 10 years, adjusted to current prices. This PE, divided by its long-term average, measures the current ratio of the stock market to fair value.

Data mining The process of manipulating a set of data in an attempt to prove a hypothesis. I refer to it particularly in the context of the Fed Model.

Dividend yield The dividend per share × 100 divided by the price.

Earnings per share (eps) Net profit after tax divided by the number of shares outstanding.

Earnings yield The eps × 100 divided by the share price. It is therefore equivalent to 100/PE; for example, an earnings yield of 5% is the same as a PE of 20.

Equity Risk Premium (ERP) This is the additional return to investors from taking the risk of buying equities in preference to bonds or cash on deposit. The ERP is properly defined as the expected (ex-ante) difference rather than the observed historic (ex-post) difference.

Efficient Market Hypothesis (EMH)   states that every security's price equals its investment value at all times.

Ex-ante Used to describe intentions or expectations which may not be realized. For example, intentions to save (ex-ante) and invest (ex-ante) can differ but they must be the same (ex-post) so that when ex-ante intentions differ they cannot be realized.

Ex-post Describes the outturn of events, such as returns actually achieved in contrast to those (ex-ante) which were expected.

Fair value The price that a security, or the stock market in total, would be if it was correctly valued. It follows that price and fair value would always be the same if the EMH held.

Fed Model The claim that the value of the stock market could be ascertained from the ratio of the earnings or dividend yields to current bond yields.

Floating rate Debt on which the interest is paid with relation to some standard short-term measure, such as Treasury bills or the London Interbank Offered Rate (LIBOR).

Goodwill This is the assumed value of a company in addition to the value of its tangible and financial assets. It may simply be a turn of phrase to describe this attribute or included in the company's balance sheet.

Illwill This is my term to describe the difference between the value of a company and the value of its tangible and financial assets. It is simply a turn of phrase and is not found in companies' balance sheets.

Inefficient (or Moderately Efficient) Market Hypothes My description of the central hypothesis set out in the book which holds that price is not always equal to value but, for the stock market as a whole, rotates around value over quite long time periods of up to 30 years. It is very different from the assumption that stock markets are irrational casinos.

Intangible assets (intangibles) These are the assets of companies which are neither financial such as cash on deposit, nor physical such as plant and inventories. They are typically represented in brand names and patents, but can cover many other things.

Inventory adjustment (IVA) A rise in the current price of inventories will affect profits based on the historic cost convention; no profit in real terms has been made and this adjustment is used in the national accounts to try to allow for this difference.

Leverage (aka gearing) Measures of the extent to which companies, or the corporate sector, are financed by debt. It can be measured in many different ways, for example by netting off interest bearing financial assets from debt, and by using ratios of debt to total assets or debt to net worth.

Linear Exhibiting directly proportional change in two related quantities, which can thus be represented on a graph by a straight line.

Log numbers In some of the charts I use log numbers. This is usually done to allow the eye to recognize that the swings in the charts around their average value are balanced with the size of falls below average balancing those above. Using percentage changes, for example, gives a distorted picture because a fall by 50% requires a 100% rise to bring it back to the original value.

Mean reversion Some series, for example those claimed for q and CAPE in this book, have a tendency to move back towards their average or trend values and the further they are away from these values the stronger the tendency. Mean reversion is statistically measured by the Augmented Dickey-Fuller test.

Negative serial correlation The behaviour of a series, such as real returns on equities, in which above average past returns indicate the probability of below average future returns and vice versa.

Net worth This is the net asset value of companies after deducting the value of their financial liabilities. It is therefore the same as corporate equity. It may be shown at book value, as in company accounts, either including or excluding intangibles, or after adjusting for inflation, as in the Z1, where the figures are referred to as being at replacement cost.

Nominal returns   Returns defined in terms of current prices.

Nonfinancial companies and nonfinancial corporate sector   The corporate sector is divided between these and the financial sector. The dividing line is fairly obvious with banking, insurance and financial advice being distinguished from manufacturing and nonfinancial services. Where manufacturing companies, like GE, have financial subsidiaries their activities are split in the national accounts between the two sectors.

PE multiple (aka PE and P/E)   The price per share divided by the eps, therefore also the market value of the company, or the stock market in aggregate, divided by profits after tax.

Price of liquidity   I use this term loosely to indicate the variable reward that investors receive when they sacrifice liquidity by buying less liquid assets.

Private sector   The economy is divided into four main sectors: households, corporations, government and foreigners. The first two together comprise the private sector.

Profit margins   The gross value of output is divided into the part taken by labour, in wages, salaries and supplements such as pension contributions, and the return on capital, including depreciation, interest, corporation tax, retained profits and dividends. According to economic theory, as typically expressed in the Cobb–Douglas production function, the ratio of the amounts going to labour and capital is mean reverting around a stable average in mature economies and, as shown, this theory is strongly supported by the data.

Public sector   This comprises the government, including local as well as central government, plus nationalized industries.

q   Comes in two forms: Tobin's *q* and Equity *q*. The former is the ratio of the market value of the equity and debt of the corporate sector, usually limited because of data problems to the nonfinancial sector, to the value of the capital stock at replacement cost. Equity *q*, which is the form used in this book, is the market value of the nonfinancial corporate sector divided by its net worth at replacement cost.

Random Walk Hypothesis   This is a restricted version of the EMH which assumes that the variations in future returns from their long-term averages are independent of past returns. An example is the toss of a coin; we know that the chances of heads and tails are even, and that this does not change even if heads has come up the previous five times.

Real returns Returns adjusted for inflation.

Risk aversion The extent to which investors are prepared to accept additional risk in return for some additional return. The evidence from the liquidity price is that it is highly variable in the short to medium term.

Sharpe Ratio This is a standard way to measure the combination of risk and return. It is normally calculated by subtracting the Treasury bill rate, with the implied assumption that this represents the risk free return, from the return given by the portfolio or asset whose Sharpe Ratio is being measured, divided by the standard deviation of that return.

Standard deviation This measures the variability of distributions, for example of returns. It is the square root of the squared differences between observed returns and their average. It is the square root of the variance.

Statistical discontinuities The stock data on nonfinancial company balance sheets, published in the Z1 Table B. 102, are inconsistent with the flow data shown in Z1 Table F. 102, the latter being derived from the NIPA data. My understanding is that the difference arises because B. 102 is adjusted to conform with the data derived from companies. This produces two major differences with the flow data: one arises from changes in land prices and the other is termed statistical discontinuities. The latter have been insignificant until the last 20 years and I attribute the change to the growing use of marking-to-market in the published accounts of companies.

Tangible assets In contrast to intangibles these are the physical assets of companies, such as plant and inventories.

Variance Like the standard deviation this is a measure of the variability of distributions and is its squared value.

Variance compression This occurs when variance falls over time by more than it would if returns were random.

Zero sum game A situation in which any benefit accruing to one player must be at the expense of another.

Appendix 3

Interest Rates, Profits and Share Prices

James Mitchell

We need to do two things to ascertain the impact of changes in interest rates on share prices: first, to look at the long-term relationship, and second, to isolate the impact of changes in interest rates from any offsetting influence from the connected changes in profits.

Given the likely co-dependence of prices, earnings and interest rates, it is necessary to study their relationship simultaneously rather than separately or on a bilateral basis. This can be carried out via multiple regression analysis, specifically using so-called Vector Auto Regressive (VAR) models.

VAR models accommodate the endogeneity of the three variables and provide a flexible means of capturing their dynamics. Estimating a VAR model simply amounts to running three separate regressions in the change in the logarithm of stock prices, the change in the logarithm of earnings and the change in the logarithm of the interest rate, where each variable is said to be influenced by lagged values of not just itself, but the other two variables.

VAR models, while atheoretical, are in fact quite flexible since they "nest" many theoretical models, often used by economists, as special cases. This is helpful in the context of our analysis in Chapter 3, in which we failed to find a relationship between real bond returns and equity returns which fitted readily with theories in which the ERP is either invariable or rotates around a stable level.

A long-run relationship exists between three variables when each of the three variables adjusts to restore a steady-state relationship between the (logarithmic) levels of the variables. That is, not only do current changes in stock prices, for example, possibly (if the data support the view) react to lagged changes in stock prices (as well as changes in earnings and interest rates), but they move towards an equilibrium relationship between the logarithm of prices (p_t), earnings (e_t) and possibly the interest rate (r_t).

This approach can be used to show, if such a demonstration were needed, that the Fed Model does not work. The Fed model postulates that there is an equilibrium relationship between prices, earnings and interest rates which takes a specific form, namely that $p_t - e_t = \lambda r_t$ where λ is believed to be equal to unity. This means there is a long-run relationship between the earnings yield of a stock, $e_t - p_t$, and the yield on a bond, r_t, such that when the earnings yield is above (below) the bond yield the stock market is "undervalued" (overvalued) and prices, earnings and/or the interest rate will, in due course, adjust to restore parity.

Even if the predictability of stock price movements cannot be captured by a valuation indicator, like the Fed model or the price to earnings ratio, a VAR model in prices, earnings and the interest rate is still consistent with the possible existence of a pseudo-indicator. As discussed in Chapter 7 "volatility compression" (i.e. the known tendency for the stock market to have lower volatility at longer horizons than that implied by its shorter-term volatility) implies the existence of a pseudo-indicator which can predict the stock market. But this pseudo-indicator contains no information not in the past history of stock price movements (strictly "returns"). Therefore, the VAR model (in fact, below, the first equation of the VAR model which explains p_t) can be seen to accommodate the existence of a pseudo-indicator since it lets stock price movements depend on past movements.

Estimating a VAR model amounts to estimating the following three equations in the logarithmic first difference of prices, earnings and the interest rate:

$$\Delta p_t = \alpha_0 + \sum\nolimits_{i=1}^{p} \alpha_{1i} \Delta p_{t-i} + \sum\nolimits_{i=1}^{p} \alpha_{2i} \Delta e_{t-i} + \sum\nolimits_{i=1}^{p} \alpha_{3i} \Delta r_{t-i}$$
$$+ \alpha_4 (p_{t-1} - e_{t-1} - \lambda r_{t-1}) + e_{1t}$$

$$\Delta e_t = \beta_0 + \sum\nolimits_{i=1}^{p} \beta_{1i} \Delta p_{t-i} + \sum\nolimits_{i=1}^{p} \beta_{2i} \Delta e_{t-i} + \sum\nolimits_{i=1}^{p} \beta_{3i} \Delta r_{t-i}$$
$$+ \beta_4 (p_{t-1} - e_{t-1} - \lambda r_{t-1}) + e_{2t}$$

$$\Delta r_t = \chi_0 + \sum\nolimits_{i=1}^{p} \chi_{1i} \Delta p_{t-i} + \sum\nolimits_{i=1}^{p} \chi_{2i} \Delta e_{t-i} + \sum\nolimits_{i=1}^{p} \chi_{3i} \Delta r_{t-i}$$
$$+ \chi_4 (p_{t-1} - e_{t-1} - \chi r_{t-1}) + e_{3t}$$

where p denotes the lag length. While the first three terms on the right-hand side of each equation pick up short-run dynamics, the final term $(p_{t-1} - e_{t-1} - \lambda r_{t-1})$ captures the possibility that prices, earnings and/or the interest rate over time adjust to ensure the Fed model holds in the long run. When $\alpha_4 = \beta_4 = \chi_4 = 0$ there is no long-run relationship between the three variables. When $\alpha_4 = \beta_4 = \chi_4 \neq 0$ but $\lambda = 0$ one can reject the Fed model as a long-run relationship.

Using the long run of data for stock returns available from Professor Shiller's website, and using long-term data on 3-month commercial paper, derived from the NBER and the Federal Reserve, we estimate monthly VAR models in p_t, e_t, and r_t over the period 1871 to 2007. Choosing the appropriate number of lags in the VAR model, to ensure the model picks up the dynamic behaviour of the data of interest, is always a concern and we therefore adopt a flexible approach considering various lag lengths, denoted p. Both real and nominal data for prices and earnings are considered.

Table A1 shows the estimates of the long-run relationship. It indicates that, irrespective of the number of lags (p) in the VAR model, r_t does not play a clear role in the long-run relationship between prices and earnings. This is evidenced by the high standard errors of the estimates of λ, relative to the size of the estimates of λ themselves. The data thus provide no support for the Fed Model as a long-run explanation of stock prices.

But as discussed in Chapter 4, the absence of a long-run relationship between interest rates and stock prices does not rule out effects of interest rate changes on stock prices. To examine whether interest rate changes have predictive power for changes in stock prices we compute, at different forecasting horizons, the probability that they have predictive content for stock prices. Importantly, to isolate the impact on stock prices of changes in interest rates from any offsetting influence

Table A1. Testing the Validity of the Fed Model as a Long-run Relationship.

	Nominal prices and earnings		
	p = 2	p = 6	p = 12
$\hat{\lambda}$	0.042040	−0.16119	−0.07844
$se(\hat{\lambda})$	0.10251	0.13511	0.13508
	Real Prices and Earnings		
	p = 2	p = 6	p = 12
$\hat{\lambda}$	−0.21426	−0.18197	−0.10485
$se(\hat{\lambda})$	0.14999	0.13222	0.12253

Note: Estimates of λ along with its standard error (se).

from the connected changes in profits, we continue to model the relationship between the three variables simultaneously.

This involves re-estimating the stock price change, or "return", equation in the VAR model, with the "return" measured over different horizons, and then computing the probability that the interest rate has predictive power for returns. Since there is uncertainty about the "best" specification of this equation (in terms of the number of lags that should be included and whether a long-run relationship should be imposed, and if so what form it should take), we consider a large set of VAR models. These models differ in terms of how many lags they consider, whether they include interest rate changes in the VAR, whether they impose a long-run relationship between the three variables and, if so, whether this equilibrium is simply the price-to-earnings ratio or the Fed Model.

To arrive at a best (statistically "optimal") guess of whether interest rates predict stock price movements for each VAR model, we first compute the probability that interest rates have no predictive content. Then we take a weighted average of these probabilities over the complete set of models, with the weights reflecting the plausibility of each model as judged by how well it "fits" the data.

Since the risk associated with the misspecification of an individual model can be high, model averaging over a large set of competing models offers an elegant but convenient means of diversifying this risk. Appendices A3.1 and A3.2 provide some of the additional technical details.

When considering the probability that interest rate changes predict stock price changes, at forecast horizons up to 6 years, Chart 5 in Chapter 4 shows that the probability varies considerably depending on how far ahead one is forecasting.

Interest rate changes which, importantly, include both anticipated and unanticipated movements, are seen to have a strong effect on stock price movements 3–15 months after the interest rate change, although they have little immediate impact. But any effect disappears in the medium run, at forecast horizons of more than 18 months.

In the long run, defined as forecast horizons of five years or greater, interest rate movements do not appear to affect stock prices. This is consistent with the absence of a long-run relationship between interest rates and stock prices, although the lack of a long-run relationship does not necessarily rule out permanent effects of interest rate shocks.

Appendix A3.1 Probabilistic Inference

The probability that interest rate changes have no predictive content for stock price changes, at a given horizon h, is computed as follows.

Consider VAR models in the three variables $(\Delta p_{t,h}, \Delta e_t, \Delta r_t)$ where $\Delta p_{t,h}$ is the h period ahead "return" at time t defined as

$$\Delta p_{t,h} = \sum_{i=1}^{h} \Delta p_{t+i}$$

where Δp_t is the one period ahead "return". Of course, in defining the "return" we have ignored earnings. Using Campbell and Shiller's approximation we know that $\log(1 + R_t) = \Delta p_t + (1 - \rho)(e_t - p_t)$, where R_t is the 1-period logarithmic return. Therefore ignoring earnings is not a bad approximation when ρ is small, which it is generally believed to be (around 0.04 is common). In any case, results are little different if we define the "price" variable to be cumulated returns so that price growth forecasts are then return forecasts.

The first equation in the VAR model, the equation of concern, then takes the form

$$\Delta p_{t,h} = \alpha_0 + \sum_{i=1}^{p} \alpha_{1i} \Delta p_{t-i+1} + \sum_{i=1}^{p} \alpha_{2i} \Delta e_{t-i+1} + \sum_{i=1}^{p} \alpha_{3i} \Delta r_{t-i+1}$$
$$+ \alpha_4 (p_{t-1} - e_{t-1} - \lambda r_{t-1}) + e_{t,h}$$

which amounts to regressing the h-step ahead return at time t on information known at time t (and earlier). This is, therefore, what econometricians call an h-step ahead "projection" (or "direct" forecast) and takes a familiar, but more general, form to predictive return regressions commonly used in finance to test the predictability of stock returns.

The "fit" of the model (with reference to the data) can then be computed, with a penalty for the inclusion of many explanatory variables given that fit can always be improved simply by considering more and more variables (i.e. increasing p). We consider as a measure of fit the so-called Bayesian Information Criterion (BIC). For the interested reader, this is computed as follows

$$BIC = \ln L - \frac{K\ln(T)}{2}$$

where lnL is the logarithm of the likelihood function evaluated at the maximum likelihood estimates of the parameters in the VAR model, K is the number of parameters in the model and T is the number of observations available to estimate the parameters. Thus, we can see that the inclusion of extra parameters is penalized.

Interest rates have no predictive content for the stock market when $\alpha_{31} = \ldots = \alpha_{3p} = 0$ and either $\lambda = 0$ or if not $\alpha_4 = 0$.

Let BIC_U denote the BIC value from the (unrestricted) VAR which allows interest rates to affect the stock market, and let BIC_R denote the (restricted) VAR which imposes the restrictions that mean interest rates have no predictive content. Then the probability (conditional on the data) that interest rates have no predictive content for the stock market is given as

$$Pr\left(\alpha_{31} = \ldots = \alpha_{3p} = 0 \text{ AND } \lambda = 0 \text{ or } \alpha_4 = 0 | Data\right)$$
$$= \frac{\exp(BIC_R)}{\exp(BIC_R) + \exp(BIC_U)}$$

This probability can be computed for a given VAR model. Reflecting our uncertainty about the best VAR model, we estimate many different VAR models. They differ in terms of their lag lengths, p; we consider a range from 1 to 12. They also differ in terms of the implied long-run relationship. We consider VAR models with no long-run relationship ($\alpha_4 = 0$), as well as VAR models with both the Fed model (i.e. $\lambda = 1$) and the PE ratio (i.e. $\lambda = 0$) imposed as long-run equilibria.

Appendix A3.2 Integrating Out Model Uncertainty

The overall probability that interest rates have no predictive power for stock prices is then computed by taking a weighted average of these probabilities over the complete set of VAR models considered. The weights reflect how well each unrestricted VAR fits the data, and are again based on BIC_U. Similarly, when forecasting from the VAR model we take a weighted average of the forecasts from the different VAR models.

This approach of model averaging to accommodate (integrate out) model uncertainty is known to econometricians as Bayesian Model Averaging.

It is also important, in terms of assessing whether any predictability is in fact exploitable, to compute the probability conditional on interest rates affecting share prices (whether positively or negatively), that a fall in the interest rate leads to a rise in share prices. It is perfectly possible for interest rates to have predictive content for the stock market, as identified above, but for this predictive content to be useless to a forecaster in practice since it is unclear to them, on a probabilistic basis, whether the stock market will rise or fall after the interest rate movement. Accordingly, for each model, we computed (conditional on interest rates affecting share prices) the probability that the initial (short-run) effect of an interest rate cut on stock prices h-periods ahead is positive – this involves computing the probability that $\alpha_{31} < 0$. The overall (conditional) probability that interest rate cuts have a positive effect on stock prices is then again computed by taking a weighted average of these probabilities over the complete set of VAR models considered.

We found that there is a high conditional probability (with probabilities greater than 0.95 for real share prices and greater than 0.75 for nominal share prices) that the short-term impact of falls in short-term interest rates is helpful to the stock market with rises tending to be inimical. After nine months the impact becomes less certain but remains highly probable, with conditional probabilities remaining above 0.85 for forecast horizons up to five years or greater (for both real and nominal prices). But looking at Chart 5 we know that the joint probability that interest rates affect share prices, and that this effect is helpful to share prices, is low looking out beyond 18 months.

Appendix 4

Examples of the Current (Trailing) and Next Year's (Prospective) PEs Giving Misleading Guides to Value

As pointed out in the text, we can measure the value of a market at any given time by hindsight provided that we have sufficient subsequent data. We do this by taking the returns from any starting point for the next 1 to 30 years and averaging these returns. We then compare them with the long-term average over the whole period. Using the Shiller data from 1871 to July 2008, we can use this method for all years up to July 1978. Cheap markets are those which have given, with hindsight, above average returns and expensive ones those that have given below average ones.

Chart A1 compares PEs with hindsight value with the periods during which below average PEs were times of poor subsequent returns, i.e. overvalued markets with hindsight, shown as the vertical lines. Thirty percent of the time when PEs were below average,

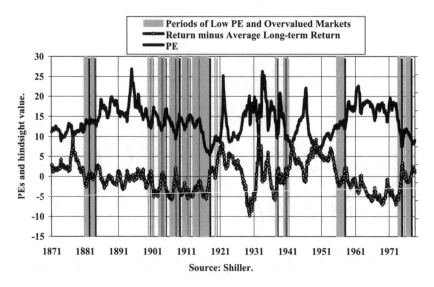

Chart A1. Showing Periods When Overvalued Markets Had Below Average PEs.

returns were also below average. (It is no surprise to find that approximately half the time – 52% – as observed, PEs were below average.)

Appendix 5

Real Returns from 17 International Equity Markets Comparing 1899–1954 with 1954–2008 and Showing Their Variance Compression

In Table A2 I show the real equity returns from the 17 international markets for which annual data since the end of 1899 are available from DMS. I also show the returns from the first half of the period available (1899–1954) and the second half (1954–2008). Negative shocks, including two world wars, hyperinflation in Germany, and the Spanish Civil War all occurred in the first half of the period. It can readily be seen that the returns in the first period, for those countries which suffered most, were much lower, relative for example

Table A2. Long-term Real Equity Returns and Variance Compression.

	1899–2008	1899–1954	1954–2008	Variance compression over 30 years 1899–2008
Australia	7.32	8.24	6.38	0.59
Belgium	1.51	−0.69	3.81	0.75
Canada	9.13	9.02	9.24	0.36
Denmark	4.67	3.42	5.96	0.32
France	3.18	1.25	5.19	0.68
Germany	2.79	−0.16	5.89	0.61
Ireland	3.38	1.41	5.43	0.45
Italy	1.89	1.69	2.10	0.21
Japan	3.76	2.08	5.50	0.92
Netherlands	4.73	3.25	6.27	0.73
Norway	3.75	3.25	4.27	0.41
South Africa	7.07	6.34	7.81	0.26
Spain	3.52	2.57	4.50	0.38
Sweden	7.24	7.20	7.29	0.49
Switzerland	4.10	3.17	5.05	0.48
UK	5.06	3.84	6.32	0.3
US	6.02	6.42	5.62	0.28
Standard deviation of returns	2.09	2.85	1.61	

Source: DMS.

to the US, than they were in the second period. Germany, for example, had a return of −0.16 in the first period and +5.89% in the second. The relative lack of negative shocks is shown by the reduction in the standard deviation of the returns from 2.85 (1899–1954) to 1.61 (1954–2008).

Countries which suffered the worst shocks were also those which had the least benefit to long-term investors from long-term variance compression.

Appendix 6

Errors in Inflation Expectations and the Impact on Bond Returns

Stephen Wright and Andrew Smithers

A6.1 Returns, Expected Returns and Inflationary Expectations

When Mehra and Prescott first set out the "equity premium puzzle", they assumed that the risk premium of equities over cash had been just over 6%, with the return on equities calculated to include reinvested income. This figure was subsequently widely quoted in both popular and academic discussions.[110] It is clear that this figure is, by a wide margin, a significant overestimate of the true historic premium, largely due to the accidental choice of the sample period.

The choice of the sample can radically change estimates of the average premium. Awareness of this fact is gradually permeating

---

[110] Confusion on this point has been common due to the tendency to misrepresent it as the premium over long-term bonds.

into academic research[111] but, since it is not otherwise widely known, we focus in this section on why this problem arises and derive more reasonable estimates of the premia over cash and long-term bonds.

Although it is common to estimate risk premia by using historic average returns, it is worth considering for a moment the problems involved in so doing. A true measure should capture the risk premium that investors are expecting to receive from equities, compared to safer assets, but this must obviously be unmeasurable. The only thing that can be measured is the returns that they have actually received.

It is evident that, even over quite long periods, realized returns need not provide any relation to the expected premium. If they did, the experience of the 1990s would have implied a risk premium of equities over cash of around 15%. This would be absurd, because rational investors were not expecting to receive such returns. A significant element in the returns they actually received was due to errors in their expectations.

This problem can only be overcome by assuming that, if a long enough period is chosen, pleasant mistakes in predicting returns, such as those in the 1990s, will be offset by unpleasant ones. Unfortunately, as we shall show, this apparently reasonable assumption does not always hold. Historic errors do not always conveniently average out at zero.

The problem is made worse by the fact that people make different types of mistakes when predicting equity returns from those they make over cash and bond returns.

The main reason why equity returns are hard to predict is the impossibility of predicting stock market troughs and peaks. In a typical bull market, even one covering a decade or more, stock returns between trough and peak can easily be more than twice the long-run average. These fluctuations thus have a significant impact on average returns over quite long periods.

Because returns, particularly over short periods, are distorted by the level of the stock market at the opening and closing dates, it is helpful to calculate them over periods which avoid such problems.

[111] See, for example, Siegel and Thaler, "Anomalies: The Equity Premium Puzzle", *Journal of Economic Perspectives*, Winter 1997, pp. 191–200.

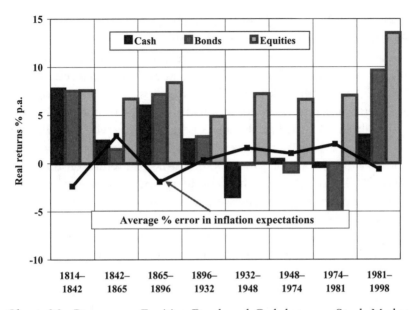

Chart A2. Returns on Equities, Bonds and Cash between Stock Market Troughs.

We have done this in Chart A2, by showing the returns for sub-samples which roughly correspond to intervals between stock market troughs.[112]

By calculating the returns between troughs, we should be able to pick periods over which expectations have begun and ended at similar levels. By this means, the average realized returns should correspond reasonably well to average expected returns.

As Chart A2 shows, the real returns on equities in the different periods are indeed quite stable. This supports the idea that the observed long-term stability of the return conforms to investors' expectations.

Our calculations were done in May 2000 and were based on data up to the end of 1998, which was not of course a time at which the

---

[112] A similar calculation could be done for stock market peaks, but there appears to be some evidence that troughs have been more consistent in nature than peaks. In particular, peaks appear to have been distinctly more extreme in the 20th than in the 19th century.

stock market hit a trough, but simply the latest data we had available. As Chart A2 shows, the real equity return for 1981–1998 was not a trough-to-trough return and was therefore anomalously high at 14.2%. With the subsequent fall in the stock market the return from 1981–2008 has come down to 7.1%, which is only a little above the long-term real return on equities and may or may not prove to be a trough in the market. In any event, this resolves the apparent anomaly. We have not, however, reworked our estimate for inflationary expectations for 1981–2008, but the real return on bonds for 1981–2008 was 7.2%, which is consistent with our original estimate that inflationary expectations were above the actual outturn.

While the swings in the stock market, between peaks and troughs, have been the main cause of fluctuations in real equity returns, the primary factor affecting historic returns on cash and bonds has, in marked contrast, been inflation.

One of the key differences between the 19th and 20th centuries was the change from relative price stability to inflation. This was clearly not predicted at the start of the 20th century and, crucially, the implied underprediction of inflation has not, thus far, been offset by an error in the opposite direction. As Chart A2 shows, unexpectedly high inflation in the 20th century was accompanied by poor returns on bonds and cash.[113]

Historically, upswings in inflation have been reliably associated with loose monetary policy, which in turn always implies low, or even negative, short-term real interest rates. Chart A2 shows that the impact of unexpected inflation on bond returns has usually been even more drastic than that on cash. This is because a move from price stability to sustained inflation raises nominal yields on a permanent basis, causing large capital losses on bonds issued earlier, when nominal yields were lower.

As discussed in Chapter 3, inflation has only had a minimal impact on real equity returns. This is confirmed by the evidence of Chart A2, which shows no relation between inflation errors[114] and the return on equities.

---

[113] It is interesting to note the poor return in the period 1842–1865, which included the Civil War, when US inflation was above the average for the 19th century.

[114] See below in Section A6.2 for an explanation as to how we derive our proxy for inflation expectations.

The effect of errors in forecasting inflation makes it harder to estimate the anticipated real returns from cash and bonds. But, as expected, the chart shows that there is a strong negative correlation between such errors and the real returns achieved. This is evident in both centuries, but is considerably more marked in the 20th. Since such errors have no impact on real equity returns they have an important impact on the difference between the returns actually achieved on equity and on cash and bonds.

The chart helps to explain how the size of the equity premium has been so often overstated and the view that it was over 6% gained currency. The data used by Mehra and Prescott ran from the end of the 19th century to the 1970s; the averages were therefore dominated by the unpredicted emergence of sustained inflation which started around the time of the Second World War, during the course of which both cash and bonds were terrible investments. Both before and after this period, however, returns on both were considerably more respectable.

Chart A3 uses only time periods in which errors in predicting inflation were small. This reduces the distortion they cause and should thus give a better feel for average expected real returns on bonds and cash.[115]

Two features are evident in Chart A3:

- Once the impact of such errors is excluded, returns on both bonds and cash are revealed as considerably more stable, and uniformly positive.
- The relative returns on bonds and cash appears to have been different in the 19th and 20th centuries. In the 20th century, long-term bonds have, after excluding the result of errors in

---

[115] Note two caveats: (a) The reliability of the chart depends on the reliability of our proxy for inflation expectations, discussed in Section A6.2, which may perhaps overstate the capacity of the average investor to exploit the degree of predictability of inflation which emerged during the 20th century. If this is the case, implied average expected returns may have been higher than as shown. (b) Unlike Chart A1, the time periods shown in Chart A2 exclude some historical data, since the *average* error has been positive (implying underprediction of inflation) – this is particularly problematic in the post-war era, a large proportion of which must of necessity be excluded.

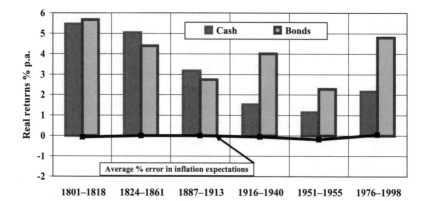

Chart A3. Returns on Bonds and Cash When Inflation Expectations Were (Roughly) Correct.

predicting inflation, consistently yielded more than cash. In the 19th century, however, the returns on both assets were similar.

This latter feature is probably due to a combination of higher credit risks on cash in the 19th century[116] and the behaviour of inflation. The combined result was that investors in the 19th century regarded the two assets as equally risky, and hence expected roughly the same returns.

While it is thus clearly impossible to make hard-and-fast estimates of historic risk premia, the evidence of Charts A2 and A3 taken together suggests that they have been very much smaller than

---

[116] Banks were more dangerous places to invest money than government bonds, up until the mid-1930s. There is therefore a problem, during the 19th century when short-term government paper was seldom available, in estimating the risk free return on cash. As for inflation, the difference may also reflect distinct differences between the two centuries. In the 20th century inflation has generally been rather easy to predict in the short term, but extremely hard to predict in the long term. In the 19th century almost precisely the reverse was the case: prices were far more stable on average, but in the short term, inflation was distinctly more volatile. On our estimates, errors in predicting inflation one year ahead in the 19th century were, ignoring signs, roughly twice as large as in the 20th.

Table A3. "Expectations-neutral" Average Real Returns, and the Equity Risk Premium.[117]

	Cash	Bonds	Stocks	Premium over cash
All relevant data	3.44%	4.16%	6.61%	3.17%
Only 20th century	1.76%	4.22%	6.01%	4.25%

the figure of over 6% suggested by Mehra and Prescott, even if the premia are measured with reference to the returns on equity in which income is reinvested and thus not available for consumption. Table A3 summarizes the information in the charts by producing weighted average estimates of "expectations-neutral" returns and the Equity Risk Premium, in both centuries, and in the twentieth century alone.

After adjusting for errors in making expectations, both bond and equity returns are remarkably stable over 200 years. There is perhaps some suggestion that equity returns, before expenses, may have been somewhat lower in the 20th century than in the 19th. This is supported by Chart A3. But this is consistent with expected equity returns after expenses being constant if, as seems highly probable, the cost of managing equity portfolios was lower in the 20th century.

Even after our adjustments, there is rather less stability in the expected cash return. It is possible that the overall average may overstate the true figure, since cash returns were more risky in the 19th century. On the other hand, our figure for the 20th century alone may possibly be an underestimate, since we may have made too much allowance for the average investor's ability to predict inflation.[118]

We conclude that, despite the uncertainty as to the expected cash return, the historic equity risk premium, using returns in which

---

[117] Cash and bond returns are calculated as compound averages over samples in which inflation expectations were realized, weighted by sample size (hence some data are excluded from averages). Stock returns are calculated as trough-to-trough compound averages (hence exclude impact of data after 1974).

[118] It is interesting to note that the average return on cash rose through the century – possibly reflecting a more gradual process of adjustment to inflation than we allow for.

income is reinvested, over cash appears to have been something like 3–4%, before allowing for expenses. After expenses, the premium should probably be decreased by at least 1% per annum. Our best estimate of the implied risk premium of equities over cash is therefore only around half the 6.1% figure used by Mehra and Prescott.

The premium over bonds appears to be around 2% per annum, hence only around 1% after expenses.

A6.2 A Proxy for Inflation Expectations

In Tables 1, 2, 3 and 4 in the main text, we show data indicating the errors made by investors in predicting inflation. The charts show the strong negative correlation between these errors and bond returns.

Clearly inflation expectations can never be perfectly measured. Some survey evidence exists for recent years, but over a period of 200 years the only way to capture expectations is to make assumptions about how a rational person would have forecast inflation at the time. A common method of doing this in academic work is to assume that expectations are no different from those that result from econometric forecasts. The measure we use takes a similar approach, but takes into account the prior expectations that a rational person might reasonably be assumed to have had.

The first stage is to carry out a sequence of econometric regressions, which forecast inflation as a function of its own past, using only the data that would have been available at the time. Of course, we do not really believe that a rational investor would have carried out such regressions, but the forecasts which result should approximate to the inflation expectations someone would have made, who expected inflation to behave in the future in a way which related to the patterns of the relatively recent past.

It is common in academic work to use these forecasts as they stand. However, this ignores the possibility that a rational person might, quite reasonably, have had some strong prior expectations about the behaviour of inflation. During the 19th and early 20th century, the most obvious expectation would simply be that of price stability. Interestingly, for the entire 19th century, such a prior view would have been quite consistent with the data. If regression equations are estimated on a "rolling" basis, using data for the 30 years before any forecast is made, it is possible to test for the overall significance of the relationships they capture. During the course of the 19th century, essentially none of the regressions have any explanatory power on standard statistical tests.[119] We therefore assume that during the course of the 19th century it would have been quite reasonable to have expected that inflation would have been zero in any given year.

Once we look at data for the 20th century, this view becomes less tenable. The estimated equations increasingly reveal a feature which has now become familiar – that inflation in any given year has a tendency to persist into the following year. However, a reasonable prior view would have been that, apart from this short-term predictability, the long-run average rate of inflation would still have been expected to be zero. It turns out that this expectation would not actually have been refutable, on standard statistical tests, until surprisingly late in the century; it cannot be rejected on a consistent basis until the 1960s. Accordingly, until this point we use a modified version of the equations, which implies that long-run expected inflation is zero.[120] Only after the mid 1960s do we assume that investors would have learned enough from history to abandon any expectation of zero inflation. Accordingly, from the early 1960s onwards, we use equations in the unrestricted form.

A6.3 Why Inflation Errors Affected Bond Returns More in the 20th Century than the 19th

The evidence as to how a rational investor would have predicted inflation in these different periods also casts light on the impact

---

[119] The equations estimated were AR(2) models including a constant. We conducted a rolling "F"-test for the overall significance of the regression in each sample. Only towards the very end of the century does this rise above its 5% significance level on a consistent basis.

[120] The test in this case is simply a rolling t-test of the hypothesis that the constant term in the regression is zero. The restricted equation is therefore an AR(2) with no constant. In principle, this specification nests a zero drift unit root process if the autoregressive coefficients add up to 1 (which would have implied that the best long-run forecast of inflation was not zero, but whatever inflation happened to be at the time); but almost invariably this specification would have been rejected.

of inflation surprises on bond returns. Assume, for simplicity, a bond that is at par – hence with yield equal to coupon. The total realized real return on the bond will be, to a log approximation, equal to:

$$ret = r - \pi + \Delta \log P_B$$

where *ret* is the one period real return, *r* is the yield, π is the inflation rate, and P_B is the price of the bond. To a reasonable approximation, this may be rewritten as:

$$ret = r - \pi - \delta \Delta r$$

where δ is the "modified duration" of the bond. For a zero coupon bond, this will equal its maturity or, at the other extreme, for a perpetuity it will simply equal the reciprocal of the coupon. Thus a "consol", trading at par with an annual coupon of 2½%, has a duration of 40 years. For finite maturity coupon bonds, the duration will always be less than the maturity.

  If we assume for simplicity that the expected real return on the bonds is constant and the nominal yield is given by the Fisher identity:

$$r = \rho + \pi^e$$

where ρ is the expected real rate, assumed to be constant, then, substituting into the expression for the return, and rearranging, it can be expressed as

$$ret = \rho - (\pi - \pi^e) - \delta \Delta \pi^e$$

  This expression brings out the crucial role of inflation expectations. If inflation expectations are simply constant over time, which according to the data would have been reasonable during the 19th century, then, with constant expected real returns, holding returns will vary one-for-one with inflation surprises. But if inflation expectations respond to inflation surprises, the impact will be greater. A very simple representation of such an adjustment of inflation expectations would be of the form:

$$\Delta\pi^e = \lambda(\pi - \pi^e)$$

This is normally taken to imply adaptive expectations, but it can also be consistent with rational expectations, if λ is consistent with the observed persistence of inflation. The greater is λ, the more rapidly expected inflation adjusts to actual inflation, with the limiting case of $\lambda = 1$ if inflation is simply a random walk.

Substituting for returns, this implies:

$$ret = \rho - (1 + \delta\lambda)(\pi - \pi^e)$$

making it clear that the more rapidly inflation expectations adjust (the higher is λ) and the more damage inflation surprises do to real bond returns. In the 19th century λ was zero, but as the 20th century proceeded and investors progressively learned more about the properties of inflation, their estimate of λ would effectively have been rising, thus increasing the damage done by inflation surprises.[121]

Note also that the equation makes it clear why inflation surprises in the 20th century may seriously distort historic average measures of the underlying expected real return, ρ. This is because the non-offsetting nature of inflation surprises means that the average inflation surprise, even over two centuries, will be positive.

---

[121] The only qualification to this was that simultaneously δ, the duration of a typical bond was falling, as nominal coupons increased. But even a smaller value of δ will imply a larger impact on bond returns, compared to the case where λ is zero.

Appendix 7

An Algebraic Demonstration that Negative Serial Correlation can make the Leverage of an Equity Portfolio Unattractive

r^e = expected return on equity in one period
r^c = expected return on cash in one period
Actual return on cash = $r^e + \varepsilon_t^e$
Actual return on equity = $r^c + \varepsilon_t^c$
$E()$ is the expectations operator with $E(\varepsilon_t^e) = E(\varepsilon_t^c) = 0$

Consider a portfolio invested in two periods in equities. The expected return is:

$$E\{(1+r^e+\varepsilon^e_{t+1})(1+r^e+\varepsilon^e_t)\}$$
$$=(1+r^e)(1+r^e)+E(\varepsilon^e_{t+1}\varepsilon^e_t)$$

The other product terms are zero because $E(\varepsilon^e_t)=E(\varepsilon^c_t)=0$

Negative serial correlation means that $E(\varepsilon^e_{t+1}\varepsilon^e_t)<0$. The return for equities over the whole time period available allows for negative serial correlation. The theoretical question is whether leverage should affect it as the empirical results show.

Suppose that of the portfolio θ is invested in equities and $\theta-1$ cash; so that when the portfolio is leveraged $\theta>1$.

Using the same approach as before, the average return over two periods is calculated as:

$$E\{(1+\theta r^e+(1-\theta)r^c+\theta\varepsilon^e_{t+1}+(1-\theta)\varepsilon^c_{t+1})(1+\theta r^e+(1-\theta)r^c+$$
$$\theta\varepsilon^e_t+(1-\theta)\varepsilon^c_t)\}$$
$$=(1+\theta r^e+(1-\theta)r^c)(1+\theta r^e+(1-\theta)r^c)$$
$$+\theta^2 E(\varepsilon^e_{t+1}\varepsilon^e_t)+(1-\theta)^2 E(\varepsilon^c_{t+1}\varepsilon^c_t)$$
$$+\theta(1-\theta)\{E(\varepsilon^e_{t+1}\varepsilon^c_t)+E(\varepsilon^e_t\varepsilon^c_{t+1})\}$$

Looking at this we can certainly say that the direct effect of negative serial correlation will be multiplied up by θ^2 which is greater than 1 in a geared portfolio. Serial correlation in the return on cash and its covariation with the return on equity will have some influence on the outcome but if, as we assume, the uncertainty on the return on cash is small, then the impact of the negative serial correlation, exacerbated by leverage, will be the dominant influence.

Appendix 8

Correlations between International Stock Markets

As Table A4 shows, the correlations between G5 stock markets are strong and have tended to become stronger in recent years.

Table A4. Correlations Using Annual Returns in Home Currencies.

	France	Germany	Japan	UK	US
1969–2008					
France	1.00	0.77	0.53	0.65	0.68
Germany	0.77	1.00	0.43	0.60	0.68
Japan	0.53	0.43	1.00	0.49	0.46
UK	0.65	0.60	0.49	1.00	0.75
US	0.68	0.68	0.46	0.75	1.00
1969–1979					
France	1.00	0.41	0.46	0.58	0.57
Germany	0.41	1.00	0.41	0.63	0.43
Japan	0.46	0.41	1.00	0.38	0.49
UK	0.58	0.63	0.38	1.00	0.75
US	0.57	0.43	0.49	0.75	1.00

Table A4. (Continued)

	France	Germany	Japan	UK	US
	1979–1989				
France	1.00	0.72	0.43	0.60	0.57
Germany	0.72	1.00	0.14	0.54	0.62
Japan	0.43	0.14	1.00	0.57	0.46
UK	0.60	0.54	0.57	1.00	0.79
US	0.57	0.62	0.46	0.79	1.00

1989–1999

	France	Germany	Japan	UK	US
France	1.00	0.87	0.39	0.47	0.40
Germany	0.87	1.00	0.37	0.50	0.41
Japan	0.39	0.37	1.00	0.27	0.14
UK	0.47	0.50	0.27	1.00	0.68
US	0.40	0.41	0.14	0.68	1.00

1999–2008

	France	Germany	Japan	UK	US
France	1.00	0.97	0.89	0.98	0.92
Germany	0.97	1.00	0.85	0.97	0.93
Japan	0.89	0.85	1.00	0.87	0.84
UK	0.98	0.97	0.87	1.00	0.93
US	0.92	0.93	0.84	0.93	1.00

Source: MSCI.

Bibliography

Batini, Nicoletta, Jackson, Brian and Nickell, Stephen (2000) "Inflation Dynamics and the Labour Share in the UK." Bank of England External MPC Unit, Discussion Paper No. 2, November.

Brunnermeier, Markus, Crocket, Andrew, Goodhart, Charles, Persaud, Avinash D. and Shin Hyun (2009) *The Fundamental Principles of Financial Regulation.* Geneva Reports on the World Economy 11, January (preliminary draft).

Churm, Rohan and Panigirtzoglou, Nikolaos (2005) "Decomposing Credit Spreads." Bank of England Working Paper no. 253, June.

Constantinides, George M., Donaldson, John B. and Mehra, Rajnish (2002) "Junior Can't Borrow: A New Perspective on the Equity Premium Puzzle", *Quarterly Journal of Economics* 117: 269–96.

Corrado, Carol, Hulten, Charles and Sichel, Daniel (2006) *Intangible Capital and Economic Growth* Federal Reserve Board, Finance and Economics Discussion Series 2006–24.

Dimson, Elroy, Marsh, Paul, and Staunton, Mike (2002) *Triumph of the Optimists.* Princeton and Oxford: Princeton University Press.

Durré, Alain and Giot, Pierre (2005) "An international analysis of earnings, stock prices and bond yields" ECB Working Paper No. 515 August.

Duus, Peter (Ed.) (1998) *The Cambridge History of Japan: Vol. 6, The Twentieth Century.* Cambridge: Cambridge University Press.

Grossman, Sanford J. and Stiglitz, Joseph E. (1980) "On the Impossibility of Informationally Efficient Markets" *American Economic Review* 70: 393–408.

Harney, Matthew and Tower, Edward (2003) "Rational Pessimism: Predicting Equity Returns using Tobin's q and Price/Earnings Ratios" *The Journal of Investing* Fall: 58–69.

Kuhn, T.S. (1962) *The Structure of Scientific Revolutions.* London: University of Chicago Press.

Lo, Andrew W. and MacKinlay, Craig (1999) *A Non-Random Walk Down Wall Street*. Princeton: Princeton University Press.

Medawar, P.B. (1972) *The Hope of Progress*. London: Methuen.

Mehra, Rajnish and Prescott, Edward C. (1985) "The Equity Premium: A Puzzle" *Journal of Monetary Economics* 15: 145–61.

Miles, David (1998) *Interest Rates from the 17th to the 21st Century*. Merrill Lynch.

Orphanides, Athanasios and van Norden, Simon (2001) "The Unreliability of Output-Gap Estimates in Real Time" CIRANO Working Papers November 2001 and subsequently in MIT Press *Review of Economics and Statistics* 84: 569–583, 2002.

Popper, Karl (1959) *The Logic of Scientific Discovery English edition*. London: Hutchinson & Co.

Robertson, Donald and Wright, Stephen (2009) "Testing for Redundant Predictor Variables" (working paper downloadable from "http://www.econ.bbk.ac.uk/faculty/wright") February 2009.

Sefton, James.A. and Weale, Martin.R. (2006) "The Concept of Income in a General Equilibrium" *Review of Economic Studies* 73(1): 219–249.

Siegel, Jeremy J. and Thaler, Richard H. (1997) "Anomalies: The Equity Premium Puzzle" *Journal of Economic Perspectives* 11(1): 191–200.

Shiller, Robert J. (2000) *Irrational Exuberance*. Princeton: Princeton University Press.

Smithers, Andrew and Wright, Stephen (2002) "Stock Markets and Central Bankers – The Economic Consequences of Alan Greenspan" *World Economics* 3(1): 101–124.

Smithers, Andrew and Wright, Stephen (2000) *Valuing Wall Street – Protecting Wealth in Turbulent Markets*. New York: McGraw-Hill.

Smithers, Andrew (1998) "Index Funds and Capital Market Theory" *Investment Analyst* September: 5–8.

Wadhwani, Sushil (2008) "Should Monetary Policy Respond to Asset Price Bubbles? Revisiting the Debate" *National Institute Economic Review* 206(1): 25–34.

Webber, Lewis and Churm, Rohan (2007) "Decomposing corporate bond spreads" *Bank of England Quarterly Bulletin* 2007 Q4: 533–541.

Wright, Stephen (2004) "Measures of Stock Market Value and Returns for the US Nonfinancial Corporate Sector, 1900–2002" *The Review of Income and Wealth* 50(4): 561–584.

Index

Page references in *italics* refer to charts and tables.